LAKANAL THE REGICIDE

Lakanal
at seventy-eight years of age

From Portrait painted by Mlle. Berriat-Saint-Prix

LAKANAL THE REGICIDE

A

Biographical and Historical Study of the Career of Joseph Lakanal

by John Charles Dawson

UNIVERSITY OF ALABAMA PRESS

0-8173-5020-9 (pbk: alk. paper)

for

Dorothy and Juliet

Après et au dessous des hommes qui ont illustré les lettres par leurs ouvrages, il est juste de placer ceux qui les ont défendues avec courage et en bravant les dangers dans des temps de deuil pour elles.—LAKANAL

Il y a eu des acteurs plus bruyants dans ce grand drame politique qui, sur la fin du dernier siècle, a changé la face de la France; il n'y en a pas eu de plus honnête et de plus utile.—PASCAL DUPRAT (1879)

PREFACE

IT WAS THROUGH AN ENTIRELY FORTUITOUS CIRCUMSTANCE FOLLOWED by a succession of happy incidents, that I became interested in Lakanal and determined to investigate his life and career.

At the close of World War I when I was stationed in Southern France as American Dean of the University of Toulouse, I made a week-end trip to the little city of Foix for the purpose of viewing the ruins of the old château of the mediaeval Counts of Foix. After viewing the remains of the château I took a walk through the town and ran across a life-sized statue in bronze of Joseph Lakanal. Never having heard of Lakanal, I asked a bystander who he was. The reply was that he was the organizer of the *Institut de France.* I then became aware that the Rue Lakanal through which I had been in the habit of walking every day in Toulouse had been named in his honor. Some time later, in rummaging through a second-hand book shop in Toulouse, I discovered a pamphlet which turned out to be the regulations concerning the organizing of the *Institut de France,* which had been drawn up by Lakanal and presented to the *Conseil* of the Directory.

At Toulouse there is an ancient custom of maintaining every Sunday morning what is called the Flea Market, where all sorts of second-hand articles, including books, are displayed for sale in the streets. While scrutinizing some second-hand books in the Flea Market, my attention was attracted to a dog-eared volume entitled "Procés ou Assassinat juridique de Louis XVI, Roi de France et de Navarre" (Paris, 1814). I purchased the book and found in it the complete record of the trial of the king. Along with the other Deputies the name of Lakanal was registered, the way in which he voted, and the remarks made by him on casting his vote.

Some time after my return to America from France my attention was attracted to the Vine and Olive Colony founded at Demopolis, Alabama, by the exiles from the Napoleonic regime in France. I discovered that Lakanal had been one of the promoters of the colony, had been called its *régulateur,* and was one of the principal shareholders to whom had been assigned 480 acres of land.

After coming to the University of Alabama as professor and head of Romance languages, I discovered in the trustees' records two letters, one written by Lakanal, and the other addressed to him offering him the presidency of the College of Orleans at New Orleans.

Through more than fifteen years my interest in Lakanal had been increasing, and when I discovered the above-mentioned letters I decided to investigate his life and career. This resulted in a paper which was read before the December 5, 1938, meeting of the local chapter of Phi Beta Kappa. In 1939 this paper was published in book form as *A French Regicide in Alabama (1824-1837)*. From that little book has grown the present longer study of Lakanal.

A number of my friends in the University of Alabama have been deeply interested in the progress of my work, and I am profoundly grateful to them for their sympathy and suggestions. Professors August H. Mason, Anne Gary Pannell, and Henrietta Thompson have read all of the chapters in manuscript, and have offered searching criticism and friendly suggestion. Deans John R. McLure and Albert Burton Moore scrutinized certain chapters, and suggested improvements and corrections. Professor Paul de Launay transcribed the Lakanal letters in the Howard Memorial Library of New Orleans, and Dr. Dan Thomas, now of Rhode Island State College, transcribed a Lakanal letter in the Dreer Collection of Pennsylvania. Professor William P. Fidler has permitted me to use passages from the unpublished memoirs of William H. Robertson. In the earlier stages of the work I was assisted by my former pupil, Mrs. Virginia Cooper Sims, who made faithful copies of certain materials in the Archives of History at Montgomery, Ala., and by my colleague Professor Jerome W. Schweitzer, who assisted in locating materials in the library of the University of Alabama. Last but not least, I owe a debt of gratitude to my friend, the late Dr. Benjamin A. Wooten, Head of Physics in the University of Alabama, for acquainting me with Demopolis, his birthplace, and introducing me to a number of descendants of the French colonists.

JOHN CHARLES DAWSON

University, Alabama,
September 1, 1947.

CONTENTS

INTRODUCTION

AFTER BEING COMPARATIVELY NEGLECTED FOR SEVERAL GENERATIONS, Joseph Lakanal received many posthumous honors. These memorials of esteem were the tribute of the men of the Third French Republic to an outstanding character of the First Republic, established by the National Convention in 1792.

In numerous towns and cities of France streets and boulevards were named for Lakanal, among them Paris, Tours, Toulouse, and Montpellier. Elementary schools received his name at Périgueux, Cette, Béziers. Secondary schools were named in his honor, such as the Lycée Lakanal at Paris and the Collège Lakanal at Béziers. At least two monuments were erected to his memory, the more imposing of which was a life-sized statue in bronze at Foix in his native Ariège.[1] The ancient adage that a prophet is not without honor save in his own country was not true of Lakanal.

Lakanal belonged to a group of thinkers at the end of the eighteenth century known as Ideologists,[2] a derogatory term applied to them by First Consul Bonaparte. When, during the period of the Consulate, Bonaparte had signed a Concordat with the Pope whereby Catholicism was restored to France, and when in 1802 he had sought to put into force the terms of the Concordat, he found a stumbling-block to his plans in the membership of the Class of Moral and Political Sciences of the *Institut de France*. In this group were to be found the most influential free-thinkers of the day: Lakanal, Garat, Cabanis, Volney, Ginguené, Mercier, Naigeon, Destutt de Tracy and others who had been consistently hostile to the Church, and who had become hostile to the ambition of Bonaparte.

By a decree of January 23, 1803, the First Consul suppressed the Class of Moral and Political Sciences of the Institute, distributing

[1]In America he has been made the central character in two novels: Charles Gayarré's *Audret Dubayet* (1882), and Emma Gelders Sterne's *Some Plant Olive Trees* (1937).

[2]See Picavet, *Les Idéologues* (Paris, 1891); Gilbert Chinard, *Jefferson et les Idéologues d'après sa correspondence inédite* (Baltimore, 1925); C. H. Van Duzer, *Contribution of the Idéologues to French Revolutionary Thought* (Baltimore,

its members among the other classes in such manner as to dissociate their group. In abolishing this class Bonaparte sneeringly referred to its members as Ideologists, a name which has stuck.

The word *ideology* as applied to these men had its origin in the title of a book written by one of their number, Destutt de Tracy: *Projet d'Éléments d'Idéologie à l'Usage des Écoles centrales.*[3] While most of the men composing the group of Ideologists were neither good writers nor profound thinkers, they played an important rôle in the final days of the era of the Enlightenment. They were the spiritual descendants of the Encyclopedists, but lacked the genius of their ancestors.

The Ideologists insisted that human progress depends upon the spread of *lumières,* a word frequently used by Lakanal. This word, meaning in English "understanding, intelligence," finds its English equivalent in "lights," as when we say for instance that a man acts according to his lights. By the exercise of the intelligence or lights, not only will the sciences progress, but the moral and social sides of life will be perfected as well.

Discarding the Cartesian theory of innate ideas, the Ideologists were followers of Locke and Condillac, believing that knowledge is arrived at through the five senses, and advocating the aid of the Baconian method of experimentation and observation. They proposed the use of the natural sciences: physics, chemistry, and natural history, in the effective development of psychology, history and sociology. They formed a bridge between the eighteenth and nineteenth centuries, and were precursors in the development of the social sciences.

The favorite tool of the Ideologists was analysis *(analyse)*. Through the process of analysis a thorough understanding of a subject was to be obtained. According to Lakanal,

> analysis ought to be the universal organ of all human knowledge, and the language of all the professors. The sciences or branches of knowledge called "higher," should be put within the reach of all men. . . . Whilst political liberty and the freedom of industry and commerce would destroy the inequality of riches, analysis when applied to all sorts of studies, would remove the inequality of *lumières;* therefore, analysis is an indispensable instrument in a great democracy.

1935); Émile Caillet, "La Tradition littéraire des Idéologues," *American Philosophical Society Memoirs XIX* (Philadelphia, 1943).

[3]Thomas Jefferson in a letter to John Adams of October 14, 1816, states:

The light that it sheds penetrates everywhere so easily that, like all the fluids, it tends unceasingly to seek a level.[4]

The influence of the Ideologists is to be seen in a number of nineteenth century writers and philosophers. Stendhal applied their principles of analysis in his novels *Le Rouge et Le Noir* and *La Chartreuse de Parme* in which the various characters indulge in self-analysis. Other nineteenth century thinkers who were influenced by the Ideologists were Sainte-Beuve, Ampère, Thierry, Auguste Comte, Littré, Renan and Taine. The often quoted thought expressed by Taine: "Vice and virtue are products like sugar and vitriol," is but the application of the natural sciences to psychology and philosophy, as advocated by the Ideologists.

While Lakanal published no books of literary value or of scientific or philosophical import, and was not a scholar in the sense of contributing original discoveries to the fields of knowledge, yet he was a man who had a thirst for learning and a wide range of interest in all that pertains to learning. Later in life, while an exile in America, he wrote a letter in which he expressed the belief that in the long period which he had devoted to study he had been able to acquire practically all the positive knowledge contained in the sciences, letters and *beaux-arts*. He says also that he has incorporated this encyclopedic knowledge in a work composed by him, and entitled: *Tableau des Connaissances humaines à la Fin du XVIIIe Siècle,*[5] a work which never saw the light of publication and the manuscript of which disappeared with his death in 1845.

As a Deputy to the National Convention Lakanal played a very minor role in the stirring political events of the times, but his previous education and experience caused him to be chosen for membership in the Committee of Public Instruction, a committee to which was confided not only educational matters, but other questions having to do with the cultural side of the Revolution. It was through this committee that Lakanal made an outstanding contri-

"Destrutt de Tracy is, in my judgment, the ablest writer living on intellectual subjects, or the operations of the understanding. . . . Bonaparte, with his repeated derisions of Ideologists (squinting at this author), has by this time felt that true wisdom does not lie in mere practice without principle." Chinard, *op. cit.*, p. 241.

[4]*Exposé sommaire des Travaux de Joseph Lakanal* (Paris, 1838).

[5]*Cf.* letter from Lakanal to J. G. Birney, Appendix 2.

bution to education and culture. It was the cultural side of the Revolution that attracted the attention of Lakanal, and to trace his career through the Convention and the earlier years of the Directory is to trace the history of cultural affairs of a period in which the interest of historians has been focussed on the stirring political events, and too little attention paid to the more peaceful aspects of that great political and social upheaval.

Preceding Lakanal a succession of men had been leaders in behalf of education and culture, addressing in turn the Constituent Assembly, the Legislative Assembly, and the National Convention: Mirabeau, Talleyrand, Condorcet, Sieyès, all of them more able men than Lakanal. However, such was the rapidity of events and the turbulence of the times, that the voices of these men produced no permanent effect. It remained for Lakanal when he succeeded them in leadership to bring to happy fruition institutions of education and culture which were the forerunners of the educational and cultural institutions of nineteenth century France.

It was not to his ability as a thinker, but to his boundless energy and aggressive spirit of action that Lakanal owed his success. His background of education in preparation for a career in the Church, his experience as a teacher of grammar, rhetoric and philosophy, his knowledge of ancient history and literature, his ability as a public speaker, all combined to make him a desirable go-between or reporter from the Committee of Public Instruction to the Convention. It was the business of the reporter to get favorable action from the Convention on projects presented to that body by the Committee. In that Lakanal was an outstanding success.

The plans outlined in the various reports to the Convention were generally the result of the thinking of the committee as a whole, but often represented the views of one or more of the members which were adopted by the committee and presented to the Convention by the reporter. Thus the reporter was not necessarily the author of the report which he presented, but he was responsible for skilfully presenting and defending the report on the floor of the Convention. Upon his skill depended the success or failure of the report in its adoption by the Convention. Condorcet, for example, who had been the first president of the Committee of Public Instruction and its most influential member, was not a success as a reporter because he suffered from a defect in his voice.

On the political side, Lakanal was an austere democrat, and remained one all his life. Had he been willing to compromise, he would undoubtedly have gone far under Napoleon. His career is quite in contrast with that of Talleyrand, whose chameleon-like qualities enabled him to occupy high place in the Revolution, the Consulate, the Empire, the Restoration, and the more liberal government of Louis Philippe.

In his profound belief in democracy and public education, and in the wide variety of his knowledge and interest in the various sciences, Lakanal is to be compared with Thomas Jefferson. The two men were of the same school of thought and possessed much in common. In his passion for public education Lakanal may also be compared to Horace Mann.

1

EARLY LIFE

JOSEPH LAKANAL WAS BORN IN 1762 ON THE SIGNIFICANT DATE OF JULY 14, in the immediate neighborhood of the little city of Foix in the Department of Ariège.[1] Foix, the ancient seat of the mediaeval Counts of Foix, is located in the foothills of the Pyrenees in the extreme southern France. The greatest of the Counts of Foix was Gaston Phoebus, whose career touches at one point that of the English Black Prince. In the later sixteenth century it was for a scion of this race, the prospective son of Diane de Foix, that Montaigne wrote his celebrated essay on the education of children.

Although Ariège produced several men who gave luster to its cultural history, such as the philosopher Pierre Bayle, precursor of Voltaire, and Frédéric Soulié, the novelist and dramatist of the period of French Romanticism, the town of Foix boasts of but two monuments to the past: one, the ruins of the castle of the Counts of Foix, the other, a monument erected in 1882 to the memory of the regicide Lakanal.[2]

Lakanal came of a substantial family of the middle class whose name was spelled Lacanal. Since all of the members of the family except Joseph were sympathizers with royalty, "more royalist than the king," after his election as a Deputy to the National Convention, Lakanal changed the *c* in his name to a *k* in order to distinguish himself from the other members of his family. His elder brother Jean-Baptiste became a well known juris-consult and *procureur du roi* at Paris. Another brother, Jérôme Lacanal, became a professor of experimental physics at Paris, while a third brother, Jean, became

[1]In the hamlet of Pujet, canton of Serres.

[2]Citizens of New Orleans contributed to the expense of this imposing statue created by the artist Picault. Lakanal, while in exile in the United States, was for a time president of the College of Orleans at New Orleans. Chapter 7 of this book is devoted to his career there.

a surgeon in his native canton of Serres (Ariège). His sister Marguerite, who was the eldest child of the family, was uneducated, not being able to read or write. There was nothing unusual about this, as the education of French girls was greatly neglected before the French Revolution. It is to the credit of the leaders of the Revolution that in all their discussions and plans for education, insistence was laid on the education of girls, although no great progress was made in that direction following the revolution.

The Lacanal family was a type of the more progressive families of the region of Ariège. The father of the family, Paul Lacanal, born about 1700, had married around 1745 Marguerite Baurès, then aged 21 years. The little house in the hamlet of Pujet in which the family was started still stands. In 1747, upon the birth of Marguerite, the eldest of his five children, Paul Lacanal is qualified on the register as a *brassier*. Later he is recorded as a *forgeur*. Among the records of the notaries of Foix and in the Departmental archives are to be found traces of his loans, purchases, transactions, and registerings.[3] Sometimes in the absence of her husband, the wife acted for him, and seems to have had a good understanding of business affairs. In one of the affairs in which she acted, her husband is recorded as *négociant*. Thus there is apparently a gradual ascension in the economic and social scale of the family. The wife died in 1766 at the age of 42. The husband survived until 1777. In 1782, when it was divided and settled, the estate of Paul Lacanal was valued at 11,450 *livres*, a sum estimated at 30 to 35 thousand francs, as the franc was then valued.[4]

As has been stated, Marguerite Lacanal had no formal schooling. At fifteen years of age, when she became godmother to her brother Joseph, she was unable to sign the official record. When the mother died, Joseph was only four years of age. The father turned over the training of the child to the local *curé*, who became his uncle by adoption. This village priest, Bernard Font, prior to the Revolution had for 40 years exercised his duties as *curé* of Serres and Bénac. He was in 1791 chosen Constitutional Bishop of Ariège. He is said to have been a man of "noble and great intelligence enlightened by a tolerant and broad mind."[5]

[3]M. Gros, "Un Coin du Pays de Foix au dix-huitième Siècle," *Mèmoires de l'Académie des Sciences—de Toulouse,* 1re Série, IX, 83-91.

[4]*Loc. cit.*

[5]Marcus, *Lakanal* (Foix, 1879), p. 7 n.

Following his early training under Bernard Font, came several years in the school of the Fathers of the Christian Doctrine *(Les Doctrinaires)* at Toulouse. At eleven years of age, Lakanal entered the *Collège de l'Esquile,* (Founded in 1551 during the reign of Henry II), one of the numerous collegiate institutions attached to the University of Toulouse. At an early age he began a career of teaching in various schools of the religious order of the Doctrinaires, occupying positions as teacher of grammar, then of rhetoric, successively at Lectoure, Moissac, Treignac, Gimont, Castelnaudary and Périgueux,—all smaller cities of southern France.

Prior to becoming professor of rhetoric at Périgueux, Lakanal pursued theological studies at Paris in the Seminary of Saint-Magloire of the Doctrinaires,[6] and was ordained a priest, although he apparently refused to perform the functions of the priesthood. When at a later period he was denounced before the National Convention during the Reign of Terror, and faced the specter of the guillotine, he wrote a letter in his own defense in which he stated categorically that he had never practiced the calling of priest, and that "during the course of the most severe illness that I have ever had in my life, they made me pass one fine morning through all the sacerdotal mummeries, from what they called confirmation to the final period of human hypocrisy, the priesthood."[7] Since then,

[6]At Saint-Magloire Lakanal had as a fellow student Daunou, who was to become later his fellow Deputy in the National Convention and fellow member of the Committee of Public Instruction. They were likewise associated in the founding and organizing of the Institut de France. During the Revolution the Seminary of Saint-Magloire was converted into an institution for the deaf and dumb.

[7]The above is based on a letter from Lakanal at Bergerac to the National Convention, a letter which was read before the Convention, 13 frimaire, 1793. Following is a further extract from the letter: "It is little in life to be sick in mind and body only one day. Since then I have been execrated by all the executioners *en étole,* as many of the old as of the new style. The deputation from Ariège to which I belong will testify that they employed in vain measures of torture to make me sacrifice to falsehood. *Je n'ai jamais messé,* etc., etc. Thus, I have never been a priest, and all that concerns that horde of jongleurs is foreign to my frank and loyal soul. I beg the National Convention to regard this step on my part, less as an abjuration of the priesthood and of the stipend that the laws have attached to it, than as a justification of the principles that I have always professed." *M. J. Guillaume, Procès-Verbeau du Comité d'Instruction publique de l'Assemblée Législative* (Paris, 1889), III, 624.

In the procès-verbal of the Convention of the date of 13 frimaire an II is the following entry: "Citizen Lakanal, representative of the people in the Departments of the South-West, sets forth the success of the manufactury of arms

he complains, he has been an object of execration to all the clergy, "both old and new style."[8]

After leaving Périgueux Lakanal in 1782 was granted the degree of *docteur-ès-arts* at the University of Angers.[9] Lakanal then became for three years professor of rhetoric at Bourges, and in 1785 was appointed professor of philosophy at Moulins, where he remained until after the outbreak of the French Revolution. While still at Moulins, he voluntarily took the Civic Oath on January 30, 1791. In this same year Bernard Font, who had been a member of the National Legislative Assembly, was appointed Constitutional Bishop of Pamiers (Ariège), and his adopted nephew, Joseph Lakanal, became his seventh Episcopal Vicar.

When Lakanal returned to Ariège he was strongly under the influence of the ideas of the Revolution, and such was his enthusiasm that he soon became the head of the Revolutionary movement in this native Department. His local leadership dates from April, 1792. He became vice-president of the Popular (Revolutionary) Society of Pamiers, and was a welcome orator in the Popular Society of Saverdun. His talent and experience in the art of public speaking were to have a large influence on his subsequent career. His Revolutionary activities led to his election on September 5, 1792, as Deputy to the forthcoming National Convention, successor to the Legislative Assembly in which body he took his seat at its

founded at Bergerac, and the happy results of his philanthropic works. He abjures solemnly the title of priest, of which he had never exercised the functions." *Ibid.* II, 791.

[8]The Civil Constitution of the Clergy was adopted December 23, 1790. By this, the Clergy became employees of the State, and were required to take an oath of allegiance to the State rather than to the Pope. Those who refused to take the oath, as many did, were referred to as "old style," while those who took the oath were spoken of as "new style."

[9]In a letter (published by Henry Jouin in *Lakanal et David d'Angers* (Angers, 1902), p. 205) dated November 27, 1837, Lakanal wrote: "It was at the University of Angers that I received the *docteur-ès-lettres* to teach at La Flèche," the famous Jesuit *college* where Descartes received his education. Following the expulsion of the Jesuits in 1762, La Flèche had come under the control of the Doctrinaires. All of Lakanal's experience in teaching prior to the Revolution was in schools of the Doctrinaires. Formerly, both Bourges and Moulins had belonged to the Jesuits, but both had come under the control of the Doctrinaires. Evidently the pre-Revolutionary degree of *docteur-ès-arts* found its counterpart in the post-Revolutionary degree of *docteur-ès-lettres.*

assembling on September 21, 1792. He was one of ten Episcopal Vicars who were chosen as Deputies.

Some forty-five years later, when Lakanal was an old man, he wrote *Exposé sommaire des Travaux de Joseph Lakanal,* Paris, 1838, a sort of autobiography in which he reviewed his activities in the National Convention and the Directory. In speaking of his entrance upon the work of the National Convention, he said:

> I was aware that men of letters are, in general, illustrious paupers, and that it was necessary to sustain them, aid them. I was aware that without this support and this help, they would go to a foreign land where they would be welcomed by neighboring governments, who know that the sciences pay their benefactors with immortality. I was convinced that this emigration would contribute in a fatal manner to discredit the Revolution. It was with this firm and profound conviction that I arrived at the National Convention. There my starting point was irrevocably fixed; the very special mission that I had assigned myself.

Whether or not Lakanal was fully conscious beforehand of the role that he was to play in the National Convention, it is a fact that nearly all of his activities there were concerned with cultural matters, and that as a result of his labours on their behalf he won the gratitude and friendship of many of the men who represented the cultural side of the Revolution.

In summing up the accomplishments of the National Convention, George Burton Adams in his book *The Growth of the French Nation* says:

> In the three years of its life it had accomplished a really great and permanent work for France, of which the establishment of the Republic was not the most important. It had devoted much time to the system of public education in France, and though it was not able to complete the work of organization, it took the first steps and established important permanent institutions. It founded the *École Normale,* the *École polytechnique,* the *Conservatoire des arts et métiers,* and the Institute of France, and the national library based on the library of the king . . . and in the adoption of a uniform system of weights and measures—the metric system.

Lakanal had a hand in all the things that are mentioned above, as well as in many others of a cultural nature.

2

DEPUTY TO THE NATIONAL CONVENTION

THE FIRST GOVERNMENT OF THE FRENCH REVOLUTION WAS THE Constituent Assembly. Its task of forming a Constitution completed, the Assembly was dissolved on September 30, 1791. It was succeeded on October 1, by the Legislative Assembly, whose business it was to apply the Constitution. The pressure of events culminating in the insurrection of August 10, 1792, caused Louis XVI and the royal family to flee to the Assembly, where they were given refuge in the gallery, while the Swiss Guards sacrificed their lives in defense of the Tuileries. This event marked the end of the monarchy. Forced by the victorious mob, the Assembly suspended the king and called for the election of a Convention, as under the Constitution no constitutional changes could be made by the Assembly itself. The king was transferred from his refuge in the Assembly to prison in the Temple.

Elections were held, and 749 Deputies were chosen to represent the various departments of the country in a National Convention, which met on September 21, 1792.

Scarcely had the Deputies to the National Convention taken their seats when the actor-Deputy, Collot d'Herbois made a motion to abolish royalty. This motion was carried, a Republic was proclaimed, and the decision was made that henceforth time should be reckoned from September 22, 1792, the beginning of the Year.[1]

Of the 749 Deputies to the National Convention, 263 had had

[1]The first session of the Convention was held on the afternoon of September 20, when the Deputies met in executive session. 371 Deputies assembled in a room of the Tuileries, and Pétion, Mayor of Paris, was unanimously chosen president. The next day the Convention met in open session in the *Manège* or Riding Academy, which remained the regular place of meeting until later when the sittings were transferred to the Tuileries.

previous legislative experience; 186 had belonged to the recent Legislative Assembly, and 77 to the prior Constituent Assembly. It was but natural that men of experience and who were well known should become the leaders of the Convention. Lakanal was unknown and without previous experience. Coming from the south of France, his sympathies would have allied him with the Girondists, so called because their leaders came from the Department of La Gironde of which Bordeaux was the capital. The incapacity, however, of the Girondists, and indeed of the majority of the delegates, for vigorous action led to the gradual supremacy of an aggressive minority led by the Montagnards (so called from the high seats occupied by them in the Convention Hall), among whose leaders professional education and philosophical sympathies had not destroyed political energy.

Although a man of education and an ex-professor of philosophy, Lakanal was not a dreamer, but above all a man of action; and he soon therefore became identified with the Montagnards, although he remained more moderate than the Montagnards in proportion as they became more fanatical. He had arrived in Paris with definite and decided convictions towards freedom and equality. He was moreover filled with a spirit of hatred for royalty, or more properly speaking, for the Bourbon dynasty, the only royalty he knew. He therefore entered wholeheartedly into the task of transforming France from a monarchy to a republic. He aspired to become a member of the Committee of Public Instruction which was appointed by the Convention on October 2, 1792, and to whose hands were to be committed all educational and cultural matters which might be presented to the Convention. Being unknown and inexperienced in governmental matters, it was but natural that he should have been overlooked at the moment of the forming of the committee only two weeks after the opening of the Convention.

More than once, critics have gloated over the fact that Lakanal was not a member of the original committee, and have used it to show that he was therefore of but little importance. To base an opinion of Lakanal's relative importance on the fact that he was not one of the original members of the Committee of Public Instruction is manifestly unfair, and it is to his credit that he received recognition for his interest in education as early as January, 1793, when he was made a member of the Committee. From that time on, although the membership of the Committee underwent frequent changes, Lakanal was repeatedly reelected to membership, and it is not certain that he did not retain his membership even during his long absence of ten months from Paris as a *représentant en mission* in southwestern France.

TRIAL OF THE KING

One of the earliest activities of Lakanal in the Convention was his participation in the debate as to whether Louis XVI could be tried constitutionally.

At the beginning of the National Convention when the first Republic had been established, there had arisen the question as to what to do with the king. In the end, the pressure of public opinion forced the Convention to bring him to trial. But prior to the actual trial there was a long controversy over the legal aspect of the case. This debate began on November 13, when a special commission of 22 members, previously appointed to examine the case, appeared at the bar of the Convention and put before that body the question: "Can Louis XVI be tried?" The most decisive argument in its influence against the king was delivered by Robespierre, who was then rising into power. Lakanal participated in the debate as to whether the king could be tried constitutionally, and his contribution to the argument was printed by order of the National Convention under the title: *Opinion du Citoyen Lakanal, Député du Départment de l'Ariège à la Convention nationale, sur la question de savoir: Si Louis XVI peut être jugé?* In this address of more than 2,000 words, Lakanal manifests himself as a disciple of Rousseau, and follows the taste of the times in drawing on antiquity for examples.

Lakanal begins his argument with the simple statement: "Louis XVI is *justiciable,* that is, he is subject to trial." He then proceeds to prove by the articles of the Constitution that to try the king is perfectly legal. He said:

I open the constitutional charter: according to Article 6 of the chapter on royalty, if the king directs hostile forces against the nation, he is deemed to have abdicated the crown. Having stated this, I will observe that on November 15, 1791, Louis the Last, furnished considerable sums to the traitor Bouillé for the formation of the counter-revolutionary camp of Montmédy. . . . November 15, 1791, Louis the Last directed hostile forces against the nation; right then he is deemed to have abdicated according to the textual expressions of the Constitution itself. . . . I read Article 8 of the same chapter on Royalty: after express or legal abdication, the king shall be in the class of citizens, and he can be tried like them for acts posterior to his abdication; therefore, since November 15, 1791, Louis the Traitor, can be tried like other citizens. . . . It is principally since the period of his legal abdication that he has summoned against us foreign war; that he has consumed the money of the Republic in feeding the brigands armed against her; that he has fomented intèrnal war, and has caused to be shed in torrents the blood of good citizens. . ."

Then follows a discussion of the inviolability of royalty, concluding:

Representatives, if you decree that Louis the Traitor is not justiciable, you will decree that the nations do not have the right to judge their mandataries; but since the peoples existed before the kings, the sovereignty of kings came into existence only after that of the peoples. And let no one tell us that by the social contract a nation ever despoils itself of the right to summon before its tribunal guilty mandataries. I will reply with the Genevan philosopher that such a contract would be illusory and nil . . . there remains then the unlimited sovereignty of the peoples over the kings.

Then Lakanal raises the question of whether or not it is to the national interest to punish the king. He concludes that it is, and exclaims:

Strike down the tyrant. If he should escape punishment, he would flee like the Parthians, while piercing your hearts; and so long as he should breathe, you would have to combat Tarquin and Italy.

To those who would excuse Louis because of certain good actions of his youth, he replies:

Who is the scoundrel whose life has been but one long crime? Nature has spared humanity the spectacle of a monster who marked his passage on earth with nothing but crimes. Greater than Louis XVI has ever been was that emperor of Rome, who out of a desire to save an unfortunate wretch, expressed the wish that he had never learned to write. Thus after having assassinated his mother Agrippina, his wife Octavia; after having caused Burrhus and Seneca to perish, Nero would still have found flatterers in the Convention of France. . . . Legislators, outraged Justice and Reason look forward to Louis on the wheel. How long will they have to groan over your culpable delays?

When finally on December 11, 1792, the king was brought to trial, three questions were put to the Convention: 1. Is Louis guilty of conspiracy? 2. Shall sentènce be referred to the people? 3. What shall be the penalty if convicted? After these questions had been decided by roll call, (adversely to the king) and the death penalty had been decreed, a fourth question arose as to whether the death sentence should not be delayed or suspended. This was also decided adversely to the king. On all these questions, Lakanal voted against the king.[2] When it came to a vote on the second question which concerned the referring of the sentence to the people in their primary assemblies throughout France, Lakanal mounted the tribune and declaimed: "If the traitor Bouillé, if the rascal Lafayette and his intriguing accomplices[3] were voting on this question, they would say *yes*. As I have nothing in common with such people, I say *no*."

The whole of the night of January 16-17, 1793, was devoted to the vote by roll call on the penalty to be exacted of the king. When it came Lakanal's turn to vote, he placed his hand over his heart and cried: "A true republican speaks little. The motives for my decision are *there!* I vote for *death!*" The theatrical quality exhibited by Lakanal on this occasion is but the outward evidence of the deep hatred which he cherished for royalty. He was an extreme republican. In his personal life he was guided by the simple and austere principles of republicanism, or as we would say to-day, democracy. His genuine hatred for royalty led him more than once to advocate extreme measures towards them, and to his dying day he was ever ready to defend his course with regard to Louis XVI. In a notebook belonging to him, and brought to light many years after his death, Lakanal records his judgment of the trial and condemnation of Louis XVI:

> Louis XVI appeared at the bar and was condemned to death. It was perfectly in order that this condemnation was regarded as a colossal crime by the men of Coblenz and Worms, by these same *Émigrés* who had erected the scaffold of their king.[4] But History, which expects no indemnity as a reward for its tears and its expirations, impartial History will not brand the 460 jurors who voted for death. This large number of voters guarantees the conscience of all. Three men seated on a platform, impelled by the instinct for blood, can cause the head of an accused to fall with passion; but it can never be shown that 460

[2]The Deputies from Ariège, six in number, voted unanimously against the king on all four questions. In the order of their election to the Convention, Lakanal stood fifth. Their names in the order in which they were called upon to vote are as follows: Clauzel, Éxpert, Vadier, Cammartin, Lakanal, Gaston.

[3]Note the lines of a then current and popular parody of some verses of the *Marseillaise:*

> "Frappez ces monstres sanguinaires,
> Ces vils complices de Motié"

The reference Motié is to Lafayette, whose family name was *Du Motier.*

[4]Many French nobles, refugees from the French Revolution, congregated in Coblenz and Worms.

judges were found, elected from all over France, perfectly united in this community of sanguinary interests. This tigerish appetite in the entrails of Man is a phenomenon of organization that can be supposed to exist in a few rare individuals, and never in the masses. These paltry appraisers of great events, men ignorant of the Revolutionists and of their epoch, have thought to reconcile by attributing to *Fear* the vote of the majority. . . . *Fear* and the *Convention!* Never shall these two words be associated.[5]

The Deputies who voted for the death of the king came to be known as regicides, and those who were still living after Waterloo were forced to flee for their lives to foreign soil. As a result of his participation in the condemnation of Louis XVI, Lakanal was destined to spend twenty-two years of exile in the United States.

LAKANAL AND PUBLIC EDUCATION

The Committee of Public Instruction which had been created on October 2, 1793, began the presentation of a report to the Convention on October 20 which concerned the establishing of an elementary school system based upon a plan which had been previously drawn up by Condorcet. Discussions on the subject occurred from time to time in the Convention until the trial of the King, which began December 12, caused other matters to be temporarily shelved. On October 22 Lakanal took the floor of the Convention on behalf of a system of education suited to the needs of the Republic,[6] urging a

national education suitable to the shaping of free men, in place of the present education which is fit only for Capuchin monks; for after having consumed the best years of life in murdering Greek and Latin we complete this undigested education by a course of philosophy similar to that which Molière gives to his *Bourgeois Gentilhomme*.[7]

[5]Marcus, *Lakanal,* p. 131.

[6]Henri Labroue, *La Mission du Conventionnel dans la Dordogne en l'an II (Octobre 1793 - Août 1794),* (Paris, c. 1912).

[7]The *Moniteur,* the official daily newspaper of the times, gives no mention to Lakanal prior to April, 1793, except to record his vote on the various questions concerned with the trial of the King. The *Procès-verbaux du Comité d'Instruction publique de la Convention Nationale,* ed. M. J. Guillaume, (Paris, 1891-1907), I, 33, mentions les Citoyens Lakanal et Massieu as reporters of a work on public education which had been presented to the Committee of Public Instruction by Chrétien-Jacques Schreiber; and again p. 42, n. 1, mentions Lakanal as reporter of a request sent for help by the *École de Ligncourt.* The name of Lakanal thus appears in connection with the work of the Committee of Public Instruction as early as the first week of November, 1792, although he did not become a member of the Committee until January, 1793.

In December, 1792, Lakanal wrote a "Discourse on National Education" which he neither delivered before the Convention nor put into printed form. An interruption in the discussion on education because of other matters which claimed the attention of the Convention prevented Lakanal from appearing before that body. Some months later, on June 4, 1793, the Convention passed a decree permitting the Deputies to publish addresses technically known as "Opinions" at the expense of the nation, but for some reason Lakanal did not take advantage of this opportunity of publishing his Discourse. The manuscript was preserved, however, and was published in the early twentieth century.[8]

This Discourse is valuable as showing Lakanal's views, some of which at least were utilized by him later in presenting plans for education to the Convention. Before going, however, into Lakanal's thought with regard to education, it will be necessary to review the work of his predecessors.

THE REVOLUTION IN EDUCATION

The revolution in education in France preceded the political revolution by twenty-seven years. The century-long struggle between the Parlements of France and the Jesuits culminated in 1762 with the expulsion of the latter. This struggle had its beginning in the middle of the seventeenth century in the contest which arose between the Jesuits and the Jansenists of Port Royal. The Jesuits were worsted by the pen of Blaise Pascal who came to the defense of his friends of Port Royal, and who in his eighteen *Lettres Provinciales* exposed the Jesuits with such devastating logic, wit, and clarity that they never recovered from the blow. The opposition to the Jesuits continued, and was led throughout the eighteenth century by the Parlements until the Jesuits were finally driven out of France.[9]

The Jesuits had control of about one hundred schools in France,

[8] *Ibid.*, v, 654-662.

[9] Almost simultaneous with the expulsion of the Jesuits came the publication of Jean-Jacques Rousseau's *Émile,* perhaps the most revolutionary book on education ever written.

and it became incumbent on the Parlements to dispose of these schools and to institute reforms in education. The most distinguished of the educational reformers in the period between 1762 and 1789, the beginning of the Revolution, were the Parlementaires La Chalotais, Guyton de Morveaux, and the President, Rolland. In 1763 La Chalotais published his *Essay* on national education or *Plan of Studies for the Youth;* Guyton de Morveaux was the author of a *Memoir on Public Education,* and Rolland's work was published in 1783 under the title of *Collection of Several Works of President Rolland.* While little was actually accomplished in the way of practical reform, the theories set forth by these men had considerable currency and formed a background for the educational theorists of the Revolution. Among the changes suggested by them were the curtailment of Greek and Latin with a greater emphasis on the study of French, the national language, the lessening of purely literary studies and the increasing of the studies in the sciences, the secularization of the teaching of morals, increasing number of lay-teachers (especially fathers), and provision for the education of girls and young women.[10]

On August 5, 1791, the Constitution had been presented to the Constituent Assembly for ratification, and with the gathering of the National Legislative Assembly on October 1, 1791, France began to live under its new Constitution. Immediately after the Declaration of the Rights of the Man and of the Citizen, the new Constitution contained the following article: "There shall be erected and organized a *public instruction* common to all the citizens, *free* with respect to the parts of education indispensable for all men, and the establishments of which shall be distributed gradually, in a relation combined with the division of the kingdom."

[10]During the Revolution the spirit of nationalism became so strong and along with it the insistence on the use of the national language that some of the Revolutionists became extremely hostile to local patois and dialects. In January, 1794, Barère in a speech before the Convention said: "We must popularize the language, destroy the aristocracy of diction. We have revolutionized government, manners, thought: let us revolutionize the language also. Federalism and Superstition speak *bas-Breton;* the Emigration and hatred of the Republic speak German; the Counter-revolution speaks Italian, and Fanaticism speaks Basque. Let us break up these instruments of error.

MIRABEAU

During the period of the Legislative Assembly the necessity of carrying out the provisions of the Constitution with regard to public instruction, produced three outstanding theorists of education. The earliest of these was the Comte de Mirabeau, the foremost orator of the Revolution whose theories and plans were not so important in themselves as that they were the views of one of the most remarkable men of the Revolution.

Mirabeau pleaded for the most complete liberty of learning and teaching. "Your sole object is to render to Man the use of all his faculties, to make him enjoy all his rights, to create public life from all the individual lives freely developed, and the general will from all the private wills." Contrary to the popular thought of the times, Mirabeau set himself in opposition to a national system of education, desiring only the loose tie of common interest that would naturally exist among the guardians and propagators of useful knowledge. For higher education, he proposed the establishment of a single *lycée national,* "which should procure for the élite of French youth the means for finishing their education." In such a school Mirabeau would have as subjects of instruction: method and grammar, public economy, moral philosophy, general universal history, geometry and algebra, mechanics, general physics, natural history, chemistry, experimental physics, physiology; Hebrew, Greek, Latin, Italian, Spanish, English, German. This vast expansion of subjects over the restricted literary curriculum of the pre-Revolutionary *collèges* dominated by the study of Latin, is of itself evidence of the revolution in education that had taken place in France, in theory at least, since the expulsion of the Jesuits in 1762.

"The chair of methods," says Mirabeau, "shall be the basis of the teaching of the *lycée national.*" Thus we see the way paved for the experiment of the Normal School of the Year III (1795). Far from being hostile to the study of classical letters, Mirabeau says "I am far from wishing to proscribe the study of the dead languages; it is desirable, on the contrary, that they be encouraged. I would wish especially that we could cause to rise again from its ashes this beautiful Greek language whose mechanism is so perfectly analytical, and whose harmonies invoke all the beauties of style. In order to appreciate well his own language, one must compare it with another, and it is the best ones that must be taken as objects of comparison."

Mirabeau had died on April 2, 1791. The Constituent Assembly had just ended its session when Dr. Cabanis, an influential physician and friend of Mirabeau, published the *Work on Public Education, found in the Papers of Mirabeau the Elder*. The book contained four essays on education: 1. "On Public Instruction, or on the Organization of the Teaching Body;" 2. "On Public Anniversaries, Civil and Military;" 3. "On the establishment of a Lycée national;" 4. "On the Education of the Heir Presumptive to the Crown." It has been established by modern scholarship that these essays were not actually written by Mirabeau, but were prepared by a ghost writer, perhaps by Cabanis himself, at the instigation of Mirabeau, who proposed to present them to the Assembly. At the time of their publication, however, they were thought to be from the pen of Mirabeau, and whatever influence they may have exerted on educational thought during the hectic period of the Revolution is to be attributed to the supposed connection with his outstanding name.

TALLEYRAND

The second great theorist of education in the Revolution was Talleyrand-Périgord, *ci-devant* Bishop of Autun. "Time marched so fast then," says Gabriel Compayré in his history of education in France,

> events were so dominating that neither the Constituent Assembly nor the Legislative Assembly could organize what they had conceived. Their work, wholly theoretical, is embodied in the remarkable reports of Talleyrand and Condorect, two men however who have scarcely any resemblance to each other: The one, the most versatile and the most supple of politicians, who died at peace with the government, after having exhausted all the honors and served all causes; the other, the most inflexible of characters, faithful to himself even upon the scaffold. And yet their pedagogical works are animated by almost the same spirit. The fact is that the breath of the Revolution, stronger than all the individual tendencies, swept all minds and hearts along in a same movement. . . In 1791, when Talleyrand presented his report to the Constituent Assembly, he was entirely won over to the new ideas, and nothing foreboded that the ex-Bishop of Autun, at that time one of the most ardent members of the Revolutionary majority, would become the complacent minister of all the governments which succeeded each other in France during half a century.

As far as any direct influence on educational legislation was concerned, Talleyrand failed to receive a favorable hearing largely through a bit of bad luck in the timing of his project, and in drawing up too long a report containing no fewer than 208 articles. In September, 1791, the Constituent Assembly was looking forward to adjournment, and its final days were not unlike the haste and pressure of the last few days of a session of the American Congress. Although, in order to get a hearing, Talleyrand reduced his project to 35 articles, which were taken under deliberation on September 25, just a few days before the close of the Assembly, the report was considered by the members of that body as of too great importance to be usefully examined at the end of the session. In the words of one of the members, Buzot, who took the floor: "When you do not have time to do well, the best thing is to do nothing at all." In spite of vigorous insistence on the part of Talleyrand, the Assembly declined to act on the report, and bequeathed it to the following Assembly. On September 30, the Constituent Assembly ceased to exist, but before adjourning had ordered Talleyrand's report to be printed and distributed. The succeeding Legislative Assembly showed little interest in the report, with the result that it never had the honor of a detailed discussion.

Talleyrand, in arguing the urgency of the educational situation on the floor of the Assembly, had insisted that that body should at least vote on a principle of law with regard to education. "You will have to decide," said he, "not the details of instruction of primary schools, but their existence." "The needs are infinitely pressing: for everywhere the Universities have suspended their operations: The *Collèges* are insubordinate, without professors, without pupils. Things must be regulated before the month of October."[11] He not only reviews the changes that have taken place in the social state, but insists on the defects of the old education. Nothing of great consequence had been done since 1762 in spite of a great deal of discussion and theorizing. Talleyrand called attention particularly to what he considered four essential vices in the old system: 1. Lack of instruction for the great majority of citizens; 2. Instruction such as it was was insufficient, improperly directed, and spoiled by all sorts of prejudices and deplorable opinions; 3. There was no re-

[11]The time for the opening of the schools.

lation, even opposition, between what a child learned in school and what he had to do when he had reached man's estate; 4. Education still followed the antiquated tendency toward a monastic spirit suited to producing men for the cloister rather than for active life.

"The new Constitution," says Compayré, "would have remained sterile, would have become a dead letter, if an appropriate education had not come to vivify it, by making it pass, so to speak, into the blood stream of the nation."

In addressing himself to the makers of the Constitution, Talleyrand calls attention to the fact that they have separated the general will, or the power reserved to the king. But this general will must be righteous, and in order to be righteous, it must be enlightened and instructed. After having given power to the people, you owe it to them to teach them wisdom. Education is the necessary counterpoise of liberty. The law, which is to be henceforth the work of the people, should not be at the mercy of the opinions of an ignorant multitude. He insists that a sense of reality be created for the two fundamental ideas of the Revolution,—Liberty and Equality.

We have seen how in America some years ago the doctrine of equality of opportunity tended to drift into the idea of equality of ability. Critics of education pointed out that our system of education was inclined to become adapted to the common level of intelligence, thus leaving too much out of account the training of those of superior mind. The problem of educating the child of superior mind has occupied the attention of many serious educators.

Talleyrand respects and reverences the superior mind, which is essential for the good of all. Although there are to be no more ignorant citizens, is that any reason why there should be no more geniuses? Let us instruct the people, he says, in order to weaken, but not wipe out the inevitable inequalities. Educate the people in order that they may preserve and increase their liberty as well as regulate it.

Education is due to all, says Talleyrand. Therefore, there must be schools in every part of the kingdom—in the smallest villages as well as in the larger cities. Teaching should be the privilege of all: no order or association shall have exclusive privilege of teaching.

Education must not only be universally distributed, but must be universal in its object. Everything that can be taught must be provided for: Schools for every branch of knowledge; although nobody can succeed in knowing every thing, every subject of learning must be provided for.

Talleyrand's plan provides four different grades of instruction, and the same care will be taken in organizing higher education as in establishing primary and secondary schools. His four steps of instruction called for (1) a primary school for each canton, thus assuring universality of opportunity for the essentials of education, (2)a secondary school for each district or arrondissement, to be located in the chief town of the district, (3) special schools scattered over the kingdom in the principal capitals of Departments for the purpose of preparing young men for the divers professions, religion, law, medicine, military art), (4) a national institute at Paris in which would be concentrated all the resources of higher education. This would be the finishing school for young men destined to devote their lives to letters, the sciences, and the arts. This suggestion was the germ from which developed later the *Institut de France,* an organization that has had a profound influence on the intellectual life of France.[12].

Elementary education shall be provided free of cost to the pupil, but not secondary and higher education. Boys of exceptional intelligence who lack the necessary funds shall be aided through the creation of national scholarships.

In the middle ages the outstanding goal of education had been the preparation of the soul for the life hereafter. In the seventeenth century, the ideal became the accurate mind joined to uprightness of heart. During the Revolution, the ideal became the shaping of the citizen for life in and participation in a democracy. According to the Revolutionists, Man is a political animal, brought into the world in order to know, to love, and to serve the Constitution. Since between the years 1791 and 1804 France was blessed with six constitutions, the question naturally arises: which Constitution?

[12]Talleyrand's suggestion foreshadows the modern graduate school. The *Institut de France* is a body composed of five learned societies, and does not give courses.

To Talleyrand the Declaration of the Rights of Man becomes the catechism of childhood. To know, to love, to perfect the Constitution are the three essentials; a fourth essential, but subsidiary to the other three, is the study of ethics and morals.

CONDORCET

The foremost educational theorist of the French Revolution was Condorcet, the great philosopher and idealist, who became a victim of the Reign of Terror. He was not guillotined, but was a fugitive, and finally died either from starvation or from poison self-administered. In Condorcet comes to a culminating point the doctrine of progress and perfectability which had grown into a veritable religion in eighteenth century France. He was a true liberal, and shared the enthusiasm and optimism of the earlier Revolutionaries.

The Legislative Assembly, feeling the necessity of rapid educational reform, charged Condorcet with the task of presenting a new report. The Constituent Assembly had no committee whose task was to deal specifically with education, but educational matters were handled under the direction of four different committees. With the ushering in of the Legislative Assembly, a separate Committee of Public Instruction was formed, and held its first sitting on October 30, 1791. Condorcet was its first president. Other members of the original Committee who will continue as members along with Condorcet into the period of the National Convention are Lacépède, the naturalist, who ultimately became Grand Master of the University under Napoleon during the Hundred Days; Arbogast, who had been *Recteur* of the University of Strasbourg; Romme, author of the Republican Calendar; Roux-Fazillac, who had fought in the American Revolution; Prieur, who, as a regicide, died in exile; De Bry, who became a Baron of the Empire; Fauchet, who died on the guillotine; and Audrein, who became Constitutional Bishop ot Finistère, and who while on a pastoral round of his diocese was executed as a regicide by a band of Chouans.

Condorcet made his report in the name of the Committee of Public Instruction on April 20 and 21, 1792. He was well qualified for the task, for he had spent the earlier years of the Revolution in preparing for publication in the *Bibliothèque de l'homme publique* five monographs on education: "Nature and Object of Public Instruction," "General Instruction for Children," "General Instruction for Men," "Instruction relative to the Professions," "Instruction relative to the Sciences." From these monographs he drew materials for his report. Unfortunately, like Talleyrand before him, his report was ill-timed, for the attention of the Legislative Assembly was at that moment absorbed in the question of war with Austria.

The reading of Condorcet's report was performed under very dramatic circumstances. On the morning of April 19, the president of the National Assembly had read from the floor, the following note which he had just received from the king:

"I request you, Mr. President, to say to the National Assembly that I expect to come there tomorrow at half past twelve.

Signed: LOUIS
Countersigned: DUMOURIEZ."[13]

The next day, April 20, the Assembly began its session at the usual hour, noon. Although it was known that the king was coming, and that his visit portended nothing less than a declaration of war, the Assembly proceeded with the regular order of the day pending the king's arrival. The report of the Committee of Public Instruction was called for, and Condorcet mounted the rostrum and began the reading of his report. At twelve-thirty, the arrival of the king interrupted the report. Louis XVI, accompanied by his ministers, sat to the left of the president of the Assembly. Dumouriez, minister for foreign affairs, read in the name of the king a report concluding with a declaration of war against Austria. At the evening session the Assembly voted almost unanimously for the declaration of war. Saturday morning, April 21, the Assembly began its session by charging the Committee of Public Instruction with the task of presenting to it the form of an address to the French people and to the army on the subject of the declaration of war which had been voted the evening before. Following this, Condorcet was invited to resume the reading of his report. The

[13]*Procès-verbaux du Comité d'Instruction publique de l'Assemblée Législative* (Paris, 1891-1907) ed. M. J. Guillaume, p. 249.

Assembly voted that the report should be printed, and put off the discussion of it.

In his report, Condorcet does not say a great deal that had not already been suggested by others. But the persuasive manner and prestige of its author gave it greater authority than any projects that had preceded it. In the preamble to his plan, Condorcet stresses the *rights* of Man in the State. Prior to the Revolution, education had stressed his *duties*. The plan proper calls for five steps of instruction: (1) Primary schools, (2) Secondary schools, (3) Institutes, (4) Lycées, (5) A National Society. The Institutes would correspond roughly to our junior colleges, and the Lycées to our senior colleges. The suggestion of an over-all national Society of Learning, which had already been made by Talleyrand, resulted during the Directory in the founding of the French Institute created by law at the instance of Daunou, but organized under the supervision of Lakanal.

LAKANAL'S "OPINION"

In his *Discourse on National Education* Lakanal followed the fashion of the moment in preparing what was technically called an "Opinion." His was but one of many such "Opinions," but whereas a number of his colleagues had the opportunity of delivering their discourses on the floor of the Convention, the trial of Louis XVI, which began on December 11, 1792, caused an interruption in the debate on education and prevented Lakanal from appearing before that body. His "Opinion," however, is of great importance in the study of Lakanal's views on education, for it contains the ideas that he was to incorporate later in his projects for education.

The Committee of Public Instruction had been formed within a fortnight of the assembling of the Convention, but it was not until the following December 1792, that the Committee presented its first report to the assembled Deputies. At that time, Lanthenas presented a report on the organization of primary schools, Arbogast reported on the composition of elementary text books, and Romme on public education as a whole. Lakanal was not yet a member of the Committee, but was elected to it in the next month, January, 1793.

Lanthenas was a physician. When the Girondists on May 31, 1793, were proscribed by the Montagnards, he was saved by Marat, who pleaded his cause: "Tout le monde sait que le docteur Lanthemas (*sic*) est un pauvre d'esprit." Isadore Geoffroy Saint-Hilaire, who was a personal friend of Lakanal and his earliest biographer, tells a similar story of Lakanal: "Let this name be wiped out," said Marat; "Lakanal thinks only of the sciences; he does not conspire." Saint-Hilaire then adds: "Justice must be rendered to all." Marat, in saving Lakanal, could not help knowing that he was saving one of his most pronounced adversaries. Six weeks before, in the permanent sitting of the 13 and 14 of April, Lakanal had voiced one of those sayings which are not to be forgotten: "I who would find the truth beautiful, in the mouth even of Marat!"[14]

Following the overthrow of Robespierre, Thermidor, 1794, Lakanal was the object of attacks of denunciation. In self-defense he published a placard entitled: Un mot de Lakanal, représentant du peuple, à quelques folliculaires qui ne sont pas avares de mots. This broadside, published by Guillaume, Vol. VI, p. 513, contains, among other things: "When I was compelled to vote on political matters, I attacked tyranny *en face*. Marat was the God of the Mountain, when I said not far from him on a roll call: 'I who would find the truth beautiful in the mouth even of Marat. . .' "

In his *Discourse on National Education* Lakanal confined himself almost exclusively to stating and amplifying his objections to various features of the reports which had been presented to the Convention by members of the Committee of Public Instruction and others. From these objections it is possible to gain some idea of Lakanal's views on education.

Condorcet had mapped out a complete hierarchy of education, the most complete ever suggested, which the Committee of Public Instruction had adopted as the basis of its reports. Lakanal feared that such a powerful corporation would prove disquieting to "the men jealous of the liberty which they have just conquered." Such

[14]Isidore Geoffroy Saint-Hilaire, *Lakanal, sa Vie, ses Travaux à la Convention et au Conseil des cinq Cents.* (Paris, 1849).

an organization of education would not be in the public interest, for it would not furnish the fusion, the homogeneity of elements necessary to weld a Republic *"une et indivisible,"* a judgment shared by many others. There is danger, suggests Lakanal,

> that this *jurande de beaux esprits* would one day stifle the national interest through the solid front that such a close corporation of educated men would present. It is not at all difficult to forsee that it will soon crush, by the weight of its superiority and pride, the outsiders who do not belong to it. There are also tyrant's in the Republic of Letters. France has not struck down her tyrants in order to raise up new ones.
>
> A second objection to the plans which have been proposed is the method of dissemination of schools over the surface of the Republic. The plan to distribute a few lycées among favored Departments is undemocratic. Each Department should have a complete system of education paralleling its political system and identical with the system of every other Department. Unless this equality of opportunity is preserved, only the citizens favored by fortune will be able to bear the expense of an education in which the poorer class will not be able to participate. National education should be cast into the mold of the constitution of the body politic in order to give young citizens the habits and practices of liberty.

A Deputy, Durand-Maillane, who had taken the floor of the Convention against the whole project of the Committee of Public Instruction, among other objections had raised the question of the teaching of the sciences. He stated that perhaps

> We are so corrupt because we know too much . . . the French people in order to be happy, have need of the sciences only in so far as is necessary to arrive at virtue. . . . The Republic's only business is to make citizens virtuous. . . . Never was Rome more happy or virtuous than when it was only agricultural.

What is meant by *virtue?* The word is a jewel of many facets, and in the eighteenth century acquired many shades of meaning. The meaning here seems to be the right-minded citizens interested in the common weal.

To the suggestion of removing from national education the study of the sciences and the arts, Lakanal retorts in his Discourse: "These apostles of barbarism fail to recognize that letters, far from being useless, cause slavery to be hated because it is degrading. Educated men do not bow easily before tyranny. If the fine arts are abandoned, fanaticism will soon raise again its altars, and servitude will cover the earth." There is a lesson in this for us of the present day (1945) when the liberal arts are in a struggle for survival against the rising tide of technology.

As early as 1763, La Chalotais had advocated the preparation of elementary books suited to the learning of branches of desirable and expanding knowledge.[15] This idea was taken up in turn by educational theorists. Lakanal advocates the composition of elementary books. However, he does not agree with the Committee on the placing of books in the hands of the pupils; the only elements that can be useful to them are their notebooks drawn up according to the oral instruction of the teacher. Through their mistakes they will acquire knowledge, just as by falling they have learned to walk. Lakanal fears that books will lead the pupil to learn only by heart, and reinforces his argument by quoting Montaigne: "To know by heart is not to know . . . 'Tis a sign of crudity to glut one's self with viands just as they have been swallowed; the stomach has not performed its operations if it does not change the form of that which has been given it to digest." Also, Lakanal does not think it at all necessary that elementary books destined for the higher grades of education shall be composed only by well-known men. "There are also charlatans in the Republic of Letters;" let the composition of elementary books be open to a general competition. Six months later, June 13, 1793, acting on a report read by Lakanal, the Convention decreed a competitive contest for the writing of elementary books. In his report Lakanal said:

> Citizens, when you shall have adopted the popular Constitution which has just been presented to you, (1) the name of Frenchman will be the most beautiful that can be borne on the earth.[16] If you then organize public instruction, the Convention will be able to appear again with glory before the bar of posterity. The columns which should support the edifice of education are the elementary books. It is important then to hasten their composition; without this measure, the citizens whose purpose it is to enter the national system of education will not be able to classify their ideas and acquire lucid notions concerning the various branches of instruction, for it is better that the heads of our young fellow-citizens remain virgin than to suffer that they be spoiled by empty or mendacious teachings which will cause them to lose forever the bent of truth.[17]

[15]Henry Thomas Buckle, the historian of civilization, says that more new truths concerning the external world were discovered in France during the latter half of the eighteenth century than during all the preceding periods put together. (*History of Civilization in England.* New York, 1859-66; 1874).

[16]The new Constitution was adopted June 24, 1793. Owing to the turbulence of the times it was suspended on October 10, and the government of France passed directly into the hands of the Convention, or rather into the power of the sinister Committee of Public Safety. It was opposition to the Constitution which had brought about the doom of Condorcet.

[17]Émile Darnaud, *Lakanal, notice biographique.* (Paris, 1874). The latter part of the paragraph quoted was taken substantially by Lakanal from his *Discourse.*

Two years later, the composition of the books and the awards of the jury had been made, at which time Lakanal presented a detailed report on the contest.

Returning to the subject of Lakanal's objections, he says that to have a regular plan of education and to have good elementary books to insure its success are not enough. The important thing is the teacher. In order to maintain a supply of the right sort of teachers the calling must be made attractive to men of character, ability, and ambition. There are three ways in which this goal may be attained: honors, financial reward, and hope of advancement.

Reward the teacher with an external decoration which he may wear in the exercise of his duties, and in national ceremonies. Let this decoration consist of an iron medal, emblem of the rigidity of Republican *mores*. Here we find in germ the Napoleonic decoration of the Palms with its two grades: *Officier d'Académie* and *Officier de l'Instruction Publique*. This honor, inaugurated by Napoleon in 1808, continued to be awarded throughout the nineteenth and twentieth centuries until the fall of France in 1940.

Lakanal argued also that the salaries of teachers should be sufficient to keep them above want. If sufficient remuneration is lacking, teaching positions will be sought only by the mediocre, who have no hope of success in any other career.

The status of primary teacher should be only temporary, and the primary field should be a testing ground where the merit and character of teachers can be observed, and from which selections may be made for the higher grades of teaching, holding out hope of ultimate employment at the top. This advancement should have the endorsement of popular approval. Teachers wishing to meet public approval in order to rise will be careful not to commit acts that will draw down upon them the disapproval of their fellow citizens.

Another form of encouragement to teachers would be to send those who had distinguished themselves, with expenses paid, to foreign lands on tours of study and observation; an idea which was later reincorporated in the organic law governing the founding of the French Institute. By studying the methods of education in distant lands, teachers would be able to illuminate the path of the legislator. Not only would such journeys profit France, but they would also be a boon to the inhabitants of the countries visited. Wherever the teachers went they would spread the gospel of liberty. The teacher-pilgrim, says Lakanal, "would spread the sacred maxims of liberty, equality and fraternity under the pines of the North, and under the palm trees of Asia. He would also visit our fellow citizens in these foreign countries, and through his influence the bonds of brotherhood would be strengthened."

Today, we are thoroughly familiar with the missionary zeal of the adherents of certain political ideologies. It was just a similar zeal on the part of the French Revolutionists for spreading the gospel of Liberty, Equality and Fraternity that caused such widespread fear and hostility among the nations surrounding France, and which caused a coalition against her. Lakanal shares the crusading spirit of the times in which he moved.

In the practical matter of financial support for a national system of education, Lakanal in his discussion reminds the Convention that a large part of the expense could be met from the proceeds derived from the endowments, buildings, lands, and other property which have been taken over by the government from the various educational establishments of the Old Régime. By providing for only two grades of instruction, primary and secondary, the additional expense per citizen would not amount to more than 35 *livres*. The national treasury for education can be aided by special taxes, as for example, on newspapers. Lakanal states that a horde of lying and calumnious sheets have sprung into life since the beginning of the Revolution, and feed off the events of the Revolution. It would only be fair to tax them for the support of education. Bachelors, husbands separated from their wives, wives separated from their husbands, unmarried women of over twenty-five, —all should be taxed ten per cent of their income for the support of education.

With the Committee's report favoring the education of women, Lakanal is in hearty agreement. "If the women had been enlightened, sacerdotal fanaticism would not have written the Revolution in letters of blood in so many unfortunate cities. The executioners *en étole* would have threatened Liberty with an impotent wrath." He then goes on to make an exalted plea for the education of women.

In its report the Committee had dealt in generalities with regard to primary education, demanding for the pupils *connaissances morales, naturelles, et économiques.* Lakanal would be more specific, and gives the following outline of knowledge to be acquired by the young pupil:

1. Reading and writing; and in these first attempts the pupils shall put nothing on paper that is unrelated to their country. By beginning to know their country, they will learn to love it.
2. Rules of simple calculation.
3. The geography of the French Republic.
4. An historical summary of the Revolution.
5. Elementary notions of carpentering.
6. Elements of rural economy.
7. The most simple and the most usual principles of morals and ethics.
8. Weekly public lectures, whose object shall be the Constitution, the knowledge and discussion of the laws. "All the citizens should derive from these instructions a religious respect, a holy enthusiasm for the Constitution of their country. From such lectures the citizen will learn that there is nothing superior to the honor of being a Frenchman."

Lakanal emphasizes physical education, again calling Montaigne to his aid: "The body must have vigor in order to obey the soul: a good servant should be robust."

As for the study of languages, contrary to the plan of the Committee, Lakanal recommends that the beginning of language study be made in the French. Its purpose should be to form good Frenchmen, not good Latins. "The aim of education should be to shape souls to the national form, and let the legislator never lose sight of the reply of the stern Spartan to the voluptuous satrap of Lydia."

In order to produce better teaching and learning results, Lakanal recommends that instruction be given a system of internal government such as to animate its activity without creating a feeling of constraint. "The academical year should be in a way a session of the teaching body. The pupils should be charged each in their turn with drawing up a report of the scholastic sitting or session; this report would afford an analysis of the various *opuscules* presented by the pupils; mention would be made of the praises and adverse criticisms that the work itself, or negligence, might have merited." The summary of these reports that the teachers would make each year would serve as a guide to the jury of awards in the distribution of prizes.

That this recommendation was incorporated into education as later developed, is shown by a statement in the Lavisse history of modern France in the chapter treating education under the Consulate: "Elsewhere they practiced the Republican discipline. The pupils corrected each others' exercises under the surveillance of the teacher, awarded by ballot the *prix d'excellence,* and voted on the matter of holiday leaves."

Lakanal's last recommendation is with regard to the attitude that should be taken toward the clergy as teachers in national education. In brief, he would not admit a member of the clergy into the teaching system unless he had first renounced his priestly calling, but when once he has done that he ought to be accepted into the ranks on the same basis as any other citizen. Lakanal expresses disapproval of the Civil Constitution of the Clergy whereby priests had become employees of the State, and proposes the complete separation of Church and State. In conclusion, he states that he is far from desiring to give the children of France lessons in Atheism, and invokes the God of Sir Isaac Newton.

Although elected to the Committee of Public Instruction at the moment of its partial renewal in January, 1793, Lakanal apparently took no active part in the work of the Committee before April 2, on which date his name first appears in the proceedings. Aside from the fact that he was a new man on the Committee, and may have remained silent for a time by design, there were two good reasons why he took no active part.

In the first place, the Committee did little, and had slight influence from the beginning of the trial of the king through the balance of the Winter and Spring of 1793. In the Fall of 1792, from a fragment detached from the general plan of Condorcet, the Committee had formulated and presented a report to the Convention on primary education. Discussion had begun and had continued during several sittings of the Convention, but with the beginning of the trial of Louis XVI had been abandoned on December 12.

From January until May, the Convention gave scant thought to the subject of education. Its attention was absorbed in turn by the trial and execution of the king, foreign war, creation of the Revolutionary tribunal, the revolt of La Vendée, the treason of Dumouriez, the debate on the proposed Constitution, and finally the struggle of the Girondists against the Parisian democracy. At last, by intervention of the Committee of Public Safety, the question of education was resumed on May 30, and the influence of Sieyès soon replaced that of the fugitive Condorcet whose arrest had been decreed. So it is seen that Lakanal would have had thus far little opportunity for active work on the Committee of Public Instruction.

THE MISSION TO OISE AND SEINE-ET-MARNE

In the second place, Lakanal was absent from Paris for several weeks on a mission for the Convention. On February 24, 1793, the Convention in the face of danger from foreign foes, ordered a levy of 300,000 men. On March 9 it decided to send into the various Departments of France 82 of its members to hasten the execution of the military measures which it had just decreed. Lakanal was one of the Deputies chosen, and together with the Deputy Mauduit repaired to the Departments of Seine-et-Marne and Oise.

When in the Spring of 1793, because of danger of foreign invasion, the Convention appointed a Committee of Public Safety, Barère, who had been elected by the largest number of votes to membership on the Committee, proclaimed:

> Liberty has become the creditor of all our citizens. Some owe her their industry, others their fortune; these their counsels, those their arms; all owe her their blood. Therefore, all Frenchmen, all sexes, all ages, are summoned by the *Patrie* to defend liberty. All the physical or moral faculties, all political or industrial means accrue unto her; all the metals, all the elements, are her tributaries. Let each one occupy his post in the national and military movement which is being prepared. The young men will fight, the married men will forge arms,

transport the baggage and artillery, prepare provisions and supplies. The women will work at clothes for the soldiers, will make tents, and will carry into the shelters of the wounded their tender care as nurses. The children will convert old linen into lint; and the old men, taking up again the mission they had among the ancients, will have themselves conveyed to the public squares. They will inflame the courage of the young warriors; they will propagate hatred of kings and the unity of the Republic. Houses belonging to the nation will be converted into barracks: The public squares into workshops; the soil of the cellars will serve to prepare saltpeter;[18] all saddle horses will be requisitioned for the cavalry; all carriage horses for the artillery; fowling pieces, swords, sabers and pikes will be useful for the service in the interior. The Republic is but a great, besieged city; of necessity France must become only one vast camp.

The program of total war outlined by Barère was carried out amidst a wave of enthusiasm which passed over France, and months later when Lakanal is sent on his second mission to Dordogne and surrounding territory the words of Barère will have their influence in the shaping of his policy in dealing with the inhabitants of south-western France.

On March 24, 1793, Lakanal reported to the Convention on his mission to the Departments of Seine-et-Marne and Oise:

"Citizens, I have just traversed with my colleague Mauduit the Department of Seine-et-Marne, and although the aristocracy is bestirring itself in all directions in order to lead public opinion astray, the citizens that this Department is to furnish for the defense of liberty are ready to fly to the frontiers."

In speaking of their expedition into the Department of Oise, and of their visit to the Château of Chantilly, he says:

The openings that have been made in the walls in order to facilitate the searches offered to our surprised gaze: towers wholly unknown, secret trap doors over deep cellars, moving stairways, and everything of a highly romantic character that fairy-land enchantment offers for frightening credulous and timorous minds.[19]

But the most precious of the discoveries that they made there was, in addition to considerable sums of gold and silver, correspondence in manuscript of the king, Marie Antoinette, Mlle Elizabeth, Necker, Calonne, Dubarry; secret plans of the campaigns of the Prince of Condé, works of Louis XV, a collection of natural history, and other documents of which it is useless to emphasize the importance and interest.[20]

[18]The French actually did dig up the earth of the cellars to obtain a supply of saltpeter, necessary in the making of gunpowder.

[19]Charles Gayarré, the Louisiana historian and novelist, devotes chapter XXV of his *Audret Dubayet* to a fictionalized account of Lakanal at the Château of Chantilly.

[20]Marcus, *Lakanal*, p. 27; *Réimpression de l'ancien Moniteur* (Paris 1847-50), XVI, 513.

Upon his return from the mission to Seine-et-Marne and Oise, Lakanal made a report to the Convention in which he recommended that a committee of two of its members should be sent to Chantilly to safeguard the interests of the Republic. This was done, and Thibaut and Bézard were appointed the two commissioners "to draw up an inventory of the papers and valuable chattels which the Château may contain." In this connection, it may be well to state that Lakanal was not without detractors. His earlier biographers incorporated into their sketches of him many things that have since been disproved, discounted, or discarded. For example, Prudhomme in *Révolutions de Paris* had treated him as an ignorant and immoral priest. Also he had been accused of having fathered the report decreeing the honors of the Pantheon to the remains of the infamous Marat. It has since been claimed that the reader of this report was Marie-Joseph Chénier, member of the Committee of Public Instruction, brother of the poet André Chénier, and author of *Charles IX,* the most popular drama of the Revolution. That the tradition lingered concerning Lakanal's connection with the honoring of Marat is shown when we peruse the words of an unsigned article published as late as the reign of Louis Philippe:

> Some astonishment has been expressed that the ministers of Louis Philippe have made no attempt to seat in the Luxembourg men who like M. Lakanal, Barère, Thibaudeau, etc., would bring there the tribute of their experience and their enlightenment. It is asserted that a person of high position to whom the proposal was made to call M. Lakanal to the royal Council of Public Instruction, replied: That is impossible; it can never be forgotten that he was the reporter of the commission which proposed to render the honors of the Pantheon to Marat!

Still another accusation against Lakanal was that of unlawfully misappropriating objects of value from the Château of Chantilly. As late as the 1840's, shortly before Lakanal's death, a repetition of this charge was intimated if not openly declared by Germain Sarrut and B. Saint-Edme in an article on Lakanal in the *Biographie des Hommes du Jour.* This article brought a reply from Lakanal:

> These acts of expropriation which were attributed to me in the first biographies which were published, are entirely imaginary. Here are the facts as they were recorded in the minute of the procedings of the Convention, sitting of March 24, 1793, and which are recounted in the *Moniteur Universal,* page 280:
>
> I was on mission in the Departments of Oise and of Seine-et-Marne, with my colleague Mauduit, Deputy of the latter Department. We were charged with pressing the extraordinary levy of the contingent that these two

departments were to furnish to our armies. In passing by Chantilly, we learned that some Commissioners of the Committee of General Security were taking an inventory in the Château. At this news, three members from the district of Senlis had repaired to Chantilly. It was with these three functionaries, with the mayor of the commune, the municipal officers, and upon their invitation, that we went together to the Château. There we found the Commissioners of General Security who had been installed there for several days. From them we received the details which, after we had withdrawn, became for us an object of deliberation. Convinced that the interests of the Republic were not sufficiently guaranteed at the Château of Chantilly, it was resolved between us that I should repair at once to the Convention, that I should make a report on what was happening at Chantilly, and that I should request that two of our colleagues should be named to replace the agents of the Committee of General Security, and in their stead to take all the measures proper to guarantee the interests of the nation. In consequence, I appeared before the Convention which, on my report, appointed Citizen Bézard, Deputy from the Department of Oise, and Citizen Thibault, Deputy and Bishop from the Department of Cantal. These two Commissioners went to Chantilly, resided there several months, and committed there at the Château all the possessory acts, all the removals which have been attributed to me, and which I could not have accomplished without the concurrence of my colleague Mauduit. We did not, we could not, commit at the Château of Chantilly, any act of authority. So long as this accusation of expropriation was limited to biographies composed to satisfy hateful passions, it deserved only contempt. To-day, when it has been reproduced by writers whom I honor, I have believed it my duty to reply, with proofs in hand.[21]

In acknowledgment of Lakanal's reply the editors of the *Biographie des Hommes du Jour* said in their own defense: "We pointed out but a single fact, and desirous that our readers should not be mistaken as to our inmost thought, we said a few lines further on that M. Lakanal remained poor, and had not derived a grain from these rich gold mines which he might have been able to exploit."

The finds at Chantilly were the object of several discussions in the Convention, and finally a decree was drawn up by the Committee of Public Instruction which passed the Convention to the effect that the Minister of the Interior, Garat, should have a building remodeled at the *Jardin des Plantes* to receive the Chantilly collection of natural history. In this connection mention may be made of a letter, the manuscript of which has been preserved among the Lakanal Papers in the Howard Memorial Library of New Orleans in which Daubenton, collaborator with Buffon and professor in the *Jardin des Plantes,* appeals to Laka-

[21]*Réclamations* addressed to Germain Sarrut et B. Saint-Edme, Rédacteurs de la *Biographie des Hommes du Jour.* Undated Pamphlet.

nal to see to it that fifty barrels which had been requested of Garat for the packing of the natural history specimens at Chantilly be sent immediately. The letter is a recognition of the readiness of Lakanal to be useful even in trivial ways in causes concerning the cultural side of the Revolution, and is but one of many instances where the most prominent scientists and learned men of the times relied upon him for assistance.

As stated, the first appearance of the name of Lakanal in the minutes of the Committee of Public Instruction is in the entry for April 2, 1793, when he, Daunou, and Romme were appointed a committee to witness "the trial of the new method of correspondence by signals." This was the signal telegraph invented by Claude Chappe, which was the forerunner of the Morse electric telegraph and the Marconi wireless. As early as March 12, Romme had announced on the floor of the Convention that the Committee had a report to make on an invention that would facilitate the transmission of messages between the Convention and the armies in the field.[22] On April 1, Romme had read the report describing the invention and its success, and recommending appointment of a committee to witness a demonstration, and also recommending an appropriation of 6,000 *livres* to defray the expenses of the test. The test was made in July, but by that time Romme had become a prisoner in the Girondist uprising in the Department of Calvados. Arbogast was appointed in his stead on the Committee.

Chappe had all the discouragements that usually beset the path of inventors, and had it not been for Lakanal there is no doubt that he would have failed. Daunou and Arbogast were guilty either of negligence and indifference, or of scepticism,—perhaps of both. Lakanal had the keenness of perception to discern instantly the importance of the invention, and threw himself wholesouledly into support of the inventor, heartening him and smoothing out the inevitable difficulties.[23] Since this was the first task assigned to Laka-

[22]Guillaume, *op. cit.*, I, 386-389, 396-397, 404; II, 3-6.

[23]At Belleville, where Chappe had first proposed to make his demonstration, the inhabitants became alarmed, and destroyed his apparatus. Chappe requested the Convention to pass a decree, the tenor of which would be such as to allay the fears of the citizens of Belleville. The Convention referred this request to the Committee of Public Instruction.

nal on the Committee of Public Instruction, it is likely that on that account alone, if for no other reason, he would have been all the more anxious to succeed. However that may be, we find the first striking evidence of that great spirit of encouragement which was to remain a dominant characteristic of Lakanal throughout his life.

In the *Exposé sommaire* to which reference has already been made, there are a number of letters addressed to Lakanal by Claude Chappe, and written during the trial and successful outcome of his signal telegraph. From these letters may be traced the progress of the test and the parts played by Lakanal, Daunou and Arbogast.

> All has turned out as we had desired and as you had forseen. I will come tomorrow to the Committee of Instruction in order to ask you to introduce me to your two colleagues Daunou and Arbogast, appointed along with you to examine my project, and to get together on means of execution. . . .[24]
>
> It seems to me that Citizen Daunou attaches little importance to my telegraphic system. Citizen Arbogast displays the same indifference. . . . If you were not there, I would despair completely of success. You will remove the obstacles so much to be dreaded from the Committee of Finance, so unfavorable to everything that concerns the sciences and letters. Finally, I am hoping strongly in you, and in you alone. . .
>
> I thank you very sincerely for the consolations that you give me; I really have need of them. What men this Cambon and this Monot are![25] I admire the courage and the calmness which you oppose to their bad reasonings, to their insulting sallies against your Committee. The sciences will never be free of obligation for the services that you have rendered them. I beg you to be persuaded that my gratitude towards you will end only with my life. . .
>
> At last, thanks to your brave efforts, to your unalterable patience, my project will be examined upon a line of correspondence suitable for giving conclusive results. You have procured the funds necessary for this preliminary test. . .

In the following excerpt Chappe refers to an effective argument used by Lakanal. Before quoting the passage it may be well to explain that Montesquieu, and after him Rousseau and Mably had all expressed the opinion that a Republic could be successful only in a small country. This idea was accepted by nearly all the Revolutionary leaders, although Brissot and Condorcet, who were familiar with the success of the Republic in America, did not share the common opinion. Since France had been forced by circumstances into

[24]Daunou was a man of literary training and tastes, and Arbogost was a mathematician. Neither was interested in the applications of science.

[25]Members of the Committee of Finance. They were interested in rigid economy due to the financial plight of the country.

the adoption of a Republican form of government, there were still many in the summer of 1793 who feared that the experiment might fail owing to the large extent of territory covered by the Republic.

I learn from various representatives and from some employees of the Committee that Citizen Daunou does not want my project, and that Citizen Arbogast does not display any zeal for its adoption. How is it that they were not struck by the ingenious idea that you developed yesterday before the Committee, and of which I had not thought? The establishment of the telegraph is, in fact, the best response to the publicists who think that France is too broad of extent to form a republic. The telegraph shortens distances and unites in some fashion an immense population about a single point. A long time ago, rebuffed on all sides, I would have abandoned my project, if you had not taken it under your protection. . .

Thanks be unto you a thousand times! You have triumphed over all obstacles; what do I say? You have transformed them into ways and means; behold me fully satisfied. The project is adopted, and the decree determines my rank and my pecuniary privileges. I can offer you only my profound gratitude, but it will perish only with me. . .

I owe you new thanks. You are inexhaustible when it comes to being useful to me. I have received the decree of the Committee which puts at my disposition the funds necessary for a trial on a large scale. I am going to busy myself with ways of execution. I shall be very attentive to keep you abreast of all my operations. I pray the creator to accept the homage of his creature.

These extracts from Chappe's letters not only bring into relief the attitude of Lakanal in contrast with that of Daunou and Arbogast, but they show the deep gratitude of the inventor toward the one man to whom he owes his success. Chappe is but the beginning of a long list of men: teachers, scientists, artists, musicians, whose lives were touched and brightened by Lakanal. Daubenton, Laplace, Lavoisier, Lacépède, Sicard, Bernardin de Saint-Pierre, Desfontaines, Lalande, Saint-Hilaire, are all names that come to mind when that of Lakanal is mentioned.

The crowning day of triumph for Chappe and Lakanal came on the 15 of Fructidor (September 2) when Carnot in the name of the Committee of Public Safety announced to a breathless Convention an official message over the completed telegraph line, a message of victory sent by the army from the town of Condé in northern France:

"Citizens, here is the report of the telegraph which has just arrived.

"Condé is restored to the Republic; the surrender took place this morning at six o'clock."

The Deputy Gossain sprang to his feet: "Condé has surrendered to the Republic: let us change the name it bore to that of Nord-Libre." (Decreed).

Cambon demands that this change of name be telegraphed to Nord-Libre. (Adopted).

Towards the end of the sitting the president of the Convention announced that the telegram changing the name of Condé to Nord-Libre has reached the army, and that in return he has received a telegram of confirmation. Thus ended the first chapter in the history of rapid long-distance communication.

SECRETARY OF COMMITTEE OF PUBLIC INSTRUCTION

The secretary's record for April 25, 1793, notes that Lakanal was chosen as one of the two secretaries of the Committee of Public Instruction.[26] Also the Committee soon began to rely on him to present reports on the floor of the Convention. His aggressive spirit together with his talents as a speaker made him a highly suitable man for the effective presenting of reports.

A twentieth century French critic, bitterly hostile to Lakanal, grudgingly pays tribute to him in his quality of reporter to the Convention, admitting that he was one of the principal ones of the Committee of Public Instruction. "That is how his name has been transmitted to us by the journals and printed matter of the time, attached to a great number of this Committee's propositions." "That is how," the critic further states, "must be understood the saying of Grégoire that Lakanal was the *Cheville-ouvrière,* or mainspring," then adding that he was one of its members that the Committee liked to choose as its interpreter before the Convention because he was glib, fluent, trained to public speech.

> He was, furthermore, a man of an extreme suppleness. He made moderate reports when the Committee was under the influence of the moderates; he made Montagnard reports after the defeat of the Girondist party; he made reports in the Thermidorian taste after the fall of Robespierre.[27]

If Lakanal is to be criticised for his suppleness and adaptability

[26]Later on he was again elected secretary, and also was president of the Committee under the Convention (August 1-September 3, 1793), and under the Directory. Robinet, *Le Mouvement réligieux à Paris pendant la Révolution,* (Paris, 1898), II, 449, prints a decree signed by the secretaries of the National Convention: P. J. Duber and Lakanal, dated August 27, 1793. If Robinet is correct, Lakanal must have been secretary of the Convention as a whole at the same moment he was Secretary of the Committee of Public Instruction.

[27]Eugène Welvert, *La Légende de Lakanal,* (Paris, 1908).

to the changing situations presented by the Convention, then all the other reporters are to be condemned likewise. And besides, however fiercely Lakanal may have ranted at times, he was a barking rather than a biting dog. His vote against the king aside, no one has ever suggested that Lakanal in his quality of Deputy ever lifted up his voice in condemning anyone to the guillotine nor in his capacity as *Représentant en Mission,* when he spent ten months at the behest of the Committee of Public Safety in installing the revolutionary program in southwestern France, did he condemn anyone to the guillotine, and he caused no more than some sixty imprisonments. This is decidedly in contrast with Carrier who was sent on a similar mission to Nantes, and who not being able to kill rapidly enough by the usual methods, drowned whole boatloads of unfortunate prisoners in the river Loire. It is estimated that Carrier slew at Nantes at least four thousand men, women and children.

SIEYES AND LAKANAL

Following the death of Condorcet, leadership in the Committee of Public Instruction fell to Sieyès. Even prior to the outbreak of the Revolution, Emanuel Sieyès had acquired renown for his various pamphlets, the most celebrated of which was the one entitled *Qu'est-ce que le Tiers État?* He had been prominent in both the Constituent and Legislative Assemblies, and was destined later to play a leading part in the Napoleonic *coup-d'État* of the 18 Brumaire Year VIII (1799), when Napoleon became First Consul, and Sieyès himself became one of the other two Consuls.

During the month of June, under the guidance of Sieyès, the Committee of Public Instruction drafted a plan for primary education, and on June 26, 1793, Lakanal reported this project to the Convention on behalf of the Committee.[28] In his preliminary re-

[28]From October to December, 1792, a project of organization of primary schools, inspired by the ideas of Condorcet, was elaborated and presented to the Convention, discussed by it, then put off indefinitely, Dec. 12, after the vote of a single article stipulating that the primary schools should form the first grade of instruction, that in them should be taught the knowledge indispensable to all citizens, and that the teachers should be called *instituteurs.* The decree of March 8, 1793, added that the payment of the professors and instituteurs of all public educational institutions should be at the expense of the nation. The decree of May 30, 1793, ordered the establishment of a school in localities of more than 400 inhabitants. This no doubt explains why Lakanal presented a plan for primary instruction *only* on July 26, 1793.

port, Lakanal discussed the subject of primary education generally, and then offered the specific articles of recommendation for the establishing in detail of a national system of public education. The preliminary report does not differ essentially from the Discourse or "Opinion" which he had prepared the previous December. Shortly after the report had been presented to the Convention, Lakanal discovered in the writing of Sieyès a discussion of education which pleased him, and which he substituted for his own preliminary report.[29]

Attacks were made on the plan of education offered by the Committee of Public Instruction, and among the objectors was Robespierre.[30] The very next day after Lakanal's report, Robespierre was elected to the formidable Committee of Public Safety in the place of Marat who had just been assassinated by Charlotte Corday. This may explain why Lakanal silently permitted his project to be shunted aside at the insistence of Robespierre, since education was included as within Robespierre's particular province as a member of the Committee of Public Safety.[31]

In rejecting Lakanal's report, the Convention resolved that a special commission of six should be appointed whose business it would be to present within a week another plan of primary education. Incidentally, it may be well to record an anecdote connected with Lakanal's report, one of few instances of humor that the writer has discovered with reference to him. The plan of education called for the celebration of a large number of *fêtes*. Among these was to be a *fête* devoted to "animals, companions of Man." When Lakanal read this item a loud laugh arose, and a boisterous scene followed. Some Deputy demanded: "What is this *fête* of the animals?" Lakanal, as quick as a flash, replied: "It is yours." The humor of the retort is obvious when it is recalled that one of the meanings of the word *fête* is "birthday."

[29]Pamphlet: *Lakanal à ses Collègues.*

[30]Harold T. Parker, *The Cult of Antiquity and the French Revolutionaries*, (Chicago, 1937), p. 162.

[31]At its sitting on July 6, 1793, the Committee of Public Instruction nominated a Commission of Six whose business would be to draw up a plan of national education. Those chosen were Jeanbon Saint André. Lavicomterie, Saint-Just, Rühl, Lakanal, Grégoire. On July 13 Robespierre presented to the National Convention the plan of education of Michel Lepeletier Saint-Fargeau.

The Commission of Six was duly appointed, and consisted of Bourdon, Coupé de L'Oise, Lakanal, Robespierre, Rühl, and Grégoire. On July 13, Robespierre as reporter for the Commission of Six read the posthumous plan of education of Lepeletier de Saint-Fargeau. Lakanal spoke neither for nor against this project which was adopted in principle by the Convention.

SAINT-FARGEAU

Michel Louis Lepeletier de Saint-Fargeau, although a former noble and *président-à-mortier* under the Old Régime, had become an ardent revolutionary and a Deputy to the National Convention. He was one of the number who voted the death penalty for Louis XVI. The very evening of the day on which judgment was pronounced on the king, Lepeletier de Saint-Fargeau, while dining in Ferrier's restaurant in the Palais-Royal, was assassinated by a former member of the king's body guard, who thus sought to avenge the sentence which had been passed on his master.[32] The dramatic end of Saint-Fargeau added greatly to the intense excitement of the moment, and his death was regarded as martyrdom for the sacred cause of the Revolution. His body was laid out in state, and the multitudes came to view the wounds. The Convention decreed to attend his funeral in a body, that the expense of the occasion should be borne by the nation, and that the remains should find their resting place in the Pantheon.[33] Marie-Joseph Chénier, the poet and dramatist, pronounced a eulogy on the deceased in the presence of the assembled Convention. The body of Lepeletier was borne to the *Place des Piques* (Place Vendôme) and deposited on the pedestal of the statue of Louis XIV. As the members of the Convention approached this temporary resting place, a funeral march composed by Gossec was played. After the Deputies had ranged themselves about the statue, the president of the Convention placed a crown of oak and a crown of flowers about the head of the "Martyr for Liberty." Following this ceremony came the funeral procession to the Pantheon, along the route of which the bloody

[32] Augustin Challamel, *Histoire-Musée de la République française* (Paris, 1857), I, 383, 392ff.

[33] Guillaume, *op. cit.*, I, 325-330; II, 31-66.

garments of Lepeletier were exhibited on the end of a pike festooned with oak and cypress leaves.

The following day the widow and her little daughter Suzanne appeared before the Convention accompanied by Félix Lepeletier, brother of the deceased. Upon motion of the president and Barère, little Suzanne was unanimously adopted by the National Convention and dubbed "Daughter of the Nation."

Saint-Fargeau's plan of education, which under the influence of Robespierre had been adopted, was never carried out, owing to the rapid movement of events. The plan, which was suited to a dictatorship rather than to a democracy, for that very reason caught the attention of Robespierre.

Saint-Fargeau's plan diverged principally from that of Sieyès and Lakanal in that it differentiated between education and instruction. Its author agreed with the Committee of Public Instruction as to instruction, but claimed that instruction should be preceded by education. He meant by education the molding of the child between the ages of five and twelve in schools where all regardless of family, rich or poor, should live in common. Great attention was to be paid to physical training, to strict discipline, to regulated hours, and above all each child was to be taught to work. No servants were to be employed. The older children were to be taught to supply the needs of the younger. Work was to be such as could be supplied on the inside, and on the outside in neighboring manufacturing or farming establishments. The life of the children was to be one of great simplicity and austerity. At twelve years of age the children were to be returned to civil life, but a certain percentage were to continue their education at the expense of the State in the Institutes, and a percentage of those completing the Institutes were to be further educated at national expense in the Lycées.

THE MUSEUM OF NATURAL HISTORY

Among the multifarious activities of the National Convention during the summer of 1793 was the suppression of the ancient academies of learning, together with the "revolutionizing" of certain other cultural institutions. Among the latter was the *Jardin du Roi* which had been created under Louis XIII, and utilized for the instruction of students of medicine. Supervised for many years by the first physician of the Court, it had finally come under the superintendence of the brilliant naturalist Buffon, who retained his position for nearly half a century until his death in 1788.

Under Louis XVI the head gardener of the *Jardin du Roi* was André Thouin, who in later years wrote a letter of introduction on behalf of Lakanal to Thomas Jefferson.[34] Associated with him were Daubenton, the aged ornithologist who had been the associate of the celebrated Buffon; Jussieu, the botanist; Haüy, the mineralogist; Lamarck, forerunner of Darwin; Desfontaines, the botanist who had enriched the collections of the Garden with specimens from the Barbary and the Atlas; the youthful Étienne Geoffroy Saint-Hilaire, who became renowned not only as an embryologist and anatomist, but as one of the line of groping evolutionists leading in the direction of Darwin, and who together with his son was to be a lifelong friend of Lakanal; and Bernardin de St. Pierre who was soon to become the new *Intendant* of the *Jardin,* and who is remembered to-day, for his touching romantic tale of *Paul et Virginie.* Acting upon the suggestion of Lamarck, who proposed to remove the odium of aristocracy from the name, the *Jardin du Roi* was rechristened the *Jardin des Plantes.* This was a happy suggestion, as it created a favorable impression on the Assembly and paved the way for a successful reorganization.

Upon the death of Buffon on April 16, 1788, the Marquis de la Billarderie succeeded him as *Intendant* of the *Jardin du Roi.* As early as the period of the Constituent Assembly attention had been called to the desirability of reform in the establishment. The Intendant called the officers together, and with Daubenton as presiding officer, drew up a project of decree to be presented to the Assembly. This project was not acted on, however, and for the moment the matter rested. In 1792 the Marquis de la Billarderie fled from France, joining the increasing

[34]Thouin was the son of a gardener and a gardener himself from childhood. He and his brothers and sisters had grown up in the *Jardin du Roi* under the tutelage of Buffon. From the status of day laborers, the family passed to that of botanists engaged in horticulture. At his father's death André Thouin became head gardener of the *Jardin du Roi,* and later, in 1793, he became professor of botany in the Museum of Natural History.

throng of *Émigrés*. In July of the same year the King awarded the place of Intendant to Bernardin de St. Pierre.

It remained for the National Convention to complete what the Constituent Assembly had left in suspense. On February 16, 1793, the Convention instructed the Committee of Public Instruction to make a report on a new plan of reorganization for the *Jardin des Plantes.* On May 14 the Convention decreed the sum of 15,000 *livres* to cover the expense of remodeling the gallery of the second floor of the building of the *Jardin des Plantes* in order to put it into a state suitable for housing the collection of natural history from Chantilly. By a later decree of June 10 the conception of the *Jardin des Plantes* was enlarged, and the reformed institution took the name of Museum of Natural History. The report leading to this enlarged creation was drawn up and read before the Convention by Lakanal. There has been some dispute as to the urgency of the movement and Lakanal's part in it. For that reason it will not be amiss at this point to quote from two differing accounts of the affair.

Deleuze, who published during the period of the Restoration a book *History and Description of the Museum* recounts the history of Lakanal's decree of June 10, 1793, as follows:

> Meanwhile, a faction hostile to order and all government, having become formidable by its victory of May 31 (over the Girondists), wished to destroy everything that might revive memories of the monarchy. An establishment whose employees had been named by the King was to be the object of its fury. The peril was imminent, and it would have been impossible to escape it, had there not been in the Convention some men of courage, who finally recognizing the abyss into which they had been drawn, desired to arrest this devastating torrent, and to prepare a return to the good by preserving the institutions useful to the sciences and the arts. Among them we must especially single out M. Lakanal, who in his quality of president of the Committee of Public Instruction exercised a great influence.[35] As soon as he was informed of the danger which threatened us, he went secretly to the *Jardin,* and inteviewed MM. Daubenton, Thouin and Desfontaines on ways to prevent it. He had them to turn over to him the *projet de règlement* which they had presented to the Constituent Assembly, and the next day he caused a decree to be passed which constituted and organized the establishment, giving it the title of Museum of Natural History.

This account differs from that of Lakanal's great friend Étienne Geoffroy Saint-Hilaire who, as stated above, was one of the employees of the *Jardin des Plantes.*[36] In a summary of the history of the

[36]The accounts of both Deleuze and Saint-Hilaire are quoted by Guillaume, *op. cit.,* I, 480-481.

Museum he mentions the circumstances which gave birth to the decree in question:

The representative of the people, Lakanal, presented himself June 9, 1793, about three o'clock in the afternoon, at M. Daubenton's. It came within my scope to introduce him to my venerable master and illustrious colleague. He was unknown to both of us. Lakanal expresses the desire to be useful to the patriarch of natural history. Explanations are made, and a decree is at once improvised and drawn up. Debated and modified that evening in the Committee of Public Instruction, this law which is destined to fix in France, and even in Europe, the destinies of the natural sciences, was carried the very next day to the National Convention and adopted. . . . The establishment feels then the effect in 1793 of the agitation of minds, and participates in the benefit from the renewal of social ideas. The National Convention and Lakanal, its organ, apply to it the then dominating thought, the unitary and philosophical views which were still lacking to it. The establishment was proclaimed *Muséum d'Histoire Naturelle.* From that time on it has had a special predilection for comparative and philosophical studies of the terrestrial universe. It is the sum of knowledge of Buffon which has been summarized and coordinated legislatively.

Lakanal had sponsored the decree by which the Convention allocated 15,000 *livres* for the purpose of preparing a place for the collection of natural history from the Château of Chantilly, with which he had become familiar on the occasion of his mission to the Departments of Oise and Seine-et-Marne. This explains naturally the visit which he made a fortnight later to the *Jardin des Plantes,* when he went to ininquire of the venerable Daubenton the needs of the institution; and while the account of Deleuze is the more dramatic, it is quite certain that Saint-Hilaïre, who was an eye-witness of the visit of Lakanal, gives a more accurate and plausible account, especially as Lakanal in the report which he made to the Convention on June 20, 1793, says nothing of "the necessity of preserving the *Jardin des Plantes,* whose existence was threatened by no one, but of the necessity of reforming the organization of it, of uprooting abuses which had become perpetuated there, and of 'naturalizing the tree of Liberty'."[37]

CASSINI AND THE OBSERVATORY

During this same summer of 1793 when the *Jardin des Plantes* was transformed into the Museum of Natural History, and ancient academies such as the *Académie Française* and the *Académie des Sciences*

[37]Guillaume, *op. cit.,* I, 481. It was rumored that the Convention intended to convert the *Jardin* into a potato patch.

were suppressed, the astronomical Observatory was revolutionized, that is to say, reorganized on a basis of equality.

The Paris Observatory dated from 1667, and the building itself was planned by the celebrated architect, Claude Perrault. In 1669 Louis XIV called to his court a well-known Italian astronomer, Giovanni Domenico Cassini, to preside over the Observatory. He remained in charge until his death in 1712. Succeeding him, his son, grandson, and great-grandson, all born in the Observatory, were in succession in charge of the establishment. They formed a sort of dynasty, and like kings were designated by Roman numerals. At the outbreak of the French Revolution Count Jacques Dominic Cassini (1748-1845), known as Cassini IV, was the Director of the Observatory.

September 21, 1792, France was declared a Republic, and very rapidly there developed a sentiment for ridding her of all her ancient institutions; if not destroying them, at least treating them *révolutionnairement,* thus transforming them to fit the ideals of the newly established Republic along the lines of Liberty, Fraternity and Equality. In reorganizing France to suit the revolutionary notions, it was inevitable that eventually the Observatory would come under scrutiny. The Observatory had been under the direct protection of the kings, and the Cassinis had been ennobled, bearing the title of Count. Thus it is seen that the Observatory and its head astronomer, Count Cassini IV, would be regarded as belonging to the hated aristocracy, and would naturally fall into disfavor with the more ardent of the revolutionists.

In the conducting of the Observatory Cassini was assisted by three young men: Perny, Ruelle, and Nouet. Cassini came under the scrutiny of Garat, Minister of the Interior, concerning the partitioning among the assistants of funds allocated to the Observatory, the question at point being the interpretation of the terms of the law governing their distribution. The matter was finally appealed to the Convention, and thus became the starting point for a democratic reformation of the Observatory, placing all the astronomers on an equal footing. This was a blow to Cassini's pride as well as a shock to his sense of the fitness of things, as the young men mentioned above were merely assistants with limited training and experience, comparable perhaps to the graduate student assistants in the modern American university. The final result was the resignation of Cassini, who was forced to undergo certain humiliations, and who later was to be arrested and thrown into prison, where he remained until after the fall of Robespierre, 9 Thermidor, 1794.

The story of Cassini belongs within the range of this book because of the part played in it by Lakanal. The correspondence between Garat and Cassini concerning the allocation of funds began in March, 1793. This had been followed by correspondence between Cassini and the Committee of Public Instruction to which the matter had been referred. During the month of August, when Lakanal was president of the Committee of Public Instruction, matters came to a head when on August 2 he presented to the Committee of Public Instruction, and later on August 31 to the Convention, a project which was adopted by the Convention.[38] By the terms of

[38]The French manuscript of the following unpublished letter has been preserved among the Lakanal Papers in the Howard Memorial Library in New Orleans. The letter is undated, but belongs apparently to the last days of July or the first day of August, 1793. It must have been written on the eve of Lakanal's report to the Committee of Public Instruction of August 2:

"Citizens: I learn that the Committee of Public Instruction is now occupied with the Observatory of which I am the head. I have believed that I owe the Committee the homage and tribute of the information and ideas that my knowledge and experience have given me. At first I had composed on this subject a long work to serve as a support and as a development of my propositions, but I have had the thought that perhaps the Committee would not have the time to read it. Therefore, I have condensed the whole into three pages here-attached; but I request that you at least be kind enough to have the patience to read to the end, and especially the essential which terminates my writing. It will be said perhaps that on this occasion I seek only to put forward my own cause and interests, but what does that matter if they are also the interests of the thing? Furthermore, those who know that the reputation of my name established for one hundred and twenty years is very independent of the Observatory and that the salary of 2,700 *livres* does not form the whole of my support, will easily believe that my intentions have been more pure and that I have easily divested myself of all small personal interest.

I am, Citizens, with consideration,

CASSINI, Member of the Academy of Sciences
and Director of the Observatory."

What Cassini means by the *essential* is a statement which he had appended to the summary in which he claimed that as all the work of the Observatory was done in common, it was essential to have a directing head and subordinates, in-the *projet de décret* an equality of rights was established between the director of the Observatory and his pupils or assistants. This led to Cassini's resignation on September 5, and since he continued to occupy his quarters at the Observatory as a matter of temporary convenience, this aroused a quarrel between him and the youthful astronomers. His place was taken by Alexis Bouvart, a future member of the French Institute, but at this time only twenty-six years of age. These four "professors, "as they were styled in the documents of the times, chose Perny as temporary director. A peremptory note from the astronomers demanded of Cassini that he vacate within a week his quarters at the Observatory. As the quarrel waxed warm, Lakanal was appointed commissioner to the Observatory by the Committee of Public Instruction. After an exchange of hostilities between Cassini and the four astronomers, on September 22 Lakanal visited the Observatory, and while in conference with the four astronomers, received a request for an interview from Cassini, to which he replied "very dryly" that he would not go to Cassini. This brought the following note from Cassini:

"The Citizen Lakanal is the representative of the people. As such, at any hour, at any moment, his ears and his heart should be open to any request from any citizen whatsoever. Therefore he can not refuse the interview which I request concerning some very simple things, things which even concern him."

Instantly Lakanal wrote at the bottom of Cassini's note: "The Citizen Lakanal is at the Observatory for public affairs. He can not busy himself with any private object. Furthermore, when any one has to see him, that person comes to him, even though he were a Count."[39] Since Cassini was already out of office, Lakanal

stead of four independent equals. In speaking of his name as established for 120 years, Cassini counts backward, not from 1793, but from the beginning of the Revolution in 1789 to 1669, the date of the appointment of his great grandfather as the first astronomer by Louis XIV.

[39]Guillaume, *op. cit.*, states that this visit of September 22 was Lakanal's last one. However, a letter of September 24, 1793, written by Lakanal apparently to the citizens of Fontainebleau, has an opening paragraph which indicates that he visited the Observatory again on September 24:

"Citizens: I was just getting ready to go to the Committee of Agriculture and Subsistances as I had promised you, when I received a letter from the C.

may have been justified in refusing to see him, as he had come to the Observatory on official business; but he was not justified in the cavalier tone which he adopted toward the eminent astronomer, especially as Cassini was much the older man, Lakanal being but thirty-one years of age at this time. Also it was within Lakanal's right to demand that a private individual come to him as an officer of the Republic, but he was wrong in the sneering reply which he made to Cassini's respectful note. Lakanal's attitude toward Cassini was owing perhaps to the testiness and arrogance of the latter's disposition. In the record of the proceedings of the Committee of Public Instruction for September 24, 1793, the following statement is made: "A member speaks of the uncivil and aristocratic attitude that he (Cassini) assumed toward a Deputy who went to visit the Observatory, and of statements which he made relative to the decree on the organization of the Observatory of the Republic." Since Lakanal was the Deputy who had been appointed to visit the Observatory, and since likewise he had been reporter of the decree which the Convention had enacted governing the Observatory, it is but natural to suppose that these words of the minutes had reference to him as Deputy, and if so, the action of Cassini was such as to arouse the hostility and opposition of Lakanal. This together with Lakanal's uncompromising spirit of democracy and his hatred of the aristocracy may explain, but not fully excuse, his attitude toward the astronomer.

Cassini, in which he invited me to come to the Observatory for pressing business. Inspector of this national establishment, I saw myself with the alternative of neglecting my duties or of going, and my choice was not long doubtful." This letter, of which only the first paragraph has been reproduced here in translation, has been preserved in the Ferdinand J. Dreer Collection, Historical Society of Pennsylvania, Philadelphia.

3

THE MISSION TO DORDOGNE

ON OCTOBER 8, 1793, JOSEPH LAKANAL WAS AGAIN DESIGNATED AS A *représentant en mission,*[1] this time to a part of southwestern France embracing the Departments of Gironde, Lot-et-Garonne, Lot and Dordogne.[2] The distinct and only purpose of his mission was to raise a levy of horses for the Republican army. This levy not only included horses, but their feed and accoutrements as well. Also by order of the Convention, Lakanal made his headquarters at Bergerac in Dordogne. While carrying out this mission with dispatch and success, Lakanal conceived the idea of creating a manufactory of arms and gunpowder at Bergerac, a project which was carried out satisfactorily and with the approval of the Convention. While he was engaged in these tasks the Convention greatly extended his powers, and he became the political representative of the Convention with instructions to revolutionize the region of his mission.

To reorganize successfully the life of the people of a large section of France far removed from Paris was the task worthy of the ability of anyone; and the success with which Lakanal dealt with the problem is an indication of the measure of the man. Not only was there a question of converting the population to the political doctrines of the Revolution, but of transforming their civilization to conform to the ideals of the Revolution economically, educationally, and religiously as well.

In preceding pages the reader has seen how the various governments of the Revolution were concerned with the subject of education, but that no practical steps had been taken for putting

[1]April 4, 1793, the Convention decreed that the *Représentants en Mission* should wear the following costume: *Un sabre pendu à un baudrier de cuir noir, placé en sautoir pardessus l'habit, une écharpe en ceinture et un chapeau rond surmonté de trois plumes aux couleurs nationales.*

[2]On the day that Lakanal left Paris for Dordogne, Danton exhorted him—"Tape dur."—André Beaunier, *Revue des deux Mondes,* T. 36 (1916).

any plan of education into execution. The Constituent Assembly had spoken of the necessity of creating public instruction, and Talleyrand had read his report on education. Condorcet had read his famous report to the Legislative Assembly, a part of which dealt with primary education; but these reports had not borne fruit. Under the Convention in the Fall of 1792 a project for the organization of the primary schools, inspired by the ideas of Condorcet, had been elaborated, presented to the convention, and discussed by it; but put off indefinitely on December 12 (beginning of the trial of the King) following the vote on a single article stipulating that primary schools should form the first grade of instruction, that in them should be taught the knowledge indispensable to all citizens, and that the teachers should be called *instituteurs*.[3]

By a decree of March 8, 1793, it was stipulated that the payment of professors and instructors of all institutions of public education should be at the expense of the nation, a measure that constitutes the beginning of modern public school systems at state expense.

A decree of May 30, 1793, ordered the establishment of a school in each locality of more than four hundred inhabitants, and compelled the teachers to hold weekly public lectures in addition to their daily teaching.

On June 26, 1793, Lakanal, as has been seen, presented a plan before the Convention for elementary instruction, but was thwarted by Robespierre, who caused the plan of Saint-Fargeau to be accepted instead, a plan destined not to be put into execution.

Thus when Lakanal was designated by the Convention on October 8, 1793, as its *représentant en mission* to Dordogne, public education was still unorganized in either fact or law.

LAKANAL'S INTEREST IN EDUCATION

When Lakanal arrived in Dordogne his sole mission was to make a levy of horses, although later his powers were very greatly extended. Yet from the very beginning he interested himself in many things that were clearly beyond the province of his mission.

[3]This explains no doubt why Lakanal presented a plan for primary education *only* in his report of June 26, 1793.

Such was his interest in education that he stretched his authority, and scarcely had he arrived in Dordogne before a meeting was held in his apartments (Oct. 21, 1793) with the Revolutionary Committee of Bergerac, and after discussion the Committee recognized "that his projects . . . of forming an institution in this city for social instruction, funds for which shall be levied on the rich, are of the most absolute necessity, since it is evident that we shall remain free only in proportion as we shall in general be educated and enlightened as to our true interests." The language is Lakanal's. Some time later in addressing himself to the republicans of his native Ariège, he will exclaim: "Tyranny in order to enslave us shut off from us all access to knowledge; public education was then in our Department a divinity without worship and without ministers." He will cry before the Convention: "You can not encourage too much the sciences; if their frightened throng were ever to withdraw from you, fanaticism would soon rear its altars and servitude would cover the face of the earth." Not only did he have a profound faith in education, but he had a keen appreciation of the role played by the teacher. "When I shall have finished my labors, I shall seek a place as teacher," he said at a meeting of the Popular Society of Bergerac on October 23, 1793; and that is exactly what he did in 1799 when First Consul Bonaparte relieved him of the governorship of the four Rhine Departments.

On the very same day that he met with the Revolutionary Committee of Bergerac, Lakanal published a decree levying taxes on the wealthy citizens of the commune of Bergerac, a part of the proceeds of which should be devoted to the temporary establishment of public primary schools. Another decree was proclaimed on October 24:

Considering that a democratic education can alone give to the minds of young citizens the fold of truth and fashion their new and docile souls to Virtue; considering that it is by education that free peoples have been able to feed into the hearts of children those lively affections which perpetuate the races of happy and brave men; considering that nothing works more powerfully for the interests of tyranny than ignorance; considering that to form citizens is not the affair of a day, and that in order to have men, they must be taught when children; considering, finally, that the National Convention has decreed the establishing of primary schools throughout the extent of the Republic. . . .

Lakanal decreed that until the definitive organization of national education, four primary schools should be established at Bergerac. Each school should be divided into two sections: one for boys, and the other for girls. In each school there should be an *instituteur* and an *institutrice*. In both sections of each school should be taught, besides reading, writing and arithmetic, the Constitution of the Republic "and everything necessary in order to fulfill the elementary social functions." Instruction was not only to be civic, but lay. In the following paragraph Lakanal announces his belief in the separation of Church and State in education: "In a democratic government, each citizen being free in the exercise of his worship, and the body of the nation knowing only the worship of the law, under penalty of dismissal it is forbidden to instructors and instructresses to entertain their pupils with any religious opinion." Equality of salary was provided for men and women. Instruction was free. Thus, in a very short time, and in advance of the country as a whole, Lakanal organized strongly primary education at Bergerac, procuring money, buildings, necessary teachers; laying down the principles of this type of education, and assuring its functioning in a regular manner.

Some of the things accomplished by Lakanal at Bergerac were frankly war measures, and hence of a temporary nature; as for example, the levying of 2,000 horses and the manufacture of arms and munitions. In his capacity of commissioner or governor, Lakanal accomplished many things which in more settled times might have had permanency and lasting importance, but which for the most part proved to be ephemeral, rapidly declining and disappearing after the final departure of Lakanal from Bergerac for Paris, where he was to spend the remaining period of the Convention and a part of the period of the Directory until the expiration of his term as a Deputy to the Council of Five Hundred in 1797.

THE MODEL FARM

Among the institutions founded by Lakanal at Bergerac was a *Maison d'Économie rurale*. Such institutions had been proposed to the Convention on October 4, 1793, by the Deputy Grégoire, and the Convention had voted the establishment of such an institution in each of the Departments. As early as December 3, 1793, Lakanal published a decree according to which there should be established at Bergerac a *Maison d'Économie rurale,* he thus becoming one of the first, if not the first of the deputies on mission to carry out the decree of the Convention. The establishing of a *Maison d'Économie,* or model farm, was no doubt a task dear to the heart of Lakanal, for in his *Discours* of December, 1792, he had included *"Élements de l'Économie rurale"* among the number of things that should be taught in the primary schools. His interest in agricultural education remained with him throughout his life, and many years later we find an echo of the model farm of Bergerac in the program for education adopted by Lakanal when he became president of the College of Orleans in New Orleans in 1822.

In Bergerac there was a garden of natural history which had belonged to an *Émigré,* Gontier de Biran. This was appropriated by Lakanal and made the nucleus around which was an establishment whose goal was to be "the cultivation of plants and the teaching of natural history applied to the advancement of agriculture, commerce, and the arts." The institution would be administered by a commission of citizens versed in a knowledge of natural history. A part of the buildings should be reserved for a library "composed of books on anatomy, mineralogy, chemistry, botany, zoology and travels." Correspondence was to be established with analagous institutions situated in different parts of the Republic, and Lakanal took it upon himself to obtain for the institution correspondence with the Museum of Natural History at Paris.

While the decree which had been fostered by Grégoire looking toward the establishing of model farms limited itself to one such institution for each Department, Lakanal dreamed of establishing one in each cantonal capital of the region over which he presided. However, so far as is now known, the model farm at Bergerac was the only one actually established.

Shortly after the death of Lakanal in 1845, Berriat-Saint-Prix read a paper at Paris before the Academy of Moral and Political Sciences concerning the model farm founded by Lakanal at Bergerac. "The purpose was to construct a sort of model farm where there would be a special intent to train good farmers, either by giving them new knowledge with the aid of a course in practical agriculture, botany, mineralogy, physics, or by developing methods acquired, or by simplifying routine methods." Berriat-Saint-Prix goes on to say that the beginnings of this model farm were successful.

All the most perfect instruments and stocks of the best trees and shrubs had been collected in a vast nursery. The expansion and acclimatizing of foreign plants would have been facilitated by the choice of seeds sent by the Museum of Natural History with which its creator, M. Lakanal, had put it into correspondence. There was no question here of vain speculations. Already at the request of our confrère, the illustrious Daubenton had sent to Bergerac a skillful gardener whose initial efforts for a year gave the most splendid expectations.[4]

Nearly forty years later, when Lakanal is spending years of exile at Mobile, Alabama, as a cotton and sugar-cane planter, we find him corresponding with his friend Saint-Hilaire concerning the flora of the region of Mobile and asking for seeds to be sent him of French plants from the Museum of Natural History.

In the report which Lakanal will make on December 16, 1794, to the Convention, looking to the founding of secondary institutions of learning which came to be known as *Écoles Centrales,* he will say:

Why have agriculture, commerce, and the arts and trades never had their schools? Why have they been left to the routine of instinct or the interest of cupidity? Did we believe in the impossibility of reducing them to principles? Or did we think that in this *genre* mistakes were without consequence and perfection without value? You will avenge the arts and trades, agriculture and commerce. . . .

We have seen how Lakanal fathered the decree relative to the establishing of the Museum of Natural History. In his report on Jean Jacques Rousseau (Sept. 15, 1794) we shall see him stressing the Genevan philosopher as the friend of Nature, and in the various programs which he will submit to the Convention devote a large part to the study of the natural sciences; and we shall see him later persuading the Council of Five Hundred to transform the garden of the *ci-devant* Cordeliers at Rodez into an establishment of public instruction for the purpose of teaching natural history and botany.

The economic importance of agriculture did not escape him by any means . . . as is proved by numerous *mémoires* that he will write in the United

[4]Berriat-Saint-Prix, [Extrait des] *Annales de La Société royale d'horticulture de Paris*, 1846; Labroue, *op. cit.*, p. 260-263.

States, where he will live long years as a planter. He will carry to the United States the works of Adam Smith, of Forbonnais, of Burlamaqui[5] as well as the five volumes of the *Journal d'Économie publique* of Roederer, concerning which he will communicate with Jefferson . . . and it is from America that he will send to the Academy of Moral and Political Sciences the summary of his observations on the temperature, flora, agriculture of the United States, the manners and customs of the American plants, etc:[6]

FÊTES

One of the prominent manifestations displayed by the men of the Revolution was their partiality for *fêtes,* or holiday festivals and celebrations; not noisy popular rejoicings without aim or object, but civic festivals in which a double goal was pursued: "a philosophical goal, by arousing in crowds sweet and sacred emotions, in order to develop in them lofty sentiments; a political goal, by appeasing the dissensions of the citizens through the reciprocal communication in the midst of public enthusiasm of noble and generous ideas and impulses." Such festivals had been advocated by Rousseau.

In the plan of education which Lakanal had presented to the Convention on June 26, 1793, the thought of civic festivals had been stressed. His wide scope of authority in Dordogne gave him opportunity to make use of the psychological effect of emotions engendered by public festivals. Within a few weeks after his arrival at Bergerac Lakanal announced a *fête civique,* stating that the object of this patriotic ceremony would be "to honor old age, misfortune, courage, men who have died for liberty, and to render public worship to all the republican virtues." The festival was to be terminated by a civic banquet to which all the friends of liberty and equality in Bergerac should be invited. Such was the success of this first *fête* organized by Lakanal that a member of the revolutionary Committee of Bergerac referred to it with the words "sublime" and "memorable," and in a document addressed to the Convention, the general Council of the Commune of

[5]Forbonnais was a French economist; Burlamaqui was a Genevan philosopher, publicist and moralist, for fifteen years professor in the University of Geneva; then he became a member of the Council of State, author of *Principes du droit naturel* (1747) and *Principes du droit politique* (1751).

[6]Henri Labroue, *op. cit.*, p. 257.

Bergerac announced the celebration of this festival, which he qualified as "brilliant," in honor of the martyrs of liberty, stating that Lakanal was present, and that thousands of voices repeated the cries of *Vive la République! Vive la Montagne!*

Such was the success of the first festival that Lakanal some two months later proclaimed a new festival which he called the *Fête auguste de l'Amitié,* the solemn festival of friendship. Attached to this festival was a pet idea of Lakanal: the abolition of law-suits and the settling by arbitration of actions at law. In this he is the forerunner of our modern arbitration boards. However such an idea might appear, there was ample need for something to be done with regard to the slow moving and corrupt practices of the law, as is evidenced by a report made to the Convention on January 12, 1793, by Carnot, who together with two other Deputies, Garrau and Lamarque, had been sent on a tour of investigation into southwest France which included Dordogne. In his report Carnot said:

> The greatest of the evils which afflict the people at this moment is the refusal of justice, or the so wasteful slowness which is worse than a formal refusal. . . . There are laws, too many perhaps, but they are not executed, often through the carelessness of public officials, more often still by the discouragement and the disfavours with which they are saturated, and sometimes also because the laws, either obscure or contradictory, can not be executed.

Carnot noted the complaints of the expensiveness of law procedure, the prevarications of the magistrates, the arbitrariness of the police courts, etc.

Lakanal, in his efforts to secure civil justice, had the happy thought of referring all cases before the courts to selected arbiters, who having nothing to gain since they would be serving out of a pure spirit of patriotism, would not only be fair, but would speedily clear up all cases brought before them for arbitration. In order to secure his end as speedily as possible, he sent out a proclamation accompanied by a decree of seven articles, inviting the inhabitants of the territory under his jurisdiction to terminate by the way of arbitration the cases at law which divided them, and that too before March 10, 1794, the day on which was to be celebrated in all the communes of the Department of Dordogne "the august Festival of Friendship."

Such was the success of the plan that Lakanal, in a letter to his friend Sieyès on July 3, 1794, wrote: "I can not refuse myself the pleasure of addressing to you two decrees, one of which put an end to 6,027 lawsuits." The crying need for some relief from the laws plus the generous feeling engendered by the Festival of Friendship had produced a miracle, and the settling of so many legal cases in so short a time was a great triumph for Lakanal. Further testimony of his success is to be seen in the fact that the Festival of Friendship became the subject of popular songs. In one, sung to the tune of the *Marseillaise,* the final stanza is devoted to Lakanal:

". . . Toi qui, terminant nos discordes,
Nous réunis par ton amour,
Du bonheur que tu nous accorde,
Lakanal, jouis à ton tour.
A ta voix renaît l'abondance;
Tu nous rends la gloire et la paix;
Mais les plus doux de tes bienfaits
Nous touchent moins que ta présence. . ."[7]

In addition to the holiday festivals when certain republican virtues were celebrated, or the remembrance of an event or of a man, there were certain minor festivals inaugurated by Lakanal known as work festivals *(travaux de fêtes).* The most outstanding festival of this nature was the work festival planned by Lakanal for the quick repairing of the highways. In his proclamation of January 27, 1794, Lakanal announced: "Before the sun has left the horizon three times, the work will be ended. All the roads of Dordogne will be repaired at the same time. That will be a unique and sublime example which the National Convention will learn of with enthusiasm."

In his instructions to the citizens of the various communities of Dordogne, Lakanal said:

This day, forever memorable, the representative of the people and all the public officials, adorned with the external marks of the law, spade in hand, will give the example of work to all the citizens. . . . The evening before a discharge of musketry, repeated from post to post, will announce in all points of the Department the day for the consummation of this great work. That day the entire population of Dordogne will line up *en masse* on the roads; the men will go and find stones, break them, dig the ditches; the women and children will load the wheelbarrows,

[7]Published originally in the *Journal d'Instruction populaire* at Sarlat, An II of the French Republic. Reproduced by Henri Labroue, *op. cit.,* p. 211. A note attached to the original publication stated that Lakanal had crossed out the above stanza, but that in his absence the stanza had been restored.

spread the broken stones; the old men will encourage the workers by their presence and their approbation. Men and women, young and old, rich and poor,—all will work.

The inhabitants of Dordogne entered into the spirit of the thing, and regarded the three days spent in mending the roads as holiday picnics. In a communication addressed to the National Convention, the citizens of Bergerac, after describing the work accomplished during the three days, added: "Public spirit has gained more from these three days of *fête* than from learned instruction. Equality has been real and within the grasp of those who had not felt sufficiently the effects of it. Food was shared in common. The rich furnished food for the poor. The work was the same for all."

Lakanal not only succeeded in getting all the roads mended, but he gave the inhabitants of Dordogne a genuine lesson in equality and fraternity, thus illustrating in a very practical way the meaning of the watchwords of the Revolution.

As stated previously, the original purpose of Lakanal's mission to southwestern France was to make a levy of horses for the Revolutionary army, a mission that at his own request was enlarged to cover the founding of establishments for the manufacture of arms and munitions. The third step was investing him with full Revolutionary powers by the Convention. Under the authority granted him it was his duty thoroughly to transform the territory to the aims and ideals of the Revolution. This he sought to do through public address and the founding of a press, through the appointing of revolutionary committees, and the sending out of Civic Apostles who were to work individually among the people, explaining and clarifying the Revolution, but with the further purpose of acting as spies, which reminds us of the present-day (1945) Gestapo. Perhaps a certain amount of spying was essential to the success of his administration.

As representative of the Convention Lakanal had full authority over his district, and the only recourse against his conduct and rulings was by making complaints directly to the National Convention. On several occasions such complaints were made, necessitating hurried trips to Paris by Lakanal. In every case he came out victorious over his detractors and retained the full confidence of the Convention.

In the course of the ten months spent by Lakanal in Dordogne we find him occupied with such questions as the administration of the Department, the districts and the municipalities; his relations with the Revolutionary Committees, and with the Popular Societies; his efforts to govern through the medium of public opinion, and in this last connection he says: "I do all with the lever of public opinion, nothing with the blade of the guillotine." The fact is that throughout his mission he did not shed a single drop of blood. This is the more remarkable when we consider that his mission covered such a length of time. Usually the Deputies on mission were sent out for a limit of three months for civil duties and six for the army.

The religious side of the Revolution engaged the attention of Lakanal, and we find him occupied with his relations with the Protestants, with the Catholic priests, his benevolence toward patriotic priests, his surveillance over suspected ones, his attacks on counter-revolutionary priests, his efforts to laïcise the spirit of the public and the *mores,* and his attitude toward the property of *ci-devant* ecclesiastics. We learn of his attitude toward criminal and civil justice, the policing against counter-revolutionaries, his pursuit of several Girondist Deputies who had been condemned to death by the Convention, and who had taken refuge in the territory governed by him; his control of arrests and setting prisoners at liberty, as well as of some sixty arrests he was forced to make in carrying out his duties. We see his efforts to cope with pauperism and famine, and the relief measures undertaken by him, which did not differ greatly from the relief measures in the United States of a few years ago. We learn of the cuttings of wood supervised by him for the French Marine, of his method of levying and collecting taxes, his handling of public works, such as mending roads, building bridges, and making rivers navigable, and also the part he played in carrying out the will of the Convention in the tearing down of the feudal châteaux of La Force, Badefols and Tiregand.

It must be kept in mind that Lakanal had arrived in Paris with little or no experience of public affairs; that his activity in the Convention was very limited before the Spring of 1793, and that in the months intervening before his departure for Bergerac in October,

1793, he was overshadowed by other men, particularly Sieyès and Robespierre. Perhaps fear of Robespierre caused him to welcome leaving Paris *en mission.* It may have been a coincidence, but was perhaps the result of design, that he was assigned to a territory with which he was familiar and where he was already known. He had taught in some half dozen schools of the Fathers of the Christian Doctrine in southern France, notably at Périgueux, which lay within the district over which he was to have jurisdiction. And although the Deputies sent *en mission* were usually limited to three months on civil missions and six months on military missions, Lakanal remained in Dordogne ten months, leaving hurriedly for Paris upon arrival of the news of the fall of Robespierre. Fear of Robespierre may have caused him to prolong his mission to ten months; and had it not been for the death of Robespierre there is no doubt that he would have continued his stay in Dordogne, for he left Dordogne fully expecting to return. However, the removal of Robespierre and the quick shifting of political affairs caused him to remain in Paris.

4

AFTER THERMIDOR

ON ARRIVING IN PARIS FROM DORDOGNE, LAKANAL APPEARED BEFORE the bar of the Convention on August 8, 1794, where he made a short speech of explanation and justification of his return:

> Citizens,[1] in the alarming position in which the National Convention finds itself, I considered that I should leave momentarily the duties which you delegated to me in Dordogne and surrounding Departments, in order to give you an account of the public spirit in those regions. The National Convention is an object there of veneration and love. The execration of the new tyrants whom you have just struck down is in proportion to the public confidence they had had the artfulness to usurp. Everywhere the people have passed rapidly from indignation to scorn for the conspirators, and from scorn to forgetfulness of their memory, concerning themselves only with you and the country. As for me, I had determined to make use of the guns from the new manufactory which I have just established in order to exterminate the new Pisistratus and his vile hired assassins.[2]

The last sentence is evidence of the strong feeling of Lakanal against Robespierre, and it would be wrong to attribute wholly to political ex-

[1]Guillaume, *op. cit.* IV, 936-937.

[2]On the 9th Thermidor (July 27, 1794) the National Convention declared Robespierre and certain other revolutionary leaders as outlaws. A few hours later they were captured, and on the 10th Thermidor (July 28, 1794) without the formality of a trial Robespierre and twenty-one of his followers were guillotined. The next day seventy more victims, and on the following day twelve more, were executed. The men who overthrew Robespierre came to be known as Thermidorians. The fall of Robespierre marked the end of the Reign of Terror.

The course of Robespierre is summed up by Bertrand Barère in his *Memoirs* (Eng. Translation, London, 1896):

"Thus the course of Robespierre is summed up: first he took possession of the 31st of May, which had been organized by Danton, who feared this tyrannical violation, the work of his hands. Some days later, Robespierre treated Danton as a usurper, and usurped his place. He exterminated the representatives whose liberty and eloquence he feared; he no longer consulted those who remained, but his club. His powers increased in a frightful manner, when he seized the censer on the 20th of Prairial, and the last remnant of civil liberty on the 22nd. Immediately, he usurped the power of the people, ruling the Convention by fear, the government by denunciations at the club, the city by terror, the laws by violence, and the revolutionary tribunal by his secret sources of information. He usurped all power, terrified every will—for a time he absorbed the Republic in himself. But the Convention recollected on the 9th of Thermidor for four hours that it was invested with national power, and Robespierre was not."

pediency the course which he was to follow with regard to the adherents of Robespierre. Paul Dupuy, who wrote a centenary history of the *École Normale* says that Lakanal's long absence in Dordogne had made a new man of him: "Type of the perfect Thermidorian, nobody pursued with more vehemence, and sometimes with more injustice, the memory of the vanquished with whom he had been allied."

Considering the fact that he had spent all his life in southern France, and considering the liberality of his views in cultural matters, the sympathies of Lakanal would naturally have been toward the ill-fated Girondists, but the Girondists were philosophers rather than men of action, and could not hold the sympathy of Lakanal, who was above all a man of action. In a notebook discovered many years after his death Lakanal had expressed his opinion of the Girondists:

> The deputation from La Gironde was distinguished for its talents, its urbanity, its social qualities, so precious when France is enjoying the calmness of peace. But these estimable men would not have saved France in the state of crisis in which she was, if they had had the power in hand. Neither oratorical talents nor social qualities were the things with which to oppose a furious enemy. . . . In ordinary times, in times of peace, I would much prefer the party of the Gironde to its fiery adversaries.

LAKANAL PROTECTS SICARD

Lakanal identified himself with the Montagnards because the Mountain was the party of decision and action. He never became a rabid Montagnard, and was never in sympathy with Robespierre.

Following the death of Couthon, who along with Robespierre, Saint Just, and several others, suffered execution by the guillotine, there was found among Couthon's papers a very compromising dedication written by the Abbé Sicard, the celebrated instructor of deaf mutes. Lakanal heard about it, and hastened to the new Committee of Public Safety. In the words of his early biographer, Isidore Geoffroy Saint-Hilaire, "He will try to stifle the affair. He is introduced into the office of his colleague, who is absent. Lakanal does not hesitate an instant; the fatal page is torn out, and when his fellow-member returns: 'You have no longer anything against Sicard,' says Lakanal. 'I am the only guilty one.' The fellow-member becomes angry at first; it is an abuse of confidence that the Committee will punish! . . . But his anger does not last long: he seizes Lakanal by the hand and says to him: 'You are always the same.'"

That same evening the Abbé Sicard came into possession of the page of dedication to Couthon, and he wrote a letter to Lakanal:

When I wrote those lines to the Conspirator Couthon, he enjoyed the confidence of the entire Republic, and he was still known only for a patriotism that no one could suspect without himself being accused of incivism. No matter, I would have been judged after the events as if I should have foreseen them, and I am indebted to your watchful friendship for having turned aside this storm. You have already received the reward of this noble action while performing it. What you shall find in my heart will be eternal. What a friend you are; And how fortunate one is to be loved by you! . . . Did you remove my manuscript from the house of that scoundrel Couthon? This piece which you sent me was the first page of it. How humiliated I am to have been thus deceived on his account; but then all France was deceived too.

On the back of this letter, says Saint-Hilaire, were these words written by Lakanal: "I saved his life by exposing mine greatly. He was one of the most celebrated men of Europe, and certainly one of the most useful."[3]

PRESIDENT OF THE COMMITTEE OF PUBLIC INSTRUCTION

Following the death of Robespierre, the National Convention on August 24, 1794, reorganized the revolutionary committees, and Lakanal was elected to the Committee of Public Instruction. On September 3 the Committee chose him as president. Lakanal was the most important man on this new committee.

Now that military victories had made France safe without, and the events of the 9 Thermidor had brought an end to the Terror within, the Convention could look forward again to planning and

[3]This is but one of the examples where Lakanal protected his friends. When Garat had been denounced to the Committee of General Safety by Dumont du Calvados, Lakanal courageously defended him. The scientist Lacépède was grateful to Lakanal and acknowledges his help: "The Citizen Daubenton has informed me of all that you have done for my return to the Museum and for my personal safety." As for Daubenton, it was upon the report of Lakanal that the Convention decided to have published at public expense 4,000 copies of the aged naturalist's *Traité des Moutons.* The astronomer Lalande in a letter expresses his gratitude to Lakanal for the 3,000 francs which the latter had procured for the furthering of Lalande's astronomical studies. Also Bernardin de St. Pierre thanks him for 20,000 *livres* which he has been instrumental in procuring for him.

establishing facilities for public education. In rapid succession the Committee of Public Instruction presented to the Convention projects for Normal Schools, Primary Schools, and Central (secondary) Schools. All of these projects were adopted and put into execution.

The idea of training schools for teachers goes back to the seventeenth century, but the name Normal School dates from 1774 when the German Felbiger drew up a plan of education for Maria Theresa which was entitled: *Allgemeine Schulordnung für die deutschen Normal-Haupt- und Trivialschulen. . . .*" From the time of the expulsion of the Jesuits in 1762 the idea of institutions for teacher training was in the air in France. Definite expression was given to this idea by Bernardin de St. Pierre in the 14th of his *Études de la nature,* where he outlines a plan for national instruction, but states that before undertaking the project, men to preside over it should be trained. In 1789, in his *Voeux d'un Solitaire* he says: "Before establishing a school for citizens, we ought to establish a school for teachers. I am struck with astonishment that all the arts have among us their apprenticeship except the most difficult of all, that of forming men. The National Assembly should give careful attention to such a necessary establishment."

From the moment of the formation of the Committee of Public Safety and the rise of Robespierre, the Committee of Public Instruction had been subordinate to the Committee of Public Safety, and it was under just such a situation that the Committee of Public Instruction drew up and presented to the Convention projects for the founding of normal schools; and it was an application of a revolutionary method created by the Committee of Public Safety which became the model of the Committee in conceiving the form and functions of the normal schools.

The first application of this method by the Committee of Public Safety had been in the year II (February, 1794) for the manufacture of saltpeter and guns. The famous *École des Armes*" was truly the prototype of the Normal School." Each district throughout France sent pupils to Paris appointed by the administration. The duration of the instruction was limited to three *décades,* thirty days. The courses for powder and saltpeter were conducted in the amphitheatre of the Museum of Natural History, where later the courses of the Normal School were to be held. After finishing their courses the pupils returned to their districts and organized the making of powder and arms; that is to say, they taught others how to do what they themselves had learned at Paris.

THE NORMAL SCHOOL

The following June the Committee of Public Safety proposed to the Convention the second application of the revolutionary method,—the foundation of the *École de Mars,* and the same day it announced formally the third,—the *École Normale,* or Normal School. In an address Barère, member of the Committee of Public Safety, said:

> The delay occasioned in public education by the shocks and duration of the Revolution will be strongly felt in a few years, and we are forced to perceive from afar a considerable gap in the needs of the Republic for all employments. This object has long since attracted the attention of the Committee of Public Safety, and it has sought the quickest means of preparing defenders, officials and good citizens. The Committee has thought that it should on the one hand set up in Paris a school where teachers could be trained, in order that they then might be scattered throughout all the districts of the country.

Thus it is seen that the object was quickly to "revolutionize" the youth of France just as the armies had been revolutionized.

Within a few weeks after the decree establishing the *École de Mars,* Lakanal writes from Bergerac to the National Convention on July 17, 1794: "Thirteen gun barrel makers, a proportionate number of platers, trimmers, mounters, forgers of bayonettes, etc., gathered together *en école normale* (in normal school) were trained at the same time, and their work yields in nothing to the best artists."[4] Incidentally, it may not be amiss to mention that Lakanal himself was not averse to vocational learning and underwent a brief apprenticeship at Tulle.

As early as July, 1793, Léonard Bourdon and Grégoire had familiarized the Committee of Public Instruction with the term Normal School, and that is no doubt the source from which Lakanal received the expression which he applied to his occupational training schools in Dordogne. In all probability Lakanal was the first to apply the name normal school to actually existing institutions in France.

[4]Guillaume, *op. cit.*, IV, 833.

Lakanal became the leading member of the Committee of Public Instruction, second in cultural matters only to Garat, the new national Commissioner of Public Instruction. Garat had played an important role throughout the Revolution. Former member of the Constituent Assembly, he had been Minister of Justice after the massacres of September, and had refused to prosecute the authors of it. Becoming Minister of the Interior in March, 1793, he had abandoned the Girondists in the affair of the 31 May; then, under the pretext of bad health, he had quit the ministry in August. Friend in succession of the Girondists, of Danton, and of Robespierre, he nevertheless did not escape arrest, and was imprisoned at the height of the Terror just long enough to be able to count himself as one of its victims. Under Napoleon he was a member of the Senate, was made Commander of the Legion of Honor, and then Count of the Empire. In 1814 he voted for the abdication of Napoleon, and in 1815 during the period of the Hundred Days, although badly received by Napoleon, he was elected to and served in the Chamber of the Hundred Days. He was a member of the French Institute, and during the second Restoration was deprived of his membership because of his participation in the Napoleonic government of the Hundred Days. When under Louis Philippe the Academy of Moral and Political Sciences was revived, Garat was restored to membership. Following his death which occurred at the end of 1833, Lakanal, at that time an exile in America, was restored to membership in his place.

Lakanal read the report of the Committee of Public Instruction on the establishing of the normal schools on October 30, 1794. The preliminary essay to this report had been prepared by Garat, and in it the author declared that the most brilliant hope and the most universal expectation had been for a plan of education which would place the whole nation in a state to exercise its democratic sovereignty. The ancient prejudices which had been destroyed had left a void in the minds of the French, and it was the task of education to fill in this void with sound principles and truths. The Constituent Assembly had lacked the force and the courage to solve the difficulties of the situation. In attempting to prepare the Constitution it had tried to conciliate two irreconcilable forces: Royalty and Liberty. Having joined two opposite and hostile spirits in its laws, it could no longer know just what genius or bent should be given to the nation. So when a plan of carefully worked out education was presented to the Assembly for consideration, that body had listened to the reading of the report as if it were the membership of an academy listening academically to a philosophical essay, and action was deferred in favor of the succeeding Legislative Assembly. All of those who were foresighted and of penetrating judgment perceived that the Legislative Assembly would never give a new national education to France, for the simple reason that education holds such a place in the warp and woof of a nation that any constitution must be so framed, education for the constitution and the constitution for education, that both are abortive if they are not the product of the same minds, the same genius.

At the behest of the Legislative Assembly a vast plan or program of education was outlined. A genuinely philosophical spirit coordinated all human knowledge into a plan of public education. But it was not to the interest of a king to support such a broad plan of enlightenment. Either such education would overturn the throne, or the throne would corrupt education. "It was a curious and instructive spectacle," says Garat,

> to see the Legislative Assembly seeking in all directions ways of setting aside the executive power of the Constitution without appearing to destroy it, and ways of finding an executive power of education, more worthy of its confidence, without appearing to create it . . . the throne destroyed brought a cry of joy to France and a cry of fright to the despots of Europe. The National Convention appeared, and the plan of education of the Legislative Assembly as well as that of the Constituent Assembly was no longer anything more than a tract or pamphlet.

From its beginning, the National Convention had been faced with foreign war; and the task of building up an army and triumphing over her enemies without, whilst enduring the horrors of the Reign of Terror within, prevented any consistent action with regard to education. Several attempts were made in that direction, but each was in turn abandoned; so that it was not until the reaction of Thermidor, when triumphant over the enemy without and having become more tranquil within, the Deputies of the Convention could turn their attention to the creating of institutions suited for the fulfillment of the ideals of the Republic. "Externally," says

Garat, "we have a regular course of victories, and internally we are no longer agitated except by the need of repairing the injuries committed against justice and of closing the wounds inflicted on humanity."

"In the Normal Schools," continues Garat,

it is not the various branches of knowledge which will be taught, but the art of teaching them. On leaving these schools the pupils will need not only to be well informed, but be men capable of instructing. For the first time on earth Nature, Truth, Reason and Philosophy are going to have a seminary also. For the first time the most eminent men in every species of knowledge and talents . . . men of genius are going to be the schoolmasters of a people; for you will put into the chairs of these schools only men who are called to them by the uncontested splendor of their renown in Europe. It will not be number, but superiority which will serve. It is better that they be few, but that they shall all be the elect of science and reason. All must appear worthy of being colleagues of the Lagranges, the Daubentons, the Berthollets, whose names come to mind immediately when we think of these schools in which are to be shaped the restorers of the human spirit. We propose to you to call from all parts of the Republic, around these great masters, citizens appointed by the constituted authorities whom their talents and their civism have distinguished the most. Already full of love for the knowledge which they possess, inflamed by a new ardor from the honorable choice that will have been made of them, delighted to hear discussed what they love most by men whose reputation they regard as the last word in human ambition, their progress in the art that they shall study will have a rapidity that can neither be foreseen nor calculated.

After reading the preliminary report Lakanal presented a *projet de décret* which was adopted by the Convention. This provided for the establishment in Paris of a Normal School "to which will be summoned from all parts of the Republic citizens already educated in the useful sciences, in order to learn under the most skillful professors in all the various subjects the art of teaching." The duration of the Normal course was set at four months. The methods acquired these four months were to be transmitted by the students to the various communities of the country. Thus from the parent Normal at Paris a multitude of centers would be established throughout France for the instructing of methods of teachers.

The branches of knowledge to which teaching methods were to be applied were: reading, writing, arithmetic, practical geometry, history, and French grammar. The methods were to be traced in the elementary books adopted by the Convention and published by its orders. The project also called for two representatives appointed by the National Convention to serve as a connecting link between the Normal School and the Committee of Public Instruction of the Convention. This was really an extension of the principle of *représentant en mission*. Lakanal and Sieyès were appointed as the representatives, but Sieyès declining to serve, at Lakanal's request the Deputy Deleyre was chosen in his stead. Deleyre was an elderly man, 69 years of age. Lakanal was less than half his age, very active and aggressive.

The subjects and the professors in the Normal School were as follows: Mathematics, Lagrange and Laplace; Physics, Haüy; Descriptive Geometry, Monge; Natural History, Daubenton; Chemistry, Berthollet; Agriculture, Thouin; Geography, Buache and Mentelle; History, Volney; Moral Philosophy, Bernardin de St. Pierre; Grammar, Sicard; Analysis and Understanding, Garat; Literature, La Harpe.

It is evident that the original intention of the founders of the Normal School was to train teachers in methods of teaching very elementary subjects in the primary schools. However, by the time the professors had been procured, the idea of training teachers for elementary schools had been largely lost, and a group of the most distinguished scholars of France had been employed to lecture on a wide variety of subjects. One of the chief reasons for the failure of the Normal School was that these professors taught subject matter instead of methods of teaching to a large group of students who were poorly prepared to understand them.[5] Another reason

[5]At the meeting of the National Convention of April 16, 1795, the Deputy Romme, member of the Committee of Public Instruction and author of the Republican Calendar, spoke on the question of the École Normale as follows: "I believe that the aim of the Normal School has absolutely failed. The pupils are composed of two sorts of men: the first are very well informed on certain parts, and very little so in others. The second are not so (well informed) in any. The latter especially expected to find in the lessons of their professors elementary notions. They have found in them only academic notions. One of the greatest vices of this instruction is that the professors presuppose in their pupils an advanced knowledge. On the other hand, it was thought that the attention of these young men could be sufficiently sustained to follow, in the same sitting, several very different objects, and which pass very rapidly before their eyes. The professors themselves would not be capable of this attention. This School can be very useful for those who already have knowledge, it is no good for those who do not have it. If they had occupied the distinguished men who direct it in composing elementary books, they would have spread throughout the Republic more instruction than they have done in establishing the School. How can you form good teachers, put uniformity into

was the overcrowded condition of the amphitheater where the lectures were held. Approximately 1,400 students assembled at the Normal School in an auditorium suited for only half that number. Still another cause of failure was the temporary nature of the enterprise. Four months had been fixed as the length of the term. Like the vocational schools which had been organized for training in war skills, the Normal School was treated "revolutionarily" as a quick process of training. A final cause of failure was the heavy expense attached to maintaining the establishment.

The experiment lasted for only one term of four months, and was then abandoned. However, what it attempted was not in vain, for a few years later Napoleon established the *École Normale* on the sure foundation on which it rests to this day. More than to any one else the credit of being the father of the Normal School goes to Lakanal. From the Normal School at Paris such institutions have spread over the world.

Before leaving the subject it may be of interest to note that the first Normal had its detractors even before it started. When Lakanal in his enthusiasm spoke of it as a "metropolis of human knowledge and learning," one of his fellow Deputies with whom he had been associated on the Committee of Public Instruction and on his mission to Dordogne, Charles Gilbert Romme, author of the Republican Calendar, retorted: "Metropolis of organized charlatanry!"

The epitaph of the Normal School is contained, perhaps, in the stanza of a *pot-pourri* of verses composed by one of the students:

"Allez-vous-en, gens de l'École,
On ne peut rien faire de vous:
L' enterprise était trop folle;
On ne peut rien faire de vous:
Allez-vous-en
Très Promptement

the teaching, give to national education a very pronounced character of republicanism if you do not put into it harmony and uniformity. First should have been composed the books which were to have served in teaching, and which should have been submitted to the Committee of Public Instruction, after which they could think of forming the teachers. As I see in the present institution only organized charlatanism, I demand the suppression of it." Guillaume, *Ibid.,* VI, 96.

Reprendre votre premier rôle;
Allez-vous-en planter vos choux."[6]

The attitude of at least one of the students towards Deleyre and Lakanal is reflected in the following epigrams:

Deleyre est un puits de science;
Comme il préside la séance!
Savez-vous bien ce qu'il fait là?
Il arrive, il dort, il s'en va:
Le lendemain il recommence.[7]

A nos leçons un pédant de collège
En belle chaire est venu s'installer.
Par un décret il a le privilège
De ne rien dire et de beaucoup parler.
Il règle tout; sur lui tout doit rouler.
Il distribue et louange et reproche,
Exalte ceux qu'il faudrait ravaler;
Bref, mon pédant est la mouche du coche,
Qui nuit, bourdonne et croit tout faire aller.[8]

PRIMARY EDUCATION

On June 26, 1793, as has been previously stated, Lakanal made his report on primary education, but that report was set aside in

[6]Take yourselves off, men of the School;
Nobody can do anything with you;
The undertaking was too cock-eyed;
Nobody can do anything with you.
Take yourselves off
Very quickly
Resume your first role;
Go on off and plant your cabbages.

[7]Deleyre is a well of knowledge. How he presides over the session; Do you know what he does there? He arrives, he sleeps, he goes away: the next day he begins afresh.

[8]A college pedant has come to sit in a privileged seat. By a decree he has the right of saying nothing and of talking much. He regulates all; all must revolve around him. He distributes both praise and blame, exalting those whom he should disparage. In short, my pedant is the fly on the coach, who is in the way, buzzes about, and thinks that he is making everything go. Allusion to La Fontaine's famous *Le Coche et la Mouche*.

favor of Robespierre's report on Saint-Fargeau's plan of education. Owing to the rapidity of events Saint-Fargeau's plan was never carried out, nor was the plan of the Deputy Bouquier which had been adopted subsequently ever executed. Thus the way had been left open for a new report on education, and on November 15, 1794, Lakanal again presented to the National Convention a project for primary education, which was essentially the same as his report of June 26, 1793. The preliminary discourse contained some ideas which were in advance of his times.[9] His insistence on physical education, including swimming, his generous attitude toward the teacher, his suggestion that education should in some manner cover the whole of life; and especially his enthusiasm for equal education of women with men—all mark him as an advanced thinker on the subject of education.

Lakanal's idea that education should extend throughout life is a forerunner of our modern ideas on adult education. Not only did he advocate adult education in his preliminary report, but during his stay in Dordogne he attempted to put his ideas into practical effect, and it must be said, with considerable momentary success, however ephemeral the final results of his efforts may have been.

In his preliminary discourse Lakanal had said: "We have not thought that the education of women should be less cared for than that of men. If women had been enlightened, sacerdotal fanatisicm would not have written the Revolution in characters of blood in so many unfortunate cities. The executioners in priestly stole would have threatened liberty with an impotent wrath. Let us render to this interesting portion of the human species all her rights to glory. Ah, how can a virtuous citizen fail, who finds in a modest companion the learning and understanding which make up the charms of

[9]Lakanal had read this preliminary discourse before the Convention, but when it came to printing the report as a whole, he had substituted for his preliminary discourse an essay on education by Sieyès. In a pamphlet: *Lakanal à ses Collègues* he explains his action as follows: "I was engaged in touching up my discourse for the press, when I saw in a journal, drawn up by the celebrated publicist (Sieyès), a faithful and illuminating exposition of the motives which had guided the Committee of Public Instruction. I did not hesitate to give this precious work in the place of mine. When you have found the good, to seek something else would be to seek the bad." Although Lakanal did not publish his own preliminary discourse, it was preserved and has been published by Guillaume, *op. cit.*, V, 662.

enlightened societies! A woman who joins education to virtue unites the qualities of both sexes."

Still another idea advanced by Lakanal has quite a modern ring:

> The national schools can be considered as so many partial families. They will govern themselves on the plan of the great social family. This mode of organization will easily assure order in the schools and the success of studies. It will impose on the pupils a daily activity, and will leave nothing to the arbitrariness of the teachers; it will render useless cruel punishments which it will proscribe forever; the degraded slave obeys the threatening scourge, but the heart of childhood is made for friendship.

Thus we find Lakanal foreshadowing the modern conception of student government.

The next day, November 16, 1794, the Convention passed a decree adopting the report on primary education. Primary schools were to be distributed over France according to population, one school to every thousand inhabitants. The subjects to be taught were reading and writing; the Declaration of the Rights of Man, and the Constitution of the French Republic; elementary instruction in republican morals and ethics; elements of the French language, both oral and written; the rules of simple calculation and carpentering; the elements of geography, and the history of free peoples; instruction in the principal phenomena and the most usual productions of nature. In addition, learning the *Recueil des actions héroïques* and the songs of triumph.[10]

Teaching was to be conducted in the French language. Pupils were to be instructed in exercises conducive to preserving health and developing the strength and agility of body. Military exercises were to be conducted under an officer of the National Guard. Swimming was to be taught in such localities as were suitable for this exercise. Other gymnastic exercises, such as running, wrestling, etc., were included in the program.

[10]The Convention proposed to publish *Annales de la République*. A part of this plan was to record heroic deeds performed by citizens of the Republic. On December 7, 1793, the Deputy Grégoire read before the Convention the first number of a *Recueil des traits héroïques et civiques*. This title became finally: *Recueil des actions héroïques et civiques des républicains français*. . . . On January 2, 1794, the Convention decreed that the issues of the *Recueil* should be sent to the municipalities, armies, Popular Societies, and to all the schools of the Republic; that they should be read publicly every ten days, and that the teachers should be required to teach them to their pupils.

Several times during the year the pupils, accompanied by their teachers, were to visit the nearest hospitals. On those same days they will aid in their domestic and rural tasks the old men and the parents of the defenders of the country. "From time to time the pupils must visit the factories and workshops . . . in order that they may have some idea of the advantages of human industry, and awaken in them a taste for the useful arts." A part of the pupils' time was to be spent in manual labor of different kinds.

Thus it is seen that Lakanal was not only the father of the normal school, but of the primary school as well. The next step in Lakanal's vision for education in a democracy will be the creation of secondary schools suitably distributed throughout the length and breadth of France.

THE CENTRAL SCHOOLS

On 26 Frimaire (Dec. 16), 1794, Lakanal made a report in behalf of the Committee of Public Instruction to the Convention concerning the establishing of schools for education above that provided by the primary schools. These institutions of higher training were to be called *Écoles Centrales,* and as implied in the title were to be centrally located, at least one to each Department. These schools maintained by the State were to replace the ancient *collèges,* most of which had been under the management of the various teaching orders of the church.

The following excerpts from Lakanal's preliminary address not only throw light on the nature and purpose of the *Écoles Centrales,* but illustrate as well the character of Lakanal's ability as a writer and as a speaker, for even to-day after the lapse of a century and half, the reader experiences a certain warmth from his eloquence:

> . . . But for the glory of the *patrie,* for the advancement of the human mind young citizens specially gifted by nature must find a sphere in which their talents may have full scope. Whatever may be the station or accident of their birth, whatever may be their fortune, the nation possesses herself of their genius. She molds them for herself rather than for themselves. She makes of them at her expense a Euclid or a Dalembert, a Quintilian or a Rollin, a Locke or a Condillac, a Drake or a La Peyrouse. She assembles for this great work all of her resources, because employing them in that fashion is less to consume them than to multiply them. She does not consider the expense of such an establishment, because she knows that it is

essentially bound to her physical and moral existence, as the armed force is to her political existence. . . . She will not defer this organization to more favorable times, because the times are marked by irresistible necessity! Tyranny has devoured the most celebrated geniuses. The torches of the sciences, half extinguished, scarcely illuminate a few isolated and solitary individuals, and if you do not hasten to relight them, the Republic will be lost in darkness.

. . . All the arts, all the sciences, are connected and interlaced; but there are some which have a closer connection than others. There are others which are so to speak superior, and which draw into their orbit a train of subordinate arts which are as their satellites. They are made to reflect mutually their light. Thus physics, chemistry, anatomy, natural history, although each has its own particular sphere and existence apart, are grouped around medicine; and you will not found schools useful for this until the others have their professorships and their class rooms. They are the members of a same body. The lack of one alone stops or hinders the action of all the others.

We have for a long time neglected *belles-lettres,* and some minds desiring to be regarded as profound, consider this study as futile. If they had observed the march of the human mind, they would have seen *belles-lettres* constantly rising as the dawn of the sciences. It is they which open the mind to the light of reason, and the heart to the impression of sentiment. They substitute morality for instinct, they polish peoples, they exercise their judgment, they render them more sensitive and at the same time more docile to the laws, more capable of great virtues. Among the peoples of antiquity who made their mark in history letters took the place of all the sciences. They had almost no true knowledge, but they were lettered. They had poets, orators, moral writers, and they were great in the eyes of the world.

The illustrious philosopher of Geneva, contemplating the corruption of enlightened peoples, came to the conclusion that letters had corrupted them. He should have said that they had been corrupted, not by letters, but in spite of letters which in that state of decadence still modified the action of vice, and relighted in the soul from time to time the torch of honor. Yes, even to the abuse that has been made of them, all proves the good usage that might have been made of them.

Encourage then the study and perfecting of *belles-lettres.* Revive the ancient tongues in order to enrich ours with their treasures. The authors of antiquity express the sacred love of country, the enthusiasm for liberty, and that virtuous hatred which every sensible being owes to the oppressors of humanity. Draw to you the principal languages of the modern world. That is the only way in which yours can be perfected. And your ideas will not be extended, nor will they be rectified except by the importation of all the foreign ideas. Then poetry, music, eloquence, which act so strongly on a free people, will take on the character which they should have and which they have never had; then, in place of Anacreon you will have Tyrtaeuses and Homers; in place of Isocrates you will have Demosthenes; especially if through your institutions the great principles of republican morality become popular, and if your divine legislation ceases to be the science of the small number.

In general, the necessity has been felt for these branches of instruction . . . but why have agriculture, commerce, the arts and trades, never had their schools? . . . You will avenge the arts and trades, agriculture and commerce, for this forgetfulness of nations: not by going like the kings to place a protecting hand on a given day on the plowshare. This empty ceremony degrades what it seems to elevate. But you will assign instructors who will shorten and assure the march of industry. Experience demonstrates the utility of these kinds of institutions. . . . Agriculture dates from the early days of the world, and it is still at an immense distance from perfection. The plow pushed at random has never been preceded by the torch of reflection. And if it is more flourishing along the banks of the Thames, it is because the grateful *patrie* has her eye on the farmer; and the first who sowed the acorn, whence come the vessels of the line, has obtained eternal statues.

It is greatly to the interest of the country to assure itself that the mathematics be cultivated and fathomed, because they give the fold of truth, because without them astronomy and navigation no longer have a guide, civil and naval architecture no longer have a rule, the science of artillery and sieges no longer a base.

Nothing in a word that has any degree whatsoever of public utility should be neglected in your system of free education, not even drawing, which up to the present has been considered only with relation to painting, but which with regard to the perfecting of the senses accustoms the eyes to seize strongly the features of nature, and is so to speak the geometry of the eyes, as music is that of the ear.

Following the preliminary report from which excerpts have been quoted, Lakanal presented to the Convention *projet de loi* in three chapters for the establishing of the *Écoles Centrales*. Only the first of these chapters is of interest to the modern reader. For the teaching of the sciences, letters and arts the project called for the establishing of Central Schools throughout the Republic, distributed according to population: one school for every three hundred thousand inhabitants. It provided one professor for each of the following subjects: mathematics, physics and experimental physics, natural history, method of the sciences or logic and analysis of sensations and ideas, political economy and legislation, philosophical history of peoples, hygiene, child delivery, diseases of women in childbed and those of infants, arts and trades, general grammar, *belles-lettres,* ancient languages, living languages (the most appropriate for a given locality), the art of drawing. In all the schools the lessons must be conducted in French. Every month the professors must give a public lecture on matters concerning the progress of the sciences, letters and arts most useful to society. In conjunction with every Central School there must be a public library, a garden and cabinet of natural history, a cabinet of experimental physics, a collection of machines and models for the arts and trades.

The *Écoles Centrales* were established, and Lakanal participated personally in supervising the founding of nineteen of them.[11] When Bonaparte established the *Lycées* as a part of his educational system, the Central Schools were either transformed into *Lycées* or abandoned.

LAKANAL AND ROUSSEAU

In September, 1794, the Convention decreed that the remains of Jean Jacques Rousseau should be transferred from their resting place at Ermenonville to Paris, and placed among the honored dead in the Pantheon. The previous year the Convention had decreed that the Vale of Montmorency where Rousseau composed his *Émile* should henceforth be called the Valley of Émile.[12] The day set apart for the removal of Rousseau's body should have a program of exercises suitable to the occasion. A plan presented by Lakanal was adopted. This philosophical celebration was to begin at the Tuileries and end at the Pantheon. It took place in October, 1794.[13] The inhabitants of Ermenonville traversed the twenty miles to Paris as an escort for the coffin of Jean-Jacques, which was concealed under a bower of shrubs and flowers. In the *Grand Bassin* of the Tuileries had been formed an artificial island in imitation of the *Ile des Peupliers,* the resting place of Rousseau's body at Ermenonville. The cortège was composed of musicians, botanists, artisans and artists. It preceded the funeral car which bore the coffin covered over with a blue cloth strewn with stars. To the sound of music interspersed with selections from Rousseau's own musical works, the

[11]The Central Schools were at the beginning of the Consulate in full development (Lavisse, p. 322). The rapidity with which they had surmounded their initial difficulties, frequently under the most unfavorable conditions, was truly surprising. Opened at the beginning of 1796, sometimes only in 1797, they were almost everywhere completely organized when the Consulate succeeded to the Directory. Each had a library, a botanical garden, a laboratory and scientific collections. The professors were regularly to the number of 9. They taught general grammar, ancient languages, belles-lettres, history, legislation, mathematics, physics and chemistry, natural history, drawing.

Speaking of the teachers, Lavisse says: "Never, perhaps, has France had a more remarkable teaching personnel as a whole than that of the Central Schools.

By decrees of Napoleon in 1802-03 45 lycées were created, and the Central Schools were abandoned in 1803-04.

[12]*Mercure français,* No. 119, Nov. 9, 1793.

[13]Paul Lacroix, *Directoire, Consulat et Empire* (Paris, 1884), p. 195.

coffin was deposited on a platform around which the women who had read *La Nouvelle Héloïse* and the men who had perused the *Émile* vied with each other in doing homage to the remains of the romancer and philosopher. Such was the exaggerated sentimentality of the moment, all the bystanders burst into bitter tears of sorrow over the corpse of poor old Jean Jacques who had died sixteen years before.

In the week following the celebration, a report by Marie-Joseph Chénier included a paragraph concerning the Rousseau celebration:

> In the festival celebrated in honor of J. J. Rousseau the details were natural and unaffected, the emblems easy to grasp, the groups skilfully distributed and suitable for the type of celebration. The inscriptions were not disfigured by a barbarous language, nor by the jargon of *bel esprit*. The music was neither noisy nor ostentatious. The melodious romances of Jean-Jacques, the books which represented his genius; those Genevans who lived with him and whose fathers witnessed his birth; those farmers companions of his last days, confidants of his last thoughts; those children, those mothers who with the book *Émile* in hand, addressed to the great man their grateful homages; those three Republics, intermingling their flags and swearing alliance with each other over the sacred pages of the *Contrat social;*—all filled the soul with a religious melancholy, with a delicious and profound sentiment worthy of the good, the sensitive Jean-Jacques, worthy too of the French Republicans repairing the faults of their enslaved ancestors, and rendering homage to the memory of a liberator of the human race.

This quotation not only throws light on the Rousseau celebration itself, but is an indirect compliment on Lakanal's planning and management of the celebration.

The removal of the remains of Rousseau to the Pantheon brought a keen revival of interest in his life and works, which explains the following entry in the proceedings of the Committee of Public Instruction for October 2, 1794: "The citizens Lakanal and Goujon will proceed to Ermenonville and into the valley of Émile *(ci-devant Montmorency)* in order to obtain there all the information they can gather concerning the person and the works of the immortal J. J. Rousseau."

The widow of Rousseau, Thérèse Levasseur, had been granted a pension of 1,200 *livres* by the Constituent Assembly.[14] The Convention raised the pension to 1,500 *livres*. When a *conventionnel* had moved

[14]Guillaume, *op. cit.*

that "the widow of J. J. Rousseau be invited to be present at the transfer of the ashes of her husband," Lakanal opposed the motion, saying: "According to the information which I received in the places where Jean-Jacques spent his last years and in accordance with the sentiments which he seems to have experienced in the last days of his life, I believe that the Convention has done enough for the widow of Jean-Jacques in granting her a pension." "The Convention passed to the order of the day," says the record, which is a way of saying that the Convention agreed with Lakanal.

On September 25, 1794, Thérèse appeared before the bar of the Convention for the purpose of offering a packet containing a manuscript of Rousseau which bore on its cover the notation that it was not to be opened until 1801. After discussion, the Convention decided to open the packet, and called for a report of its contents for the next day. Lakanal was appointed to scrutinize the manuscript and to make the report. In his report he stated that the manuscript was that of the *Confessions,* more correct and more carefully done than the manuscript which had served for the publishing of his works, and while it would no doubt serve a useful purpose whenever a new edition of the *Confessions* should be published, the differences between it and the printed edition were not sufficient to justify its publication at that moment. One of the statements of Lakanal in his report is worthy of quotation: "The reading of the manuscripts of the author of the *Contrat social* and the *Émile* affords naturally a reflection that has not been voiced up to this time in the various judgments formed on the character of the works of this great man. His first draft in composition is always an ingenious thought, but he effaces it subsequently in order to substitute sentiment for it. In all the erasures of his works, the language of the heart is substituted for that of the mind." Continuing, Lakanal expresses the opinion that there are still private portfolios of the manuscripts of Rousseau that have not yet enlightened Europe. "The art of enjoying these treasures," he says, "is by properly distributing them, and it is especially the regenerated French whom it behooves to possess the works of the philosopher who produced the Revolution of Liberty."

Soon after this, Lakanal presented to the Convention several manuscripts, "fifteen cahiers written entirely in the hand of this great man." They had been offered by the Citizeness Masuyer, wife of one of the Deputies. Presumably, the manuscripts were turned over to Lakanal for examination, for on October 19 he appeared before the tribune of the Convention and pronounced the following words:

> I come to offer to the National Convention and to my country the fruit of my researches upon the manuscripts of J. J. Rousseau, inserted up to this time in private portfolios. Here are fifteen *cahiers* written entirely in the hand of this great man. They include several pieces which have never appeared in print and the germs of the principal products of his genius. In them are to be seen the first draft of the thoughts of this philosopher and the modifications they underwent before arriving at that admirable perfection of style which is to be found in all that left his pen. It would be an excellent treatise on the art of writing. I count on offering you soon the original of the work of the Genevan philosopher on the government of Poland. It was communicated at the time by the author to Necker, who had it copied in a fair hand. This work is all the more precious in that there are found in it several important passages which have not been printed, because they appeared to smack too strongly of despotism. The text, denatured in all the editions, is here in all its purity.[15]

This report was accepted, and on November 2, 1794, the Committee of Public Instruction charged Lakanal with the duty of having the necessary labors performed in order to extract from the various manuscripts of J. J. Rousseau the works which were not yet printed, so as to deliver them to the public; and with the further task of having engraved the various portraits and drawings with which to enrich this collection.[16]

In the article "Rousseau" in the *France littéraire* (1836) Quérard, says Guillaume, inserted the following note:

> M. Lakanal, member of the National Institute, had proposed to publish, in one volume in-12 and one volume in-4, several manuscripts of Rousseau, extracts from those collected in the library of the Committee of Public Instruction, and in several other literary depositories. These manuscripts formed seventeen *cahiers* of twenty pages each. Two included considerable additions to the *Contrat social,* three additions to *Émile,* three to *La Nouvelle Héloïse,* two to the *Confessions,* two to the writings on music, one including general views on agriculture, commerce and finances; two containing notes on the personages cited by the author; and the key of his writings or nomenclature of names that are indicated in them

[15]*Ibid.*

[16]On Nov. 8, 1794, the Committee appointed Lakanal and Deleyre to examine and report on a manuscript which had been found in the effects of the late Hérault de Séchelles, who had been guillotined. . . . This was a French translation of the works of Francis Bacon. Five days later, at the instigation of Lakanal, the Convention passed a decree authorizing the Committee of Public Instruction to publish this translation of Bacon's works.

only by initials. To these extracts M. Lakanal proposed to join a great number of letters written by the philosopher of Geneva to several scholars, men of letters and artists, who had been kind enough to communicate them to him and permit him to give them to the public. But the editor not having obtained subscriptions to cover the expenses of the enterprise, M. Lakanal did not publish these manuscripts.[17]

Guillaume also quotes from a certain Morin: "What became of the manuscripts which Lakanal had extracted from those collected in the library of the Committee of Public Instruction? . . . It must be believed that Lakanal to whom they were intrusted for the publication which he projected, neglected to return them, and that at his death these precious documents were probably scattered, perhaps even destroyed."

OTHER ACCOMPLISHMENTS

The career of Lakanal in the National Convention has been traced, but there are several things that have been omitted and that should have mention. To him goes the honor of causing to be passed a copyright law protecting the property of writers, composers of music, painters and designers.[18] This law was a generation in advance of such a law passed in England at the urging of the novelist Bulwer-Lytton. The laws of 1791 protecting dramatic works had lapsed. Lakanal had them restored. He also favored a law that was passed against defacing or destroying historical and artistic monuments. In this connection Lakanal is said to have coined the word *vandalisme,* a word which not only gained currency and won a place in the French dictionary, but also finds its cognate in the English language.[19] It may be of interest to note that Lakanal also coined the word *édémenter,* which although it did not become popular, would have filled a useful place in the language. By it Lakanal meant to simplify rather than to abridge or make a résumé. He used it in discussing the preparation of elementary books for use in the schools.

[17]*Ibid.,* VI, 945.

[18]Paul Lacroix, *op. cit.,* p. 273.

[19]In an address at the inauguration of the statue of Lakanal at Foix, September 24, 1882, Paul Janet said: "Sa proposition de décret contre les actes de *vandalisme* (expression dont il est l'auteur) commis à cette époque contre les monuments des arts. . ." In the Lavisse "Histoire de France Contemporaine" the statement is made that Grégoire (a fellow member of Lakanal on the Committee of Public Instruction) boasted of having coined the word *vandalisme.*

Lakanal was instrumental in the establishing of the *Lycée des Arts,* a forerunner of the *École Polytechnique,* the school of living oriental languages, and he also sponsored the creation of the Bureau of Longitudes.

5

DIRECTORY TO RESTORATION

FOLLOWING THE ADOPTION OF A CONSTITUTION, THE CONSTITUENT ASsembly had dissolved on September 30, 1791, in favor of the Legislative Assembly, which in turn yielded to the National Convention of September 21, 1792. The immediate declaration of a Republic made it essential that France should be provided with a new Constitution suitable for a Republic. In the summer and fall of 1793 a new Constitution had been prepared and adopted, but was not put into practice because of the exigencies brought about by the Reign of Terror. It was not until after 9 Thermidor and the subsidence of the Terror that the National Convention could again turn its attention to the perfecting of the Constitution and the adopting of insitutions of a permanent rather than a temporary or revolutionary nature. This was the moment to which may be applied an American writer's tribute to the accomplishments of the National Convention: "It first of all European governments outlined a system of public education in which were included public schools, manual training schools, technical schools, universities, a conservatory of arts, museums, and a polytechnic institute."[1] The institutions mentioned are owing in their origins more to Lakanal than to any other one man. If, as has been said, Carnot was the organizer of victory, it may also be said that Lakanal deserves to be considered the initiator of public instruction distributed in conformity with the needs of a democracy. Napoleon was but a continuator of Lakanal in his educational views and policies.

In the Year III (1795) the Constitution was adopted, and the Convention gave way to the Directory. France was henceforth, for a few years, to be governed by five Directors and two Councils. These Councils were composed of 250 and 500 members respective-

[1]Shailer Mathews: *The French Revolution* (Paris, 1912), p. 249.

ly. To the Council of the Ancients belonged married (or widowed) men of forty years of age or over, and to the Council of Five Hundred belonged men under forty years of age. The Council of Five Hundred had the duty of initiating laws, and the Council of Ancients that of approving or rejecting the laws proposed by the larger body. Lakanal was among the number of Deputies who entered into the Councils of the Directory. Owing to his age, 33, he automatically became a member of the Council of Five Hundred.

ORGANIZES THE FRENCH INSTITUTE

One of the early tasks performed under the Directory was the perfecting of the French Institute which had been incorporated into law in the new Constitution. The formation of a national Institute had been suggested by Talleyrand, endorsed later by Condorcet, and incorporated into law in the Constitution by Daunou. The task of finally organizing the Institute fell to the Directory. The *règlements,* the set of regulations governing the organizing of the Institute, was drawn up by Lakanal.

When it came to the choice of the first membership of the Institute, it was decided that one-third of the members should be chosen by the Directory, and that this one-third (called the *tiers-électeur*) should in turn elect the remaining two-thirds of the membership. Lakanal was invited to present a list of names for the *tiers-électeur,* although, of the forty-eight names submitted by him only one-half, or twenty-four, were chosen. Among those rejected was Lakanal's friend, Du Pont de Nemours, who was considered too strongly royalist in his sympathies. A few years later, following Napoleon's rise to power, in 1799, Du Pont de Nemours became an exile in America where he founded the Du Pont family.[2]

When the one-third of the membership of the Institute had been chosen, and when it in turn had begun the process of selecting the remaining two-thirds of the membership, Lakanal was elected a member of the Class of Moral and Political Sciences. He was also appointed one of the two secretaries.

[2]Du Pont de Nemours went back to France in 1803, and returned to America after the downfall of Napoleon.

THE CONSTITUTION

The role of Lakanal in the Revolution was predominantly a cultural one. During the period of the Convention his participation in the trial of Louis XVI, the political side of his mission to Dordogne, and his contribution to the discussion of the new Constitution form the more important aspects of his political activities. On the subject of the Constitution, he made an address at the bar of the Convention. The closing paragraph of this address runs as follows:

> I believe this plan useful to liberty if this Directory, central point of execution, is circumscribed within well defined limits; if its functions are clearly enunciated. I demand: (1). That there be added to the Constitution a chapter concerning the relations of the executive power and the legislative power. (2). That in this chapter shall be specified the prerogatives of these two powers. (3). I demand the delivery of these observations to the Commission of Eleven[3] to which I shall communicate a work that I have prepared on the real functions of the executive power.[4] Lakanal's proposition was not adopted. His work concerning the functions of the executive power was lost. It would be interesting to know just what views he held on the subject.

Elected to the Council of Five Hundred, Lakanal on January 21, 1796, took the oath of hatred to royalty prescribed that day for all the members. Accompanying the formula: "I swear hatred to royalty," Lakanal made the following motion: "The Council has ordered that all public officials sign the oath that they have taken.[5] You know to how great an extent since the beginning of the Revolution we have made light of loyalty to oaths. I demand that an authentic document attest and preserve them; that the *procès-verbal* (proceedings) of this meeting be individually signed by all the members and deposited in the archives." This proposition was adopted. Among the names signed were those of Boissy d'Anglas who became Senator and Count of the Empire, then Peer of France under the Restoration; Cambacérès, who became Arch-Chancellor of the Empire, then Prince, then Duke of Parma; Sieyès, who became Senator and Count of the Empire. There could be mentioned many other names of men who forgot their oath of hatred to

[3]This has reference to the committee on the Constitution. Marcus, *op. cit.*, p. 83.

[4]*Réimpression du Moniteur.*

[5]Marcus, *op. cit.*, p. 93.

royalty, and who throve and prospered under the Empire and the Restoration. It is to Lakanal's credit that he remained true to his republican principles, although his staunch adherence to these principles brought ruin to his public career. Had he fallen in with the trend of the times, he would no doubt have gone far under Napoleon.

Two days after his motion concerning the oath of hatred to royalty, Lakanal again took the floor in a flood of indignation against the *jeunesse dorée,* the *muscadins* of the Directory, who by devices escaped conscription in the army and troubled the tranquillity of the capital, whilst the sons of the *sans-culottes* and the peasants fought like lions on the frontier.

> You celebrated day before yesterday the anniversary of the Republic. It can rest only on the ruins of all privileges and all abuses. I am going to denounce to you one that for a long time has nourished indignation in the bottom of my heart, and which must be eradicated at the roots. I am going to denounce to you that throng of dishonored youth, included in the conscription, who have not yet expiated at the frontier the shame of having done nothing for their country. In vain does the legislator strive to rally them under the banner of Liberty. Their labors until now have produced only the triumph of the guilty and the flouting of the laws. The cause of these affronts to the national will, you will find it in a throng of female solicitors, the opprobrium of their sex; you will find it in the corrupting influence of the feasts where shines the gold stolen from the Republic; you will find it in the criminal slackness, in the corruption and want of patriotism of the agents of execution, and principally of the health officers of the whole Republic. Especially on them must a pitiless eye be cast. They go about distributing bundles of certificates of sickness to young men, who every day gamble without shame in our public places, and who in the evening, gathering at the public spectacles, insult the national authority and boldly mock the songs of our triumphs. . . . The cowards must either go and serve the Republic on our frontiers, or the Republic must vomit them from its womb. . . . I demand the formation of a commission charged with proposing to you a method of early and sure revision of all the certificates delivered by the councils or officers of health.[6]

The Lavisse history of France treats the Muscadins at considerable length, and it will not be amiss to quote a few lines: "These gentlemen of the gilded youth, *ci-devant* fops, to-day *"collets noirs"* and *"bas blancs"* who are sometimes called *"jacobins blancs,"* and commonly "Muscadins," were the cocks of the walk. There were among them slackers. . . . The general headquarters of the Muscadins was in the

[6]*Ibid.*, pp. 94-96.

Palais-Royal, which had become again the center of luxury, elegance, gambling, speculation, and of prostitution. . ."

Lakanal's proposal was adopted by the Council of Five Hundred, but its effects scarcely outlasted the echoes momentarily awakened in the Assembly. The wind-mill at which he was tilting was real, but his victory was as elusive as that of Don Quixote.

Under the Directory Lakanal appeared frequently before the Council of Five Hundred in behalf of measures of minor importance. On November 5, 1795, he read a report and submitted a resolution concerning the elementary books, the preparation of which had been entered in a competition, and was successful in obtaining action favorable to the publishing of some of these books.[7] On January 31, 1796, he secured the appointment of a commission to facilitate the teaching of botany. Other measures put forward by him and adopted were a resolution relative to the pay of librarians in the Central Schools, the rectified *règlement* of the French Institute, putting the Observatory of Lacaille at the disposition of the Bureau of Longitudes, the maintenance of the Central School of the Department of Hérault at Montpellier, and the addition of a national garden to the Central School of Aveyron.

On May 19, 1797, Lakanal was included among the outgoing members of the Council of Five Hundred. On April 17, 1798, he was reelected from the Department of Seine-et-Oise. He declined to serve, was again elected, and a second time declined. Marie Joseph Chénier was chosen in his place. In declining the honor the second time, Lakanal declared: "When hostile armies were at the gates of the capital I accepted the perilous duties of representative of the people; to-day, when the Alps and Pyrenées are leveled under the triumphal marches of French armies, I withdraw apart with my books and a few friends, the only blessings that my heart covets."

COMMISSIONER OF THE RHINE DEPARTMENTS

"But soon new dangers called him to new sacrifices." In the disastrous year of 1799, when Italy was evacuated and lost, when

[7] *Réimpression du Moniteur.*

the English were disembarking in Holland, when the Russians were penetrating Switzerland, when the Austrians were marching on the Var and on the Rhine, at a moment when France was threatened from all sides, Lakanal was sent by the Directory to the frontier of the North as Commissioner General of the four Departments of the Rhine: Rhin-et-Moselle, Roer, Sarre, and Mont-Tonnerre.[8] These four new Departments on the left bank of the Rhine which treaties and victories had joined to France, had been badly administered. With signal success Lakanal undertook to eradicate the abuses, giving these Departments a strong administration, and pursuing with inexorable integrity those whom he called *pillards,* that is to say, unworthy officials who oppressed the region, greedy army contractors who feathered their nests at the expense of the army. Some of these officials he removed from office by public decrees which covered them with shame and ignominy, and threw the damaged merchandise of others into the Rhine. It is said that one day he caused to be poured into the river so many casks of adulterated wine the waters of the Rhine below Mayence ran red. The inhabitants of the region were greatly impressed by the energy displayed by him, and especially by his attitude in the face of the enemy. When Prince Charles marched upon Mayence at the head of 30,000 men, and when the civic officials were counseling retreat, Lakanal said: "The cowards can flee. My duty is to save the place. I remain."

A letter signed by the leading public men and citizens of Mayence and addressed to the heads of the Directory at Paris, contains the following: ". . . Men who have all to fear from the return of their tyrants . . . who have property and families: these men, Citizen Directors, have need of a guarantee, and this guarantee they will find only in the nomination of a civil commissioner for the garrison of Mayence. But he must have given certain pledges to the Revolution and to the Republic, and he must have acquired the honor of being inscribed on the list of proscription by absolute royalty. Such a man, Citizen Directors, (and we believe we have found him in the person of the Citizen Lakanal, Commissioner of the Republic in our Departments), clothed with the power of op-

[8]Marcus, *op. cit.,* pp. 97-100.

posing his veto to the decisions of a council of war, of preparing vigorous and obstinate defense in case of attack, and of not capitulating in any case without stipulating for all the patriots and for their families and their property, such a man alone can tranquillize us, and determine those among us, who by the nature of their employments should remain at Mayence in case of siege, not abandoning their posts, and exposing themselves to all the perils for the safety of the Republic."

THE COUP D'ETAT OF BONAPARTE

While Lakanal's vigorous administration attracted to him many friends and partisans, it also brought him many enemies who did not fail to complain and to denounce him to the Directory. In the midst of these recriminations came Bonaparte's *coup d'État* of 18 Brumaire. The 22 Brumaire (Nov. 12, 1799), less than four months after Lakanal had assumed the duties of Commissioner General, Cambacérès, Minister of Justice informed Lakanal that he was expected to retain his post temporarily, and that he counted on his fidelity.[9] But Lakanal was lukewarm to the *coup d'État,* and in reply to Cambacérès he did not conceal his opinion that the *coup d'État* was the beginning of a dictatorship and the abolition of the representative system. In retaliation Cambacérès read to the Consuls a long report concerning the attacks directed against Lakanal, and the justification which the latter had presented in answer to his enemies. In the end, Lakanal was recalled. In this connection he received the following letter from Bonaparte:

General Bonaparte, First Consul of the Republic, to the Citizen Lakanal, Commissioner of the Government in the four Departments of the left bank of the Rhine.

The important services which you have rendered to so many distinguished men will earn in all times rights to the esteem of men. You can count on the desire that I have of giving you proofs, etc.[10]

Thus Bonaparte held out the olive branch to Lakanal, and there

[9]Cambacérès was a Deputy to the National Convention and member of the Committee of Public Safety, Deputy to the Council of Five Hundred, and one of the five Directors. He became Minister of Justice 2 Thermidor An VII, a post occupied until 3 Nivôse An VIII, when he replaced Sieyès as Second Consul. He was Chancellor of the Napoleonic Empire.

[10]Marcus, *op. cit.*, p. 99.

is no doubt that if he had approved Napoleon's ambitions, he would have had the friendship and patronage of the First Consul, and it is interesting to conjecture, as indeed some of his admirers have done, that he instead of Fontanes might have become the head of the French educational system when it was reorganized in the period of the Empire.

Henry Jouin, a French scholar who wrote a monograph on the friendship between Lakanal and the sculptor, David d'Angers, reproduced one of Lakanal's letters and remarks: "In secondary education the study of Greek does not precede the study of Latin. Why? If Lakanal, accepting the offers of the First Consul, had been Grand Master of the University of France from 1808 to 1815, the programmes would no doubt have been different from what they were as enacted by Fontanes."[11]

As has been stated, Lakanal left the Council of Five Hundred in 1797. From then until the second Restoration (1815), with the exception of the four months spent at Mayence as Commissioner General of the Departments of the Rhine, he occupied positions relatively unimportant.[12] From 1797 to 1804 he was a professor of ancient languages in the Central Schools of the Seine, schools whose founding he had assisted in supervising. From 1804 to 1809 he was one of the administrators of the Lycée Bonaparte with the title of Procureur-Gérant (Économe). From 1809 to 1815 he was Inspector of Weights and Measures for the four Departments of Seine-Inférieure, Oise, Eure and Somme. None of these positions was of a national scope, but as Inspector of Weights and Measures he performed a significant task in putting into practice the metric system which in 1801 had been adopted by law, but the execution of which had remained in abeyance.[13]

VILLARCEAUX

Westward from Paris, in the direction of Rouen, near the town

[11]Henry Jouin, *Lakanal et David d'Angers,* (Angers, 1902).

[12]In a notebook discovered years after Lakanal's death appears the following notation made by him: "When a man has drunk for a long time in the cup of power, it is very difficult for him to enter again into the class of citizens."

[13]Marcus, *op. cit.,* p. 100. Labroue, *op. cit.,* Introduction.

of Magny, Lakanal purchased the presbytery of Villarceaux, where he made his home dividing his time between his official duties in Paris and the enjoyment of country life. When earlier in the Revolution the clergy had been dispossessed by the government, church houses and lands were sold at a small price to the citizenry of the Republic. Lakanal no doubt purchased Villarceaux at small cost from the government. Joseph Bonaparte likewise possessed an estate formerly belonging to the church at Mortefontaine, not far from Paris, where he lived until his flight to America after the battle of Waterloo.[14]

Lakanal lived at Villarceaux with his wife and one or more children. The date of his marriage is unknown, and nothing is known of his wife further than that her maiden name was Marie-Barbe François, that she died at Mobile, Alabama, in May 1836, and was buried in the cemetery at Ganon Bend, now known as Garrow's Bend.

That Lakanal was married while living at Villarceaux is attested by a letter, still extant, which Madame Lakanal wrote to Madame Morand, wife of the professor of legislation in the Central Schools of Paris. Lakanal's friendship with Morand had begun when they were colleagues at Moulins, and was destined to continue throughout life. Morand accompanied Lakanal on his mission to the Departments of the Rhine. Many years later when he was in exile in America, Lakanal wrote a letter in which he referred to Morand as his *fidus Achates*. In another letter Lakanal mentions being detained at Villarceaux by the illness of "three sick ones." This led certain French scholars to conjecture that he had a wife and two children. That he had one child, a daughter, is certain. Her name was Alexandrine, and she married Lucien Charvet in New Orleans.[15]

When Lakanal became Inspector of Weights and Measures his

[14]The *Procès-verbal of the Committee of Public Instruction* of August 26, 1794, contains the following entry: "L'Inventaire du jardin du ci-devant château de Morfontaine, appartenant ci-devant au nommé Durney, frappé du glaive de la loi." Joseph Durnier. former treasurer of foreign affairs, had been condemned to death 28 Ventôse (March 18).

[15]Two letters among the Lakanal Papers in the Howard Memorial Library in New Orleans mention the daughter Alexandrine.

headquarters were in Rouen. He divided his time between Rouen and Villarceaux. He became a member of the *Société d'Émulation* of Rouen, a body established in 1793 "for the progress of the sciences, letters, and arts." Similar socieies were founded in numerous places in France.

As stated, Lakanal had been elected to membership in the French Institute in the Class of Moral and Political Sciences. Among the members of this group as has been stated in the Introduction, were the most influential free-thinkers of the times: Volney, Garat, Ginguené, Cabanis, Mercier, Naigeon and Lakanal, whom Bonaparte sneeringly dubbed *"idéologues"* (ideologists). The word *idéologie* had come into current usage from a book: *Projet d'Éléments d'Idéologie à l'Usage des Écoles Centrales,* written by Destutt de Tracy, who was likewise a member of the Class of Moral and Political Sciences. These so-called ideologists were all men who had been hostile to the church and to the ambition of Bonaparte. For this reason Bonaparte reorganized the Institute, suppressing the Class of Moral and Political Sciences. The members of this Class were distributed in other Classes in such manner as to dissociate their group. Lakanal was transferred to the Class of History and Ancient Literature.[16]

In 1802 was founded the Legion of Honor, of which Bonaparte in his capacity of First Consul was the head. Lakanal was chosen as a legionnaire, but refusing to take the oath which accompanied the appointment, his membership was not recorded. He did, however, receive the insignia of the order, and the decoration was preserved by his widow for many years after his death.

"Of all the acts of the Consulate," says Aulard in his history of the French Revolution, "the one in which the contemporaries saw especially a return to the customs of the monarchy, was the law of May 19, 1802, which created a Legion of Honor." As to how the decoration was at first received is reflected in the following passage quoted by Aulard:

[16]In the reorganization effected in 1803, the Institute was composed of four divisions instead of three: Class of Physical Sciences and Mathematics, Class of French Language and Literature, Class of History and Ancient Literature, Class of Beaux-Arts. The Class of History and Ancient Literature was a substitute for the Academy of Inscriptions and Belles-Lettres of the Old Regime.

> M. Réal could not at the first moment show himself to us without blushing. I found Garat at Fouché's, the lapels of his coat carefully folded across, in order that there might not be seen on the breast of a philosopher the too unequivocal sign of the vanity of a courtier; but the pitiless Fouché made a joke of forcing Garat to uncover it for me. In a few days people became accustomed to it; in a few months they came to the point of envying it.[17]

It is not strange, then, that Lakanal with his hatred of anything that smacked of the monarchy, should refuse to subscribe to the legionnaire's oath. His action was consistent with his republicanism.

Nevertheless, the next few years were to witness the transformation of the Consulate into the Empire and the transition of Bonaparte into Napoleon. With the development of Napoleon's far reaching plans for education and cultural institutions, Lakanal seems to have become somewhat reconciled to the Emperor, and aspired to play a larger role in the educational efforts of the times. In a letter supposedly addressed to Fontanes whom Napoleon in 1808 appointed Grand Master of the University, Lakanal cried out: "Let me cease being a helot in the Republic of Letters. Do what you will with me, but deign to do something!"[18] That there was opposition to him is shown by a letter which he addressed to the Emperor protesting against the calumnies of which he was the object. As to what these calumnies were we do not know, and can only conjecture. The fact that he was one of the regicides, that he had remained so strongly republican, that he was a Deist and vigorously anti-clerical, that he had recently joined the order of the Masons (Sept. 20, 1807), all of these things were calculated to make bitter enemies for him.[19]

Lakanal did not succeed in his plea for advancement, and on September 24, 1808, he addressed to Fontanes his resignation as *Procureur-Gérant* of the Lycée Bonaparte, declaring that he wished henceforth to belong only to the truth, and that he preferred Liberty to the Uni-

[17]The quotation is from the memoirs of Mme. de Chastenay.

[18]Lafranc, *op. cit.,* Introduction, p. 29.

[19]Labroue, *op. cit.,* Introduction, p. 29, asks rhetorically if the unfavorable reports of which Lakanal complains may not have been because of his personal conduct, citing as his authority E. Welvert, "Lakanal en Amérique," published in *Feuilles d'histoire* Oct. 1, 1910, p. 370. What Welvert has to say is contained in a footnote and without any supporting evidence. He states that Lakanal caused great scandal at the Lycée Bonaparte by keeping a mistress there, and that this mistress gave birth to a child in 1807. Welvert is an exceedingly bitter critic of Lakanal.

versity; adding that temporarily he would continue in his duties, which he did until 1809, when he was relieved and then appointed Inspector of Weights and Measures. Upon his retirement from the School System, Fontanes granted him a pension of 3,000 francs.

THE RESTORATION

Following the death of the Dauphin on June 8, 1795, the Count of Provence (brother of Louis XVI) who was in exile at Verona, had hastened to issue a manifesto announcing his succession to the throne of France as Louis XVIII. In this manifesto, among other things, he had declared his firm intention of avenging the death of his brother by punishing the regicides without mercy. Intervening events had postponed the ascent of Louis XVIII to the throne until after Napoleon's first abdication in 1814. While in 1814 no action was taken against the regicides, there was agitation of the question, and a book was published in Paris whose title was: *Procès ou Assassinat juridique de Louis XVI.* In this book the records of the trial were faithfully reproduced, together with the record of how each of the Deputies to the National Convention had voted on that momentous occasion, as well as the remarks made by each one in casting his vote.

Lakanal became uneasy, and began converting his property into cash, selling Villarceaux, which must have brought the larger portion of the 30,000 francs which he accumulated as a fund to support him in exile in case it became necessary for him to flee from France. The return of Napoleon from Elba must have reassured him, but the defeat at Waterloo together with the approach of the Allies toward Paris gave him grave concern.

> The events which led to the second Restoration found him (Lakanal) in a modest position. His name, naturally above all, to be inscribed first on the lists of proscription, he made his preparations for exile. The hostile armies were at the gates of Paris. Some former members of the national assemblies had gathered at the home of Barras. They discussed ways and means of making a last effort to spare Paris the shame of a second occupation. But the sinews of all attempts of this kind, money, were lacking. M. Lakanal was present at this meeting. He had with him a modest sum, which however was his whole fortune, and which was to aid him in his exile. He offered it for the execution of the projects which were in course of deliberation, and which had no further result than having given rise to this noble offer.

These words were spoken in 1845 at the tomb of Lakanal by his friend and physician, François Lélut, who added: "Lakanal was praised for his devotion. A tear came into the eye of Cambon who shook his hand, but all these projects stopped there." The sum mentioned by Lélut was thirty thousand francs ($6,000), the whole of the amount which Lakanal had been able to accumulate in view of his approaching exile.

When later several lists of proscription appeared in succession, the name of Lakanal did not appear on them, the reason being no doubt that he had not subscribed to the *Acte additionnel* as the Napoleonic constitution adopted during the Hundred Days had been called.[20] It is true that he had continued to hold his place as Inspector of Weights and Measures, but that had been due to an oversight on the part of the Restoration government and was not to be considered as evidence of adhesion to the restored Napoleon. The ire of Louis XVIII was directed against those who had actively aided and abetted Napoleon in the period between his return from Elba and the catastrophe at Waterloo.[21]

However, even before the first proscription list appeared on January 16, 1816, Lakanal was already on the high seas bound for America. His departure was no doubt hastened by the trial and execution of General Labédoyère and Marshal Ney, as well as the condemnation to death of Lavalette. Labédoyère had been in charge of Grenoble, and when on his triumphal march from Cannes to Paris, Napoleon had arrived at that place, instead of opposing him, Labédoyère threw open the gates of the city and welcomed him with open arms. Marshal Ney had been sent from Paris at the head of troops to intercept and capture Napoleon. Ney boasted

[20]The Additional Act was voted upon by the people of France during the Hundred Days with a majority of 1,500,000 to 4,206.—Duruy, *Histoire de France* (Paris, 1866), p. 653.

[21]On January 12, 1816, Louis XVIII issued an ordinance from the Tuileries containing seven articles, one of which concerns the regicides: Those of the regicides, who in contempt of an almost boundless clemency, voted for the Additional Act, or accepted offices or employments from the usurper, and who by so doing, declared themselves irreconcilable enemies of France, and of the lawful government, are forever excluded the realm, and are bound to quit in the space of one month, under penalty of the punishment enacted by the 33rd article of the penal code. They can not possess any civil right in France, nor any property, title or pension granted to them of favor.—*Niles' Weekly Register,* March 16, 1816, p. 42.

that he would bring Napoleon back to Paris in an iron cage, but when the two men met Ney's heart melted, and he joined with the Emperor. Lavalette had been general postmaster under Napoleon during the period of the Empire, and when the news arrived in Paris that Napoleon was on the march towards the city, Lavalette hastened to the post-office, and finding the Bourbon postmaster Ferrand in the act of flight, he took over the post-office, and was in full charge when Napoleon reached Paris. For these acts these three men had been condemned to die; but owing to the fidelity and ingenuity of his invalid wife, Lavalette had escaped from the *Conciergerie* on the eve of the day on which he was to be executed. Spirited out of Paris and rushed to the northern border by some sportively inclined Englishmen, Lavalette barely reached Belgian soil before the signal telegraph sent a message to detain the party at Valenciennes. A dense fog prevented the message being delivered in time to intercept the fugitives. A hue and cry was raised over the escape of Lavalette such as had probably never been known before in France. The ultra-royalists were in dire rage, the police were frantic, the royal household tremendously upset. In spite of every search, every precaution, every threat against those who might harbor the fugitive, every inducement in the way of reward for his capture, Lavalette had got away. It was in the midst of this turmoil that Lakanal took to flight.

Following the execution of Marshal Ney in December Richelieu drew up a motion proposing the banishment of the imperial family, and the thirty-eight persons named in the Ordinance of July 24, but the commission greatly extended the number of exceptions to amnesty . . . Regicides must be punished as having revolted, not against the laws of the state, but against the laws of nature. In a conflict between a moderate ministry and a chamber strongly regicide, agreement was made more difficult by the escape of Lavalette, which the ultras regarded as proof of revolutionary machinations. The exile of the regicides was passed with a majority.

LETTERS OF INTRODUCTION

By December, 1815, Lakanal's mind was definitely made up to flee, as he assembled a number of letters of introduction to men in America. On Dec. 15, 1815, the United States Consul-General Warden at Paris addressed the following letter to General Mason of Virginia:

> I beg leave to introduce to you Mr. Joseph Lakanal, member of the French National Institute, Member of the Legion of Honor, Officer of the National University, and General Inspector of the new Metrical System of France; who enamored of American freedom, bids adieu to his native country, and proposes to spend the remainder of his days as a peaceful cultivator, on the banks of the Ohio. Favored by fortune, he has collected a considerable sum for the purchase of lands; but this is of minor importance to the United States compared with his superior talents, acquirements, and ardent zeal for every useful improvement. To state all that he has done in the foundation and progress of the celebrated scientific and literary institutions of Paris would fill a volume. His long and useful services have been often acknowledged by their most distinguished members; and he carries with him many written and printed monuments of their esteem and regret. A person so highly gifted must be a valuable acquisition to the country in which he resides.[22]

Thouin, who had been head gardener of Louis XVI, keeper of the *Jardin du Roi,* the name of which had been changed to the *Jardin des Plantes,* and with whom Jefferson had had correspondence upon agricultural and horticultural matters, wrote to Thomas Jefferson as follows:

> Permit me to present to you one of our learned confreres, M. Lakanal, member of the department of history and ancient literature of our Institute, a man to be recommended by his morality as well as by his learning, to whom our scientific institutions owe many debts. He leaves our old Europe, in which civilization seems to be retrograding, to settle with several of his friends, in Young America, which is called to such high destinies, and where society already offers to its happy citizens, liberty, tranquility, and good fortune.[23]

On December 28, 1815, the Marquis de La Fayette addressed to Lakanal the following letter on the eve of his departure for the United States:

> I feel grateful for the sentiments you have expressed relative to me; and I regret that your sudden departure should prevent the verbal expression of my feelings.
>
> Not being acquainted at this time with the public men of Kentucky, you may make use of this letter in a way which will meet your views, by presenting it to Mr. Madison, to Mr. Jefferson, who live in the upper part of Virginia; to General Nevils of Pittsburg, one of my aids-de-camp; to Mr. Clay, who is known in all the western states; as well as to Mr. Monroe and Mr. Crawford. Those gentlemen will be eager to favor your views. My regret

[22]From the *Courrier de la Louisiane,* May 31, 1822.
[23]Reeves, *op. cit.*

for the losses of France are mitigated by the idea that they will benefit the United States.

The friends of freedom need not however despond. They may carry with them the consoling hope that its cause is not lost in Europe;—and in France less than anywhere else. All that is great and useful in the Revolution will, I trust, be preserved.[24]

Accompanying the above letter La Fayette addressed the following introduction of Lakanal to Thomas Jefferson:

The bearer of these lines is Mr. Lakanal, Member of the French Institute, Officer of the University, and Inspector General of the New Metrical System, who abandons these functions and a handsome treatment to become a settler in the State of Kentucky. He has for several years been in the Representative Assemblies of France, and is going to seek in the U. S., Liberty, Security, and Happiness. I can not procure for him a greater gratification than by introducing him to you, and I know you will find a pleasure in favouring him with your advices and recommendations for the part of the Country where he means to settle himself and family.[25]

FLIGHT

Just at the moment when the hue and cry after Lavalette reached its climax Lakanal fled to Le Havre, where on or about January 9, 1816, he took ship for America. When a few days later the king's lists of proscription were published Lakanal's name did not appear on them, so that his exile, as he later claimed, was voluntary. However, his escape did not remain unnoticed, and he was the object of a search by the government police, who reported that he had fled to Milan. This is some indication of the secrecy surrounding his departure. By the Ordinance of March 21, 1816, he was deprived of membership in the French Institute by virtue of being a regicide, and also his retirement pension of 3,000 francs was suspended by the Commission of Public Instruction on June 25, 1816, "as not having been granted in conformity with the rules."

[24]*Courrier de la Louisiane,* May 31, 1822.

[25]La Fayette wrote his letter in English. Note his linguistic slip in translating a French word into an English one similar in appearance, but different in meaning. He translates the French *traitement* as *treatment,* when he should have said *salary* or *remuneration.* Reeves, *op. cit.*

6

LAKANAL IN KENTUCKY

THE TRADITIONALLY ACCEPTED DATE OF LAKANAL'S ARRIVAL IN AMERICA has been the year 1815. In every reference he ever made to his arrival in America Lakanal placed the date as 1815. In a manuscript preserved among the Lakanal Papers in the Howard Memorial Library, New Orleans, Lucien Charvet, his grandson, says that his grandfather sailed from France in 1815 on the "Salem" under Captain Destibéchau. However, a letter from Lakanal to Julien de Paris[1] was postmarked at Le Havre January 9, 1816, and this has been accepted as the date of his departure from France by several recent historians. In searching through the files of the *Courrier de la Louisiane,* the writer discovered two of the letters of introduction which Lakanal brought with him to America. One from Consul Warden bears the date of December 15, 1815, the other from La Fayette is dated December 28, 1815. This shows most conclusively that Lakanal did not leave France before 1816, and the postmarked date of his letter from Le Havre may be accepted with assurance as the approximate date of his sailing for America.

Even before the disaster of Waterloo, Lakanal, as we have seen, had quietly made preparations to leave the country, converting his property into cash. Before leaving France he had arranged for a farm on the Kentucky side of the Ohio river at its junction with the Kentucky river just opposite the village of Vevay, Indiana. During the year 1815 he had secured passports, and on or about the ninth of January, 1816, he set sail. He was accompanied by his wife Marie-Barbe François, his young daughter Alexandrine, and possibly a second daughter of whose existence there is no positive proof. He carried with him 30,000 francs in money, his books and scientific apparatus, his correspondence with well known men of

[1]Julien de Paris was *homme de confiance* of Robespierre, and through him had been appointed in 1793 *commissaire adjoint* for Public Instruction.

the Revolutionary period, together with his letters of introduction. Since the passage of the Atlantic by sailing ships required from thirty to forty days, or even more, according to the state of the weather, he must have landed in New York near the end of the month of February. Immediately he presented himself at the office of the French Consul with his passports and other official papers. He remained for a month in New York in company with Joseph Bonaparte, Regnault de Saint-Jean-d'Angely, and Lescallier, all like Lakanal fugitives from the *clemency* of an irate Louis XVIII. These four formed a group which Lakanal describes as composing the Institute of America.[2]

BEAU PAYS!

To every inquiry addressed to him by Lakanal on the subject of the Ohio Valley, American Consul Warden would exclaim: "Beau pays! beau pays!" Thus encouraged by the Consul, and greatly influenced by a book of his countryman Francois-André Michaux, son of the André Michaux who had been sent to this country by Louis XVI in search of plants and trees which might be added to Versailles, and who became the founder of the botanical gardens at Charleston, South Carolina, Lakanal set out for Kentucky.

"I envisage the borders of the Ohio from Pittsburg to Louisville as bound to become within 20 years from now the most populous part of the United States and the most traficking; it is also the part to which I would not hesitate to give the preference for fixing my place of abode."[3] Thus spoke Michaux.

[2]In a letter to Baron Bignon (Feb. 26, 1838) concerning his *Histoire de Napoleon* which had just been published, Lakanal said: "Ayant vécu un mois à New York avec le comte de Survilliers, Regnault de Saint-Jean-d'Angely, Lescallier, nous formions l'Institut d'Amérique, et nous agissions, loin de la vieille patrie, comme on sera aux Champs-Elysées." Lakanal and Joseph Bonaparte had been colleagues in the same class of the Institute, and it is to be presumed that the others mentioned belonged to that or some other class of the French Institute. Joseph Bonaparte assumed the name of Count of Survilliers, from a village on his estate of Mortefontaine.

[3]Michaux's book appeared in 1804, was republished several times, and was translated into German and English, the English translation appearing in 1805. The edition which Lakanal saw was that of 1808. The writer has had access only to the English translation, in which the above passage does not appear: *Travels to the Westward of the Alleghany Mountains, in the States of the Ohio, Kentucky, and Tennessee in the year 1802.* The above passage was quoted by Mignet.

In order to understand better Lakanal's decision and the route he took to arrive at his destination, it will be well to dwell for a moment on Michaux and his book. Michaux made several journeys in the interest of securing plants and shrubs, and among such journeys was one of three and a half months from Philadelphia to Lexington, Kentucky, Nashville and Knoxville, Tennessee, through western North Carolina, down to Charleston, South Carolina.

Michaux gives in detail the route he pursued. Leaving Philadelphia on June 27, 1802, he passed through Lancaster, York, Carlisle, and to Shippensburgh, 140 miles from Philadelphia. From Shippensburgh to Pittsburgh was a distance of 170 miles. After leaving Shippensburgh he passed through Strasburgh, crossed the river Juniata, on to Bedford Court House, West Liberty-Town, to Pittsburgh.

From Pittsburgh Michaux went on foot to Wheeling, a journey of two days. On July 18, he and his companion, a Mr. Samuel Craft of Vermont, purchased a pirogue or canoe and paddled from Wheeling to Marietta. From Marietta they went to Gallipolis, a distance of 100 miles, after four days of navigation. The Ohio has frequent islands, and as their pirogue approached the islands the water became shallow, and in the words of Michaux, "the rapidity of the current becomes extreme, the canoe is carried along with the velocity of an arrow, and it is only in proportion as we recede from the islands that the bed increases in depth, and the current is less rapid." One of the regicides who had fled to this country and who was drowned together with some companions in the Ohio river while on the way to the French Vine and Olive Colony in Alabama, was Garnier de Saintes.[4] This unfortunate Frenchman was no doubt a victim of his inexperience in handling a pirogue in the swift currents of the river.

From Gallipolis, Michaux and Craft went to Limestone, (now Maysville), Kentucky, where they hired a conveyance for the cross-country journey to Lexington, a distance of 65 miles. This journey consumed two and one half days, and was made via Washington, Springfield, Mays Lick, Millersburgh, Paris, and to Lexington.

[4]See Chapter 7.

VEVAY

Lakanal must have closely followed the route of Michaux, as he speaks of making botanical explorations from Philadelphia to Pittsburgh. He no doubt made a similar journey down the Ohio in a pirogue, but instead of stopping at Limestone, he must have continued on the river as far as Cincinnati, and from there by land on the northern bank of the river to his destination, Vevay, Indiana; inasmuch as he speaks of exploring that stretch of country for plants and mastodon bones.

That Lakanal made a very leisurely journey from New York to Vevay, Indiana, is to be inferred from the fact that it was not until July 20, 1816, that his arrival was announced in *Niles' Weekly Register*: which quoted the weekly published at Vevay: "M. Lakanal, a distinguished French gentleman (member of the national institute of France, and of the legion of honor), remarkable for his republican principles, has lately arrived here with his family. He has purchased an estate on the bank of the Ohio, two miles above Vevay, on the Kentucky side. M. Vairin, a professor of mathematics, has also arrived from France, with a part of his family—he has purchased a farm on the river, one mile below Vevay. May happiness attend them in our land of liberty—their adopted country."

Vevay had been settled in 1805 by a group of French-speaking peasants from the neighborhood of Vevey in the canton of Vaud in Switzerland, the scene of the grape gathering at Clarens. This most charming picture of rural life was drawn by Jean Jacques Rousseau in his *Nouvelle-Héloïse.* Vevay had been selected as a county seat in 1814, and by 1816 contained 75 dwellings, 8 stores, 3 taverns, 31 mechanics, 2 lawyers, 2 physicians, a carding machine, and a library of 300 volumes. Mail arrived 3 times a week. Says *Niles' Register* of July, 1816; "The site is said to be beautiful and it promises to become the center of the wine business of the West, the grapes raised here being of a very superior quality."

"The promised introduction of the culture of the vine procured a special law in favor of the Swiss settlement on the Ohio."[5] That no deed of land to Lakanal is of record in the county court house of

[5]Letter from Thomas Jefferson to George Flower, Sept. 12, 1817.

Gallatin County, Kentucky, is to be explained by the fact that he must have occupied a government grant. Since the government made such grants, usually at two dollars per acre, on long term payments, Lakanal, who remained in Kentucky only six years, must in the end have relinquished his land before making final settlement.

LAKANAL AND JEFFERSON

Evidently, one of his first acts after reaching his new home was to write to Thomas Jefferson enclosing his letters of introduction from Lafayette and from Thouin of the *Jardin du Roi.*[6]

In the communication which accompanied his letters of introduction, Lakanal wrote to Jefferson:

Your Excellency:

I have the honor to address you a letter which I had hoped to have the inestimable benefit of presenting to you personally; but events over which I have had no control have changed my plans. Here I am upon the banks of the Ohio, upon an estate which I have just purchased: Gallatin County, in the vicinity of the French colony of Vevay. In this pleasant retreat I shall divide my time between the cultivation of my lands and that of letters. I purpose writing the history of the United States, for which I have been collecting materials for the past ten years. The spectacle of a free people supporting with obedience the salutary yoke of law will lessen the grief which I feel in being exiled from my country. She would be happy if your pacific genius had guided her destinies. The ambition of a single man has brought the enraged nations upon us. My country, prostrate, but struck by the wisdom of your administration, wishes for such as you of the new world to raise herself from her ruins. I hope that in writing your history and that of your predecessors, more or less illustrious, the picture will prove the painter and that, sustained by the beauty of my subject rather than by my own ability, I shall be able to say with a poet of antiquity at the close of my work, 'Exegi monumentum aere perennius.'

Deign, your Excellency, to receive the tender and respectful homage of your very humble and very obedient servant,

LAKANAL, *of the Institute of France*
and of the Legion of Honor.

This letter was answered by Jefferson from Monticello on the following July 30:

Sir:—Your favor of June 1, with the letters it covered was received a few days ago only; and had your worth been less known, the testimony of my friend Lafayette would have been a sufficient passport to my esteem and services. The affliction of such a change of scene as that of Paris for the banks of the Ohio, I can well conceive. But the wise man is at home every-

[6]For these letters of introduction see previous chapter.

where, and the mind of the philosopher never wants occupation. I weep indeed for your country, because, although it has sinned much (for we impute of necessity to a whole nation the wrongs of which it permits an individual to make it the instrument), yet its sufferings are beyond its sins, and their excesses are now become crimes in those committing them. We revolt against them the more too, when we see a nation equally guilty wielding the scourge, instead of writhing under its infliction at the same stake. But this can not last. There is a day of judgment for that nation, and of resurrection for yours. My greatest fear is of premature efforts. It is an affliction the less for you, that you now see them from a safe shore; for to remain amidst sufferings which we can not succour is useless pain.

I am happy that in your retirement the subject to which you propose to avert your mind is an interesting one to us. We have not as yet a good history of our country, since its regenerated government. Marshall's is a mere party diatribe, and Botta's only as good as could have been expected from such a distance. I fear your distance from the depositories of authentic materials will give you trouble. It may, perhaps, oblige you at times to travel in quest of them. Should your researches bring you into this section of the country and anything here be worth your notice, we shall be glad to receive you as a guest at Monticello and to communicate freely anything possessed here. With every wish for your happiness in the new situation in which you are placed, I salute you with perfect esteem and respect.

THOS. JEFFERSON

M. Lakanal of the Institute of France and Legion of Honor.

From early youth Lakanal had devoted himself to teaching, and therefore could not have had that training and experience essential to becoming a successful farmer, and even if he had had a background as a cultivator in France, he would have had to undergo a drastic readjustment to accommodate himself to the life of a Kentucky farmer of the early nineteenth century.

The French historian, Mignet, wrote a biographical sketch of Lakanal in which some glimpse is afforded of the exile's expectations and disappointments in Kentucky. Since Mignet was a personal friend of Lakanal, he had had abundant opportunity to hear him relate his experiences.[7] Under the encouragement of Michaux and the enthusiastic exclamations of Consul Warden, says Mignet, he thought he would find orange trees in full growth.

Although distrusting the poetic descriptions of M. Chateaubriand, and not expecting to see bears either on the banks of the Ohio or on the shores of the Mississippi, balancing themselves above cradles of vines and intoxicated with grapes, he did at least expect to encounter the vine. What was his surprise when on this privileged soil he harvested only corn, hemp and

[7]Mignet, *Notice historique sur la Vie et les Travaux de M. Lakanal.* (Paris, 1857).

certain cereals, without being able to make grow there properly a single vine-stock imported from Europe; when under a climate so vaunted, he underwent winters of seven months, and saw the thermometer reach thirty-three degrees Réaumur below zero! To make the disillusionment worse, the only large market open to the sale of the products of his plantation was three hundred leagues away in the opulent city of New Orleans. . . . In order to get there it was necessary to descend the Ohio and the Mississippi, the *Belle-Rivière* and the *Père des Eaux*. But the *Belle-Rivière* was blocked at Louisville by a chain of rocks called the *Rapides,* which prevented at one point navigation, and the return had to be made with difficulty through the savage tribes of the Chickss-was [Chickasaws] and the Chocklaws [Choctaws].

That Lakanal could not have been closely attentive to farming is indicated by the frequency with which he set out on long journeys, each of which must have required months for accomplishment. From his own statements in various of his letters, we learn that during the time of his residence in Kentucky, he went down the Ohio and Mississippi to New Orleans, that he made at least two journeys to South Carolina, and that in company with J. A. Pénières, one of his former colleagues in the National Convention and like himself numbered among the regicides, he explored the West as far as the headwaters of the Osage river near the present town of Sedalia, Missouri, then the outpost of civilization, seeking a suitable site for the French Vine and Olive Colony which settled ultimately in Alabama. It is also possible that he journeyed to this colony in Alabama, and likewise that he visited Joseph Bonaparte near Philadelphia.

An undated letter gives details of Lakanal's trip through the West with Pénières:

You know that after the disasters of 1815 the American congress granted four townships (2,304 acres each) to the French refugees, with the privilege of choosing them where they should judge it to be most suitable to their interests, nevertheless in the land office, or lands that the government had not already disposed of. Our compatriots assembled at Philadelphia named me, along with Pénières, my former colleague in the National Convention and in the Council of the Five Hundred, to traverse the United States in all directions and determine the most suitable location for our future colony. Full of strength, courage and enthusiasm, we pushed, my good comrade and I, our investigations almost to the headwaters of the Missouri, towards the Rocky mountains. It was there that Pénières, constantly botanizing, constantly picking up from the ground little shining pebbles, suddenly cried out: 'I've got an opal;' I snatched it quickly from his hands, crying: 'I'll keep it for Mme. Geoffroy Saint-Hilaire,—for the "better half" of my best friend.'[8] 'Just as you say,' replied Pénières. . . . On my return to New Orleans I had this find polished and mounted in a ring by a jeweler named Redon. . . . I beg

[8]For account of Saint-Hilaire see Chapter II.

you to have Mme. Geoffroy Saint Hilaire accept this little offering which derives some value from the circumstances in which I found myself. It belonged to the Indian tribe of the Osages which I had just traversed. Would you believe that on seeing us one of these savages cried out: 'Falanche babichile' (Frenchman friend), and immediately afterwards: 'Bonaparte! Bonaparte!' What a man! . . . the loss of the battle of Waterloo has not dampened in the United States the enthusiasm for this prodigy of our century.

That Lakanal's step in retiring to farm life in Kentucky far from the populous cities of the East was approved by some of his fellow exiles is attested by letters written to him in his Kentucky retreat by General Clausel and Simon Chaudron. Writing from New York, Clausel said:

You have seen Generals Lallemand, Lefevre-Desnouettes, Pénières, Garnier de Saintes, etc.; you are the only one who has acted well; it is up to us to imitate you.

The letter of Chaudron was dated January 16, 1816, a date that can not be reconciled with the facts. At that time Lakanal was on the high seas on his way to America. Chaudron's letter gives evidence that Lakanal had already been in this country for some time, and the only plausible explanation is that Chaudron by a slip of the pen put 1816 instead of 1817. By dating the letter 1817 all difficulties of understanding are removed.[9]

"My wise and illustrious master," says Chaudron,

You are opening the career, and I see with delight that my compatriots are accepting you as the salutary look-out man (*vigie Salutaire*) who serves them as a rallying point. You know through our friend M. Parmentier that all the appearances are in favor of our national establishment. I, I know that if there is occasion, I shall come and join you personally as a respectful friend. . . . My decision has been made, Monsieur and worthy Frenchman; I wish to get away from the mire of the great cities where nothing is in fashion except prejudices and pride, and where liberty and civil equality would very soon find their tomb, if there were not formed republican colonies in the interior of the country. I wish to do penance to Nature for having robbed her of forty years of my existence, and to expiate upon her maternal breast the error that I shall always reproach myself for.

The letter from Chaudron is evidently in reply to a letter which he had previously received from Lakanal and in which the latter had praised him for his poetic gifts.[10]

You overwhelm me with praises when all that I covet is your esteem and your approbation. If I were to heed your benevolent expression, I would

[9]The writer of this book came to this conclusion independently, but later discovered that Eugéne Welvert in his monograph "Lakanal en Amérique" had previously reached the same conclusion.

[10]Chaudron was known as "the blind poet of the canebrakes."

consider myself authorized to imbibe equally from Hippocrene and Pactolus, when a drop from either of these immortal fountains is all that my humble and obscure mediocrity has a right to aspire to. I do not renounce so easily your valuable consideration. I want it, and I shall have it.

That Lakanal's pen had not been idle, and that he was in bitter revolt against the tide of affairs in France, is to be seen from the following paragraph of Chaudron's letter:

"The reproof, my illustrious Master, that you gave to the infamous Fouché pleased all honest men, that is, all his enemies. I sent two copies of it to Belgium and one to Mr. Cobbett in England.[11] This whip-lashing applied from afar on a conscience already so lacerated, will make itself felt, I hope. Not millions can cauterize such wounds. Farewell, my wise and illustrious Master. I bow to you."

HENRY CLAY

As a resident of Kentucky it was but natural that Joseph Lakanal should attempt to cultivate the acquaintance of Henry Clay, the foremost Kentuckian of the times and at that moment Speaker of the House of Representatives in Washington. That he lost no time in addressing the distinguished Kentuckian is indicated in a letter which shows that he was in correspondence with Henry Clay as early as July, 1816; that in early 1817 he used his influence with Clay in behalf of the newly formed Vine and Olive Colony of Alabama, and that Lakanal occupied a prominent place in the minds of the colonists. The letter was written to Lakanal in Kentucky by Nicholas Simon Parmentier from Washington on February 25, 1817, and reads as follows:

Your letter of the third of this month, my respected friend, came to me yesterday in this capital of the free world. I was sent here by our Society as solicitor to Congress, and already by its bill of the 21 of this month the Senate has granted us a part of our demands, that is to say, 92,160 acres of land payable in fourteen years without interest. All we need now is the concurrence of the House of Representatives and the approval of the President (of whom we are very sure,—I am speaking of the President) in order that this bill may have the character of law.

Having no introduction to Mr. Clay, I made one out of the copy which you had sent me of his letter of the month of July last. His reception was

[11]Wm. Cobbett was an exile in this country from October, 1792, to June 1800; and again from April, 1817, to the end of 1819. Following his second exile, as a result of these two years, he wrote "A Year of Sojourn in America." Chaudron's letter was written while Cobbett was still in England.

that of a man who relies entirely on his popularity, and of whom the whole art is to satisfy without obliging himself. Yesterday morning I saw him again; I knew that you had written to him, he acknowledged it, received me better, but spoke to me little about your letter. That evening I met him again at a social gathering. I had then received the copy of your letter of this month and I told him so. 'In that case, oblige me by translating it to me: I am ashamed to confess it, but I have lost my French, and I can not read this letter.' It was then 11 o'clock in the evening. At nine this morning I brought him the translation of your letter, and he was able to digest at ease the most flattering letter he has ever received in his life, but the best written, and to such a degree that in spite of the excess of praises, the most republican character is compelled to yield and to swallow the pill. He said to me in smiling: 'You deserve that I use my influence for you. You did not then go to bed? You are worthy of being the friend of Mr. Lakanal. I will do all for his friend.' Ah! When I declared that you were the guiding spirit who would steer our bark to a safe port and when I accustomed each of our members to call you the Regulator of the Society, I did nothing but satisfy the impulse of my heart, and the truth, etc.

In less than a month after Parmentier's letter, Henry Clay wrote to Lakanal:

Washington,
March 20, 1817

Sir;

I was not able to reply during the session of the house of representatives which recently adjourned to the letter that you did me the honor of writing. You have no doubt been instructed of the success of the request that was made in favor of the French immigrants who desire to establish a colony on the Tombeckbee. In the choice of the individual that shall be commissioned to select the land which the colony is authorized to purchase, great care should be had that it be a person of sound judgment who knows the region well or is in a position to know it well before determining the site.

I am leaving in a few days from this city for Kentucky where I hope to arrive in April. I shall be much flattered to have the pleasure of being with you and learning the progress of your great work. Many accounts have been written on this country in the form of history, of travels, and by foreigners. But a good one still remains to be produced: the accomplishment of this task, I hope, is reserved for you.

I am with great respect, Sir, your obedient servant.

CLAY[12]

That Lakanal was in correspondence with Lafayette from his Kentucky retreat, and that he acted as an intermediary between Lafayette and Henry Clay, is illustrated by a letter written by Lafayette to Clay on October 26, 1818. In the last paragraph of his letter, he says:

This letter will be delivered by Mr. Lakanal, member of the French Insti-

[12]This letter was translated into French and published by Nigoul, who wrote under the pen name of *Marcus.* Not having access to the English original, the writer has been compelled to retranslate from the French.

tute of the Academy, and Rector General of the Medical System with a handsome treatment [sic], all which he abandons for a settlement in the neighborhood of Lexington, State of Kentucky. The high rank he holds in the scientific world, and his having been a member of our former assemblies, will recommend him to your notice. But I have presumed to engage in your name you would favor him with your good advice, and with letters of introduction to the country which he intends to inhabit. I know you will be so kind as to render him in that way, the services which I beg leave to solicit on account of his own merit and my earnest desire to oblige him. Permit me to depend upon you to ask the same favor from you friends, Mr. Monroe, Mr. Crawford, and others who may recommend him to public and private characters in the State.

Not only would Lakanal have had the opportunity of meeting Henry Clay personally in Lexington, but it is also probable that he came into contact with him in his own county of Gallatin. In a letter received several years ago by the writer from Miss Anna V. Parker, of Sanders, Kentucky, Miss Parker says:

I am very much interested in the early history of this part of Kentucky. My great grandfather, Lewis Sanders, was one of the early settlers. He was a friend of Henry Clay's, and is said to have often entertained him in his home. Henry Clay, so the story goes, made numerous trips to Vevay for his supply of wine, and stayed at the old tavern in Ghent. When on one of these trips, he was asked to suggest a suitable name for the town, he named it "Ghent" in honor of the Treaty of Ghent, Belgium.

THE NAPOLEONIC CONSPIRACY

From the letters that have been quoted, it is evident that Lakanal sought to create a friendly relation between himself and Henry Clay, and for a definite end.

The hope of the refugees from the Bourbon rule had been, that just as Napoleon had returned from Elba, in like manner he would succeed in escaping from Saint Helena and once more rule over France. But the tide of affairs in France quickly showed the impossibility of the realization of such a hope. Then the dream of the exiles became that of rescuing Napoleon, and assisting to form an empire of the Spanish speaking peoples of the Americas, whilst Joseph Bonaparte, ex-King of Spain and the Indies, would occupy the throne of Mexico. The dream was not unlike the plot of Aaron Burr (1806), and was the forerunner of the events in which the Emperor Maximilian came to a tragic end in the Mexico of the next generation.

Niles' Weekly Register for Saturday, September 21, 1816, contained the following item datelined Paris, July 24:

It is said that the unambitious character of Joseph, ex-King of Spain and the Indies, has been powerfully worked upon by a numerous body of generals who regained their fame under Bonaparte, and who having fled to America for refuge, are uneasy at the state of inaction to which they have been reduced. These persons, we are told, have urged Joseph to resume his pretensions as King of the Indies, and have offered to unite their means with those of the Insurgents of Mexico, to drive the Spaniards from their colonies, and to establish a mighty empire on the shores of the Pacific. We are further informed that nothing has prevented the immediate engagement in this enterprise but the refusal on the part of the Government of the United States to undertake any ostensible co-operation (Manufactured).

So preposterous were the contents of the item, the editor of *Niles' Weekly Register* did not hesitate to brand it *manufactured,* that is, a lie. However, later events proved that there was some substance of truth in the article. Let it be noted that if this item was published in Paris on July 24, 1816, it must have been written some eight or ten weeks earlier in America, or just about the time Lakanal had arrived in Kentucky.

Also the use of the word *ostensible* would seem to imply that while the Government of the United States might refuse to co-operate openly, it would not be above secretly encouraging the enterprise.

Lakanal had left France with the definite intention of settling in Kentucky. May he not also have come to this country with the definite intention of entering into a conspiracy on behalf of the Bonapartes? Why did he separate himself from the other colonists at Vevay, Indiana, and settle on the Kentucky side of the Ohio river? May it not have been for the purpose of cultivating more easily a friendship with Henry Clay in the hope of receiving sympathy and encouragement? Henry Clay was notoriously anti-English, and it was the English who held Napoleon in captivity. Clay had been a strong adherent of Aaron Burr until thoroughly convinced of Burr's treachery. Clay was at this time Speaker of the House of Representatives, and was logically the man to be approached in order to secure, if not active, at least passive support of the plan on the part of the American Government. Clay's interest in the struggles of the Spanish countries of America to throw off the Spanish yoke was very keen, and there used to hang (and perhaps does yet) in the legislative halls of the Republic of Columbia a portrait of Henry Clay as recognition for his interest and aid in the struggle of that country to gain its independence.

CONSPIRACIES ON KENTUCKY SOIL

When he settled in Kentucky Lakanal was no doubt aware of the fact that Kentucky had been the birthplace of four conspiracies within a generation. The fertile soil for these conspiracies was prepared by the unsettled state of the country west of the Alleghenies in the years following the close of the Revolutionary War. At the close of the American Revolution in 1782, a preliminary treaty of peace was signed with Great Britain in November of that year. However, the final treaty of peace was not signed until September, 1783. The interval between these two treaties was one of intrigue on the part of the French and Spanish to limit the boundaries of America on the westward to the Alleghenies. The purpose of this was to leave the West in the hands of the British. If this were done they would feel free to contest the territory with Great Britain by force of arms. Fortunately, the American Commissioner, John Jay, saw through the scheme. He notified the British, and the final solution was independence of the territory from Great Britain.

Following the Revolution, the years up to 1791 were spent by Kentucky in repeated efforts to gain a separation from Virginia. The fact that Kentucky was the western outpost of civilization, the unsettled state of mind with regard to the separation from Virginia, and the repeated Indian raids instigated by foreign powers, all of these combined, contributed toward making Kentucky a breeding place of conspiracies. The first of them known as the First Spanish Conspiracy, and was led by James Wilkinson, a born agitator.[13] Wilkinson advocated violent withdrawal from Virginia. At the same moment the right of the United States to navigate the Mississippi had become a burning issue between this country and Spain. The boundary between the two countries placed the lower Mississippi in Spanish territory. It was exceedingly important that Kentucky have access to New Orleans and the sea for her markets via the Ohio and the Mississippi. Gathering together a cargo of tobacco and other products, Wilkinson went to New Orleans ostensibly on a trading expedition, but in reality to make a bargain with

[13]For accounts of these conspiracies see *A History of Kentucky* by Elizabeth Shelby Kinkead (Cincinnati, 1896).

the Spaniards "to obtain the separation of Kentucky from the United States, and then to deliver the district thus separated into the hands of his Majesty, the King of Spain, to become a province of that power". The loyalty of the people of Kentucky to the United States, and their opposition to an illegal separation from Virginia caused the frustration of the conspiracy.

The second of these conspiracies was known as the French Conspiracy. In 1793, news reached Kentucky that France had declared war against England, Spain and Holland. President Washington refused to enter into an alliance with France. Citizen Genet, minister of France, had recently landed in Charleston, South Carolina, for the purpose of enlisting aid for his country in the impending war. As soon as he was aware of the agitation of the Kentuckians over the right of navigation of the Mississippi, he sent agents to Kentucky to raise volunteers for an expedition against New Orleans and the Spanish possessions. . . . He succeeded in raising two thousand men, and General George Rogers Clark accepted the commission of "Major General in the armies of France and Commander-in-chief of the revolutionary legions of the Mississippi." This conspiracy ended in the recall of Citizen Genet.

The Second Spanish Conspiracy developed in 1795 when the Spanish governor of Louisiana attempted to bribe Kentucky to secede from the Union, and to form an alliance with Spain, in order to obtain the navigation of the Mississippi. Judge Benjamin Sebastian, one of the accomplices of the former conspiracy, was approached, and he proceeded to New Orleans to negotiate with the authorities there. However, before any agreement had been reached, news came that a treaty between the United States and Spain had been effected, and that Spain had granted to the United States the free navigation of the Mississippi River.

The most daring of the conspiracies was that of Aaron Burr in 1806. Cut off from all high official attainment as a result of his having taken the life of Alexander Hamilton in a duel, Aaron Burr sought a means to gratify his ambition. The dazzling scheme which he fathered was to conquer the Spanish province of Mexico, unite it to the southeastern states, and to make New Orleans the capital of this vast territory, and himself the emperor or ruler. To arrange his project, Burr made frequent trips to Lexington and Louisville. In 1806, he was indicted in the court at Frankfort for high treason. He secured Henry Clay to defend him; but when the day of the trial arrived, the United States attorney failed to obtain the attendance of the necessary witnesses. Later, Burr was arrested in Alabama and tried in Richmond in 1807, but was not convicted because of technicalities.

LAKANAL THE CONSPIRATOR

The conspiracy entered into in 1817 by Lakanal was somewhat similar to that of Aaron Burr, except that it did not contemplate action against any part of the United States. It was part of a plan to free Napoleon from Saint Helena, make him Emperor of South America, and put Joseph Bonaparte on the throne of Mexico and the Indies. Lakanal's part in the conspiracy was confined to organizing American sympathizers who would furnish men and means for carrying out the project. No doubt he hoped through Henry Clay to secure the silent consent of the United States Government for the carrying out of his scheme.

Until the death of Napoleon on May 5, 1821, the possibility of his escape to the United States was in the minds of the Napoleonic exiles in America at least. Two distinct plots were formed in this country for the freeing of Napoleon; one in Philadelphia, and the other in New Orleans. To this day there stands a house in New Orleans built in the expection of its becoming the home of Napoleon.

Philadelphia was the scene of a plot devised by the many French refugees who had forgathered there and in nearby communities, which was to be carried out in conjunction with plotters in Brazil. A letter to the secretary of Joseph Bonaparte, intercepted by the British Secret Service, gave the first intimation of a plot, and the name of General Lallemand as concerned in it. Another clue was furnished by a letter written in French at Philadelphia, July 24, 1817. General Raoul is mentioned as one of the chief figures of the plot. Both Lallemand and Raoul were among the original members of the Vine and Olive Colony of Alabama, a history of which will be found in Appendix III (pages 186-202) of this book.[14]

There was one man in the United States who had good reason to fear the consequences of the presence of a member of the Bonaparte family in America. This was Hyde de Neuville, the Bourbon Louis XVIII's minister at Washington. Following the troubles incident to the Pretender in 1745, a member of the Hyde family fled from England to France and settled near Nevers. From him was descended Hyde de Neuville, an ardent royalist who during the trial of Louis XVI sought to influence certain of the Deputies of the National Convention in favor of his king. He had attended the Collège of Bourges where Lakanal had taught. He must have known of him there, and also he must have been perfectly aware of Lakanal's hatred of the king, for he was present when the votes were taken and must have heard the words pronounced by Lakanal when casting his vote.

De Neuville had a close watch kept upon the movements of the Count of Survilliers, the name under which Joseph Bonaparte was known in this country, and took careful note of his relations with the body of Napoleonic officers in Philadelphia and Bordentown. It was no doubt owing to this close surveillance that in August, 1817, a packet of letters addressed to the Count of Survilliers was intercepted in Philadelphia and came into the hands of Hyde de Neuville. Upon reading them, De Neuville rushed to Washington to interview acting Secretary of State Rush. Soon afterwards, when John Quincy Adams had taken charge of the Department of State, De Neuville brought the papers to him, and together they made an examination of them. The package was addressed, *A Monsieur le Comte de Survilliers, pour lui seul,*" and sealed with the insignia of the Convention, the liberty-cap on the head of a pike; surrounding the device were the words "Lakanal, Deputy to the National Convention." Within the packet were six documents in plainly undisguised handwriting, and signed by the same hand. De Neuville and Adams were both convinced of the genuineness of the docu-

[14]A full account of American plots to rescue Napoleon is to be found in McCartney and Dorrance, *The Bonapartes in America* (Philadelphia, 1939), chapter XIV.

ments. On September 12, the French minister addressed the following official note to the Department of State:

Circumstances of a very extraordinary nature have caused several documents to fall into my hands which announce the existence in America of an association organized under the name of the Napoleonean Confederacy. From these papers, which I have already had the honor to communicate to you, it results that a very considerable levy of men is on the eve of taking place in some of the Western States or Territories.

The apparent object of this conspiracy is the conquest of a Spanish province; but the real one is only known to the leaders; according to their own report, it is to cause Joseph Bonaparte to be proclaimed in Mexico, King of Spain and the Indies.

It is very painful for me, Sir, to be under the necessity of unfolding an intrigue which might possibly implicate subjects of His Majesty the King, my Master; but I still cherish the hope that among the Frenchmen whose names have been used on this occasion, there are several who, having been some time desirous of putting themselves under the protection of the government of their own country, will not have connected themselves with a project so directly opposed to the object they have in view; that others have only been misled for a moment, and that, finally, all the odium and madness of the Napoleonean Confederation will fall on some individuals, without country, without remorse, who in 1817 have audacity to employ their criminal seal of 1793, and thus proclaim the fatal part they bore in our most deplorable misfortunes.[15]

De Neuville thereupon requests that the President of the United States be made acquainted with the event.

The papers to be submitted to him consist of a letter of four pages, headed ULTIMATUM. This letter is wholly written as you yourself ascertained, in the hand of the said Lakanal, formerly a member of the Convention, and who, by the documents annexed to my letter, appears to be invested with the character of Principal Commissioner near the Executive Committee.—Of a REPORT, forming twenty-three pages, likewise in the handwriting of Mr. Lakanal.—3. A PETITION of the same Lakanal,—by which Joseph Bonaparte is requested to exercise, from the moment, his rights of sovereignty, to grant commissions, distribute crosses, ribands, to create counties, marquisates, etc., etc., and above all to confer on the petitioner 'a Spanish distinction' as 'this new mark of your gracious favor will give me', adds he, 'a degree of political importance, in the eyes of your Mexican subjects, which I venture to assure your Majesty will promote your Majesty's best interests'.—4. A vocabulary of the wandering Indians in the neighborhood of Mexico, towards Santa Fe.—5. A list of the Indian tribes inhabiting northern Louisiana, etc.—6. An enigmatical vocabulary composed of forty-columns or alphabets, with a Latin word corresponding with each letter. This vocabulary is followed by a key, beginning thus, 'In using this vocabulary, the Latin word may be written, although that language be not understood, and the following use is to be made of it'. The key concludes with

[15] Note how De Neuville strikes at Lakanal.

this article of the rules: 'Every partial correspondence should be headed with this word, 'Oratio', a prayer, because it will appear merely to be an extract, whether in express terms, or in others equivalent, of the Lord's Prayer, and because this innocent stratagem may have its effect upon the minds of the Spaniards, who are generally attentive to all religious forms'.—7. Of four covers which enclosed the packet. . . .

In the ULTIMATUM which Lakanal addresses to Joseph Bonaparte, he says:

Sire! I am charged to lay before Your Majesty the annexed documents, and to request that Your Majesty will be pleased to examine them in order in which they are presented.

I was invited to repair to Your Majesty for the purpose of making this important communication; but, being on the eve of setting out on a long and fatiguing journey, it became necessary for me to husband both my strength and my funds.

I was unwilling however to trust this important dispatch to the mail, as that conveyance would not have offered the certainty of inviolable secrecy.

The person who has undertaken to deliver these papers, to the contents of which he is an utter stranger, is not personally known to me, but he is to those who merit my entire confidence.

Throughout the whole of this important enterprise I have had no other merit, Sire, than that of conducting myself in these countries as a man of honor, and of rendering useful to Your Majesty's service, the tender and profound veneration felt for Your August Dynasty; I have already on several occasions entertained Your Majesty on these general dispositions of the minds and feelings of the people of these countries.

Deign, Sire, to transmit to me your orders, as speedily as it may please Your Majesty; as Your Majesty will be sensible of all the danger attending the smallest delay.

I repeat to Your Majesty that the common profession of our political faith is and always will be: 'The King has nothing to do in this affair; it is our unbounded devotion to His Illustrious Dynasty, which prompts us to act; we are consistent in our principles; we wish for free states only, and legitimate princes in the just acceptation which Reason gives to these words. The King neither will, nor can, surrender his rights; but he expects everything from the goodness of his cause and the attachment of the brave Spaniards, seconded by all the friends of the cause of nations, arrayed against Power imposed by Force.

I await Your Majesty's answer with extreme impatience.

I have the honor to be, Sire, Your Majesty's Most Humble, Most Obedient, and Most Faithful Servant and Subject,

LAKANAL.

In the personal PETITION, among other things, Lakanal requests a distinction at the hands of Joseph Bonaparte:

In the position in which I am placed by the momentous interests of Your Majesty, I respectfully request of you to confer upon me a Spanish distinction, which may affiliate me in some sort with that nation, with which I have been greatly conversant from my childhood, at the foot of the Pyreneean Mountains, having been born in the ancient County of Foix, now the Department of Ariège, where a part of my family still resides.

This new mark of your gracious favor will give me a degree of political importance in the eyes of your Mexican subjects, which, I venture to assure you, will promote your Majesty's best interests.

My irrevocable resolution is to make known that Your Majesty has taken no part in this great affair, and that you expect everything from the goodness of your cause, and from the good-will of the Spanish Nation."

In the Report Lakanal says: "We at first proceeded upon a small scale, because we only thought of acting with our individual means. Against the success of our enterprise, there were many numerous chances. However, we were devoted, the sacrifice was entire, we held nothing in reserve. By the progressive increase of information which sprang up on all sides, when we saw ourselves surrounded by a number of experienced associates, a project which was but indistinctly seen and was in some sort the spring of our first ideas, became a regular plan, well concerted in its ensemble and judiciously calculated in all its details." He goes on to say that the Napoleonean Confederation is to be extended to nine hundred members, armed and equipped as flankers of the Independent Troops of Mexico. One hundred and fifty of the members are to be chosen immediately as Commissioners, and who are to repair without delay to different points of the States and Territories of the West. Each Commissioner shall associate with himself as many as five individuals, known by their principles to be favorable to the nature of the undertaking, but he shall not unfold to them the ultimate object of the enterprise.

Lakanal then makes a request that Joseph Bonaparte contribute 65,000 francs toward the expense of the enterprise.

De Neuville, in great excitement, wrote the details of Lakanal's plan to the Duc de Richelieu, Minister of Foreign Affairs in France, winding up with the fear that Napoleon might escape from St. Helena, and begging that the strictest watch be kept on that island, exclaiming: "Où en serait-on si cet homme prodigieux arrivait au Méxique déjà conquis?"

When the matter of the Napoleonic Conspiracy came to the attention of President James Monroe, he addressed himself to William Lee, who had formerly been American Consul at Bordeaux and who was at this moment second auditor of the United States

Treasury. Lee was interested in the newly established French Vine and Olive Colony in Alabama, and was on the best of terms with the French officers. It was to William Lee that Jefferson had written a letter declining to draft a constitution for the projected colony. This letter is reproduced in Appendix III, p. 187.

In his investigation of the conspiracy, Lee discovered that the two Lallemands, General Charles and General Henri, together with Colonel Galabert, were at the head of the scheme. He also connects the Vine and Olive Colony of Alabama with the enterprise. When the President became convinced that there was some substance to the conspiracy revealed in the Lakanal documents, he considered the matter carefully even to the point of referring it to his Cabinet for discussion in one of its regular meetings. Since De Neuville could not prove that the Count de Survilliers had contributed to any political enterprise either in money or encouragement, and since the intercepted papers were the only basis for an investigation, and also since it would be difficult to prove that Lakanal had written the documents, although they seemed clearly to be in his handwriting, the final conclusion was that as matters stood there was no definite basis on which the government might act; that nothing short of an overt act would justify governmental interference.

No doubt, Lakanal was warned that he would be subject to arrest and prosecution if he persisted in his course of action. At any rate, the exposure of the papers seems to have had a quieting effect on him, and little is known of him during the remaining four or five years of his residence in Kentucky.

An aftermath of the conspiracy treated above, was a letter addressed by Lakanal to Joseph Bonaparte on November 24, 1817, in which he indulges in self-pity over the embarrassment which Joseph's silence has caused him, and stating that that silence had been taken by his followers for assent. "What a horrible change around me! Either I had no part in your confidence, or else I am an impostor to be unmasked and delivered up to Justice. My decision has been made; I will sell my fine estate, and I will indemnify those who have uselessly consumed both their time and their means of subsistance. I will then go to the States of the East, where I have been offered an honorable place in an institution of public education."

From the above, it is clear that Joseph Bonaparte refused by his silence to acknowledge any responsibility for the conspiracy for which Lakanal had drawn plans and assumed leadership. It is also clear that Lakanal has been discredited among those who had participated in the plot and that he was sensitive to his responsibility toward those who had spent time and money in the enterprise. His decision to reimburse them for their time and expense is a favorable commentary on the character of Lakanal, but his veiled threat at the end of the letter: "I may suggest that it is to the great interest of Your Majesty to heed my requests," if it does not smack of blackmail, at least makes a bad impression. In this letter—and this is the real purpose of the letter—Lakanal requests a short term loan of $4,000 in order that he may honor the obligations that he has assumed and in order not to fall into a dire poverty from which he was far removed when he arrived in America. In undertaking the leadership in raising means and men for the carrying out of the purposes of the Napoleonic Confederation, Lakanal had no doubt envisioned for himself a better situation both materially and socially. His disappointment must have been extreme when his plans failed. As for the institution of learning in the East to which he had been invited, we can only conjecture which one is meant. At this time Thomas Jefferson was engaged in his plans for the University of Virginia, and may have spoken to Lakanal about occupying a professorship there. However, the University did not open its doors to students until 1825, and if there was any understanding between the two men, it could only have been for the future. It is the more likely that Lakanal had been offered a place in South Carolina at Beaufort, Columbia, or Charleston. From a letter which he wrote in 1837, we learn that Lakanal had made three journeys to South Carolina, the second of which was in 1821.

What were the motives which had impelled Lakanal to espouse the cause of the Bonapartes? He had enjoyed scant favors at the hands of Napoleon, and in the letter which has been quoted in which Lakanal writes to Baron Bignon concerning his *Histoire de*

Napoléon, he states: "Napoléon me condamna à l'ilotisme (Napoleon condemned me to a state of serfdom)." There could have been little love on Lakanal's part for Napoleon; but as a choice of two evils, he preferred the Bonapartes to the Bourbons. His hatred of the Bourbon Dynasty was intense, and this had been increased by the vengefulness of Louis XVIII after Waterloo. As late as December 14, 1816, a year and a half after the downfall of Napoleon, *Niles' Weekly Register* contained the following item: "Trials are still going on in France, for real or pretended plots against the government, and execution is yet 'the order of the day'—83 civil tribunals or prevotal courts, and 24 military tribunals are busy at work to make the French 'forget the horrors of their revolution.' *The tyranny of Bonaparte is regretted.*"

It is very likely that even before leaving France, Lakanal had fallen into accord with the group in France which regretted the loss of Napoleon and which sought to bring him back to rule over them once more. As the hope of Napoleon returning to rule over France faded, the dream of rescuing him and setting up an empire in the Americas, or at least finding a home for him in the United States, grew in the minds of the Napoleonic exiles; and although Lakanal may in the beginning have shared the dream of restoring Napoleon in France, yet in this country he underwent a transformation and threw himself whole heartedly into the views of his fellow exiles.

Although the Napoleonic Conspiracy of which Lakanal was a leader failed because of the exposure of the documents forwarded to Joseph Bonaparte by him, there was an interesting aftermath in the expedition led by Generals Charles and Henri Lallemand to what is now the State of Texas, but at that time territory in dispute between the United States and Spain. Led by the Lallemand brothers several hundred Frenchmen, among whom were forty of the French settlers of the Vine and Olive Colony of Alabama, set sail for Galveston, then the rendezvous of the pirate Lafitte and his buccaneer band. After weathering storms and hardships, the French settled at what is now Liberty, a few miles from the City of Houston. Here they founded a colony along military lines which they called *Champ d'Asile.* After a few months of incredible adventures and hardships the colony disbanded, those who managed to escape returning, some to France, others to the Eastern states. The *Champ d'Asile* received a great deal of publicity in France and became the inspiration of one of Balzac's novels, *Le Ménage d'un Garçon.*[16] Lakanal did not participate in this enterprise. His unhappy experience in this country seems to have put an end to his taste for conspiracy. He remained quietly on his farm in Kentucky, and did not even take up his grant of land in the Vine and Olive Colony of Alabama, of which he had been a promoter and one of the largest share holders.

[16]In his novel Balzac speaks as follows: "The occupation of Texas by the remnant of the Grand Army was no doubt a splendid idea; but it was the men that were found wanting rather than the conditions, since Texas is now a Republican state of great promise. The experiment made under the Restoration proved emphatically that the interests of the Liberals were purely selfish, and in no sense national; aiming at power, and at nothing else. Neither the material, the place, the idea, nor the good will was lacking, only the money and the support of that hypocritical party; they had vast sums at their disposal, and would give nothing when the reinstatement of an Empire was at stake.—English translation under title of "A Bachelor's Establishment," by Clara Bell, Philadelphia 1902.

7

LAKANAL IN LOUISIANA

WHEN THE SIEUR DE LA SALLE CAME DOWN THE MISSISSIPPI IN 1682, he took possession of the territory explored in the name of France. In honor of Louis XIV the new possession was named "Louisiana." La Salle returned to France, and sailed from La Rochelle on a new voyage with intention of settling a colony; but missing the Mississippi's mouth, he landed in what is now Texas, where, in 1687, he was murdered by some of his own followers. After the treaty of Ryswick, Pierre le Moine d'Iberville in 1697 was chosen to head another colony, which reached the Gulf coast in 1699. Near the present site of Biloxi, Miss., he built Fort Maurepas, and soon after erected a fort on the Mississippi river about forty miles above its mouth. From 1712 to 1717 the French possessions of the Missisipi valley were held as a private grant from the king by Antoine Crozat, who relinquished his rights to what was known as the "Western Company," afterwards merged with John Law's Company of the Indies. When John Law launched his famous Mississippi scheme, the company did much for the colony of Louisiana. For forty years a brother of Iberville, the Sieur de Bienville, was governor of the colony. One of his first acts was to found New Orleans on its present site in 1718. In 1763 Louisiana passed into the control of the Spanish. Wrested from the Spanish by Napoleon, the 885,000 square mile territory was purchased from France for $15,-000,000 by the United States during the administration of Thomas Jefferson in 1803.

Very soon after its founding New Orleans was confronted with the problem of education of its youth.

As early as 1727 a company of Ursuline sisters had migrated from France to New Orleans, and had established a French convent whose chief occupation was to become the education of girls. Although Bienville made efforts to establish an educational institution for boys, his plans failed.[1] The change to Spanish rule proved unfavorable for creating educational institutions, and it remained for the coming of American rule for any definite plans to be made for education; and after a tentative period of hesitation to be put into execution. This hesitation was due no doubt to the attitude of the French inhabitants of the region. Explored and settled in the time of Louis XIV, the civilization of Louisiana was thoroughly French of the seventeenth-century type; the sort of education desired was the kind of seventeenth-century education which in France produced the *honnête homme.* In the *Essays* of Montaigne we find the first development of the French conception of the *honnete homme.* This conception arrived at its fullest perfection around the middle of the seventeenth century, and was closely akin to the English ideal of the "gentleman," though it came to stress the social graces rather than moral rectitude. The strongly orthodox religion of the reign of Louis XIV came with the colonists and remained a strong force in the mother country, and as will be seen had a decisive influence on Lakanal.

This attachment to the French culture and language was increased by certain circumstances resulting from the transfer of the colony to the United States. Under the French and Spanish dominations, the Créoles had cleared and broken up for tillage thousands of acres of rich alluvial lands on the two banks of the Mississippi and on the banks of its more or less marshy tributaries, and at the same time they had collected large gangs of slaves. American control brought from the North a considerable number of energetic colonists, some of whom were fortified with sufficient capital to permit them to purchase plantations and slaves. This rivalry increased considerably the value of the land and the negroes—two commodities in which the Créoles abounded. The Spaniards had suppressed free trade; the Americans abolished all restrictions. The result was not long delayed: the 'Kaintucks' descended the river by thousands on broad flatboats loaded with lumber, wheat, potatoes, and flour for the market of New Orleans, which became a lively and flourishing port. The admission of Louisiana to the States of the Union in 1812 only increased this prosperity. The Créoles became rich, and thanks to their wealth possessed leisure. Thus the period of the pioneers closed.

In advance of this wave of influence towards the South, the rich planters had engaged tutors and governesses for their children; the practice was now general; young men and women from France, when they were unable otherwise to supply their wants after arriving in Louisiana, were generally chosen

[1]C. Gayarré in his *History of Louisiana* states that Bienville first approached the Jesuits of Louisiana with regard to undertaking the building of a college, but they refused on the ground of not having sufficient means. He then appealed to the king, Louis XV, whose response was that the colony was of too little importance for such an instituiton.

to fill this position. It is said that even Jerome Bonaparte, later king of Westphalia, was among the number of these tutors. At New Orleans the boys attended schools where only the French language was spoken, and where the professors were often refugees from Santo Domingo following the insurrection of the blacks, or exiles from France for political reasons; the girls who made any pretense of belonging to honorable families were educated in the Convent of the Ursulines directed by French nuns. These Créole children not only heard French spoken to the exclusion of any other language in their homes, but during the years when children are most receptive they received from their tutors and governesses[2] French ideas and mental outlook.

This Gallicization was extended further, for the sons of the richest Créoles were usually sent to France in order to complete their classical studies. French thought, French art, French literature, imbued them to such an extent that they brought back to Louisiana an authentic French culture, imitation of the culture in favor at Paris. Upon returning to their country, these men were in the habit of importing from France their books, their wines, and even their ideas; and that is the reason why the Créoles, although living under American government, were always in heart and mind more closely attached to France than to the United States.[3]

From this statement it can be seen that New Orleans of the earlier nineteenth century was largely inhabited by descendents of French colonists of the period of Louis XIV, Louis XV, and Louis XVI. Added to these there was a layer of *émigrés,* both lay and ecclesiastic, fugitives from the French Revolution. The heart of the population consisted therefore of people who were *ancien régime,* "friends of the Throne and the Altar." When Napoleon was overthrown, hopes ran high in New Orleans that under Louis XVIII Louisiana would again become French. Thus there was in the years following Waterloo a strong resurgence of French nationalism under the influence of a spirit of royalism.

The ideals of the reign of Louis XIV had entered to such a degree into the shaping of Louisiana and the molding of New Orleans, that the city was throughout the eighteenth century thoroughly French, in spite of the Spanish occupation of the last third of the century. The sort of education in demand there was one that should be French and guided by religion. The school of the Ursuline nuns met with great popular favor for this very reason,

[2]The French of the text reads: *maîtres et maîtresses.*

[3]Edward Larcoque Tinker: *Les Écrits de Langue française en Louisiane au XIXe Siècle. Essais biographiques et bibliographiques* (Evreux, 1932). The quotation, which has been translated, is from the Introduction, pp. 3-4.

and for the same reason there was difficulty in starting any plan of general higher education.

Since there were no opportunities for higher education for boys, the young men of French descent attended the schools of France. What began as a necessity, later became a long-established custom and fashion. To be educated in France bestowed a certain amount of prestige. On the other hand, the small American population sent its sons to the schools of the North in the United States.

Although with the transfer of Louisiana to the United States in 1803, the official language necessarily became English, for a long time it was the official language in theory rather than in practice. Part of the success of the men in power in governing the State was largely due to the fact that they never attempted to proscribe the use of the French language. As late as 1880 it was permissible to make speeches in the French language in the two legislative chambers. Depositions were made in French before the courts; the law prescribed that interpreters be provided for those who did not speak the French language.[4]

In 1804, very soon after Louisiana had passed into the possession of the United States, a group describing themselves as planters, merchants, and other inhabitants of Louisiana, placed before Congress a petition of remonstrance in which they aired their grievances. One of these grievances dealt with the difficulties which had attended the transfer of Louisiana to the United States with regard to language, as the majority of the inhabitants of the new territory knew English either not at all or only imperfectly.

> Another subject of great moment to us, is the sudden change of language in all the public offices and administration of justice. The great mass of the inhabitants speak nothing but the French; the late government was always careful in their selection of officers, to find men who possessed our language and with whom we could personally communicate; their judicial proceedings were indeed in the Spanish language; but being carried on altogether by writing, translations were easily made; at present for the slightest communication an interpreter must be procured; in more important concerns, our interest suffers from not being fully explained; a phrase, a circumstance seemingly of little moment, and which a person uninterested in the affair will not take the trouble to translate, is frequently decisive, and produces the most important effects. That free communication so necessary to give the Magis-

[4] *Ibid.* At Ville Platte, French is to this day the language of the court.

trate a knowledge of the people, and to inspire them with confidence in his administration, is by this means totally cut off and the introduction of *viva voce* pleadings into the courts of justice, subjects the party who can neither understand his Council, his Judge, or the advocate of his opponent, to embarrassments the most perplexing, and often to injuries the most serious.[5]

The *Mémoire* presented by these inhabitants of Louisiana to the Congress is a document of rare value, and reflects the views of those who signed it. We also catch glimpses of the nature of the opposition in Washington. The inhabitants of Louisiana were opposed to territorial status with a governor and other officials to be sent from Washington to be over them, officials who know nothing of the people, their manners and customs, and their language. In stating their grievance on this score the signatories said:

The third article of the treaty lately concluded at Paris, declares 'that the inhabitants of the ceded territory shall be incorporated into the Union of the United States and admitted as soon as possible, according to the principles of the federal constitution, to the enjoyment of all the rights, advantages and immunities of Citizens of the United States, and in the meantime they shall be protected in the enjoyment of their liberty, property, and the exercise of the religion they possess.[6]

The Louisianians wanted statehood immediately, but the opposition delayed the admission of Louisiana into the Union until 1812. ". . . We find the advocates of our subjection," said the *Mémoire,*

driven to an argument, at which we have before hinted. To deprive us of our right of election, we have been represented as too ignorant to exercise it with wisdom, and too turbulent to enjoy it with safety. Sunk in ignorance, effeminated by luxury, debased by oppression, we were, it was said, incapable of appreciating a free constitution, if it were given, or feeling the deprivation, if it were denied.

The sentiments which were excited by this humiliating picture may be imagined, but cannot be expressed, consistent with the respect we owe to your honorable body. We were willing, however, to ascribe it to the want of correct information, but we could not avoid wondering that it should be so very defective as to have drawn from the names of some districts in our country, an argument as to the language spoken in them, which proved fatal to an important amendment to the Bill.[7] We could not imagine what had excited the idea of our effeminacy and profusion; and the laborious planter,

[5]*Mémoire présenté au Congrès des États-Unis d'Amérique par les Habitants de la Louisiane* (New Orleans, 1804). Text given in French and English in parallel columns. The original document was evidently in French. The English translation which accompanies it in parallel is frequently faulty. *Cf.*, pp. 29-30.

[6]*Ibid.*, p. 21.

[7]Bill of March 26, 1804.

at his frugal meal, heard with a smile of bitterness and contempt, the descriptions published at Washington, of his opulence and luxury

As to the degree of information diffused through the country, we humbly request that some more correct evidence may be produced than the superficial remarks that have been made by travellers or residents, who neither associate with us nor speak our language; many of us are native citizens of the United States, who have participated in that kind of knowledge which is there spread among the people; the others generally are men who will not suffer, by a comparison with the population of any other colony. Some disadvantages as to education in the *higher branches of literature,*[8] have lately attended us, but the original settlement of the province was marked by circumstances peculiarly favorable when *science*[9] had attained a great degree of perfection, and from a country in which it flourished; many individuals possessing a property and rank, which suppose a liberal education, were among the first settlers; and perhaps there would be no vanity in asserting that the first establishment of Louisiana might vie with that of any other in America, for the respectability and information of those who composed it; their descendants now respectfully call for the evidence which proves that they have so far degenerated as to become totally incompetent to the task of legislation.[10]

THE PROJECTING OF AN EDUCATIONAL SYSTEM

In 1805 Governor William C. C. Claiborne projected a plan for a general system of education for Louisiana, which should include an academy for each parish or commune, together with a college at New Orleans. Governor Claiborne, a Virginian by birth, had received his education at Richmond Academy and at the College of William and Mary. He later studied law for three months in a private office. When the capital was removed to Philadelphia, Claiborne entered into a friendship with Thomas Jefferson. After studying law for a brief period he went to Tennessee, where eventually he was sent to Congress as the successor to Andrew Jackson, who had been elected to the Senate. While in Congress he voted for Jefferson for president, and in 1802 he was appointed governor of Mississippi Territory. From that office he was sent to Louisiana, "where he succeeded in overcoming all prejudices against

[8]The French parallel reads as follows: "Nous avons éprouvé, à la vérité, depuis peu quelques désavantages du côté de l'instruction, par la difficulté de nous en procurer les moyens."

[9]The French parallel reads: "les sciences," with the eighteenth-century meaning of branches of knowledge, rather than the more recent meaning of *science.* The word science as separate from other branches of knowledge did not come into general use until the nineteenth century.

[10]*Ibid.*, pp. 17-19.

him and became very popular with the Louisianians of French origin. The reason of his success was that he was laborious and thoroughly honest."[11]

It was no doubt his experience as a student in Richmond academy and William and Mary that gave him the general plan of academies and a college.[12] The curriculum of the college was to embrace courses in Greek and Latin, English, French and Spanish, literature, philosophy and the sciences.[13] The preamble to the legislative act drawn up by Governor Claiborne expresses nobly the highest ideals for education in a democracy. Its central theme that the only way to preserve a republic is to educate its citizens was not only sound Americanism, but a theme that had been harped on repeatedly throughout the sittings of the *Convention Nationale.*

> Whereas the independence, happiness and grandeur of every republic depend, under the influences of Divine Providence, upon the wisdom, virtue, talents and energies of its citizens and rulers; and whereas science, literature and the liberal arts contribute to an eminent degree to improve those qualities and acquirements; and whereas learning hath ever been found the ablest advocate of genuine liberty, the best supporter of rational religion, and the source of the only solid and imperishable glory which nations can acquire; and forasmuch as literature and philosophy furnish the most useful and pleasing occupations, improving and varying the enjoyments of prosperity, affording relief under the pressure of misfortune, and hope and consolation in the hour of death; and considering that in a commonwealth whose humblest citizen may be elected to the highest public office, the knowledge which is required for a magistrate should be widely diffused.[14]

The State legislature hesitated for a period of five years before putting into execution Claiborne's plan of education, a plan which received able support from the many French refugees from Santo Domingo who found asylum in New Orleans after the uprising

[11]Alcée Fortier, *History of Louisiana* (New York, 1904), III, pp. 11-12.

[12]There is a possibility that Governor Claiborne was influenced by an educational attempt in Kentucky. F. G. Davenport in his book *Ante-Bellum Kentucky* (p. 37) says: "During the first two decades of its statehood, Kentucky attempted to project a state-controlled system of education that in theory had excellent possibilities. The plan called for an academy in each county. Each academy was granted 6,000 acres of land which was to be sold to furnish endowment. It was the original intention of the State to have the academies supply well-trained students for a university that was to be at the head of the entire system."

[13]Thomas Jefferson suggested Du Pont de Nemours as the president of the projected college. Jefferson was influenced in his educational ideas by Du Pont, and it is very probable that the latter's influence entered into the shaping of the University of Virginia.

[14]Alcée Fortier, *op. cit.,* III, pp. 22-23.

of the blacks in 1802.[15] Finally, in April, 1811, the legislature passed an act creating twelve academies and a college to be administered by a board of regents, the majority of whose members were selected from among the Santo Dominican exiles. The plan of Claiborne had called for the foundation of two lotteries to provide funds for the upkeep of the university. The legislature, instead, appropriated $5,000 per year for free instruction for fifty pupils. The citizens of New Orleans contributed a site between St. Claude and Hospital Streets for the buildings and gave an additional fund of over $10,000. By the time the buildings were constructed in 1811 the available funds had been used and there remained an amount of $6,000 due to the contractors.

Nevertheless, the College of Orleans opened its doors toward the end of 1811, with Jules d'Avezac, a Santo Dominican lawyer as first president. The first year the college enrolled approximately 100 students, of whom 25 were admitted free. The debt and expense of running the college caused the legislature to authorize the university to conduct two lotteries for the purpose of raising an annual appropriation of $50,000. The board of regents took little interest in the scheme, and the sum needed was never raised. Avezac resigned and was succeeded by a professor of English named Carr. He became involved in a scandal over the handling of the finances and was dismissed. He was succeeded by Rochefort, a poet from Santo Domingo who was portrayed by his pupil Charles Gayarré in his book entitled *Fernando de Lemos.* Under him matters went from bad to worse, and in the Spring of 1821 there were only twelve students and a debt.

The University of Orleans was on the point of expiring when the legislature came to its rescue by making radical changes. The original plan of a university was abandoned officially and completely. The College of Orleans alone survived. The regents were replaced by nine administrators. Also the appropriation was in-

[15]When in 1808 Napoleon forced the king of Spain to abdicate and placed Joseph Bonaparte on his throne, the Spanish Captain-General of Cuba regarded France and Spain as in a state of war, and as a consequence a large number of French refugees from Santo Domingo who had settled in Cuba were forced once more to flee, and they took refuge in New Orleans. Their number was more than 5,000, a number increased by arrivals from others of the West Indies.

creased to $5,000 a year. A year passed by, but instead of making progress the college continued to decline. In 1822 the number of pupils was reduced to seven. Should the program of studies be changed?[16]

The subjects of study called for in the plan of Governor Claiborne were only partially followed. Under the first president the course of study was arranged for Latin, French, Spanish, English, mathematics, music, dancing and fencing. The only result possible from such a program was *"un honnête homme"* in the sense the term implied in the seventeenth century. The pupils became known 'for their classicism and for their good manners.'[17] What the community needed was not to train elegant gentlemen, but future planters, merchants and navigators. For this reason the legislature decided to change the program of studies, and with this in view Lakanal was called to the presidency.

LAKANAL AS PRESIDENT OF THE COLLEGE OF ORLEANS

Between the latter part of 1817 and the Spring of 1822 nothing is known of Lakanal further than that in 1821 he made his second trip to South Carolina. That he continued to reside in Kentucky is shown by the fact that James Workman, President of the Board of Administrators of the College of Orleans at New Orleans, addressed to him in Kentucky a letter announcing that he had been elected President of the College of Orleans. This letter, one of two documents relating to Lakanal which were discovered several years ago in the archives of the University of Alabama, reads as follows:[18]

New Orleans, March 31, 1822.

Sir:

I have the satisfaction to acquaint you that the Administration of the College of Orleans, having seen the numerous and honorable testimonials transmitted to you by their late president, Edward Livingston, Esq., have by

[16] Dolive Benoît, "Lakanal et le Collége d'Orléans." Unpublished manuscript.

[17] *Ibid.*

[18] The other document written in French is reproduced in translation elsewhere in this volume. Both documents are to be found in the records of the Board of Trustees of the University of Alabama.

an unanimous vote, elected you president of that institution. We are anxious to know when we may expect the pleasure of seeing you in the city.

I have the honor to be, Sir, with the highest respect,

JAMES WORKMAN
President of the Board of Administrators.

JOSEPH LAKANAL, *Esq.,*
Near Ghent, Gallatin County, Kentucky.

This letter is of value since it shows that Lakanal was still living in Kentucky as late as 1822, and fixes the time of his departure for Louisiana. Accepting the offer, he must have left very soon for New Orleans, for on Thursday, May 30, 1822, at six o'clock in the evening Joseph Lakanal was officially inaugurated President of the College of Orleans in the presence of the Secretary of State, the Attorney General, the Mayor, the City Council, and judges of the courts, as well as other prominent citizens. James Workman, President of the Board of Administrators, welcomed the new president, extolled his merits, and ended up by expressing the hope that "the College of Orleans will, under your directing care, become a lasting benefit and ornament to the country which you have honored by adopting."[19] After an interpreter had translated the speech into French, Lakanal replied in French in an enthusiastic if not eloquent manner. A translation into English of Lakanal's address appeared the next day in the *Courrier de la Louisiane:*

"It has at length been determined," said Lakanal,

that Ignorance and Barbarism shall not obtain their promised triumph,[20] and that the College of Orleans shall resume that rank, which it formerly held, under the direction of a president distinguished as well by his literary talents as by the engaging urbanity of his manners. An extended and systematized plan of instruction has been adopted by the administrators of

[19]The *Courrier de la Louisiane* for May 31, 1822, devoted several columns of its editorial page to the installation of Lakanal as president. The account was given in both French and English. An address of welcome by Workman states that Lakanal had arrived in this country in 1815, and that he would take out papers and become a citizen of our country. This address was followed by the response of Lakanal. Also a statement was read by Workman "To The Public" on behalf of the Administrators informing the public who Lakanal was, and based on diplomas, letters and other authentic documents. Among the extracts of letters read were those written to Lakanal by Daubenton, La Grange, Laplace, Lacépède and La Fayette.

[20]A reference to the threat of closing the College which had led the trustees to change the program and employ Lakanal.

this institution, to assure the execution of which it has been thought proper to appoint me, to act in concert with Professors distinguished by their morals and their abilities.

According as we shall be possessed of or deficient in wisdom, either a great source of knowledge will be opened for the fertilizing of every mind, or the rising generation be plunged into that abyss of ignorance and darkness in which the slaves of Despotism and Tyranny repose. The mission with which we are charged is so grand that it must extend the views of our minds; it is so noble that it is calculated to implant new virtue in our breasts. In sacrificing our time, our repose, our moral and physical faculties to our country, we hope to justify the choice which has been made by men distinguished by those useful acquirements which extend and enlarge the mind; by that probity which secures the reality of patriotism; and by that wisdom which forms the mainsprings of Republican minds. In the exercise of their high functions they have always the public good for their end; in their labors, truth for their rule, antiquity for their guide, and the suffrages of good men for their recompense. The jury of public instruction which they form is vested with as high powers as that which is convened to sit in judgment on the lives of its fellow citizens. The one is destined to repress crimes by punishment, the other, by instilling knowledge to call forth the virtues into existence. A public teacher ought to be as a father over his children, possessing all that dignity of character which represents paternal authority, and that gentleness, that patience so necessary with scholars which is calculated to represent maternal tenderness.

We have been called to the task of forming men destined to hear, to understand and to assert truths; to enjoy all the rights and privileges of nature. In the first place, then, we must establish the basis of universal morality; of that morality which teaches to man the most necessary science, the art of living well. We shall then proceed to those exact sciences, which accustom the mind to truth, and appear to be by Truth herself. Then to those physical sciences which attach themselves to the bosom of nature, to ravish from her all her treasures and all her secrets—to *belles lettres,* which augment our enjoyments in prosperity and console us in the hour of adversity; which sustained Boethius in chains, Ovid in exile—"Ingenio tamen ipse meo comitorque, frecorque!" to the ancient and modern languages those vehicles of human knowledge, and in short, to those acquirements which accompany and constitute a complete and liberal plan of instruction.

When nothing but errors and long established prejudices were taught in the schools (and some of those establishments remain), when nothing was spoken but a jargon of words without ideas, which served as a medium for replying to everything except good sense and good taste, good taste and good sense applauded when the world disdained the dust of the schools. The title of teacher had nothing honorable attached to it, when that which was taught merited no honor, and sometimes Genius herself has been seen to blush whilst disseminating in private that knowledge which her works spread with so much glory over the nations of the earth.

Now, when in those colleges, whose professors are nominated by the public authorities, nothing is taught but those truths which have enlightened mankind; now, when the eyes of men, distinguished by their virtues and their acquirements are opened upon this establishment, the proudest minds will find there enjoyment for their pride itself—no talent is too great for the College of Orleans.

By the lessons that the student will there receive, they will be disposed not to desert them, but to direct them with more intelligence. After having finished their studies in the College, these students will not repair to the cities to idle away their time, or to pass it in discoursing on nothings: No, they will dispose of themselves amongst our warehouses, in the country, on the sea, and the state will have ingenious artists, scientific agriculturists, seamen active as intrepid, and worthy of treading in the footsteps of their fathers. . . .

Europe knows and admires the warlike valor of the brave citizens of Louisiana; The British Lion has fled, trembling before the American Eagle; these high deeds of arms have resounded through the universe; but I must acknowledge that my astonishment was inexpressible, when, in a country which I thought far behind my native land, I saw men of superior order and who recalled to my mind those whom thirty years I saw shining with the greatest splendor on the national tribunal and in the academical chair. I have had the honour of sitting beside the Tronçon du Coudrai, the Debonniére, the Merlin de Douay oracles of the French bar; beside the Bailly and Pétion, incorruptible and indefatigable mayors of Paris, I find, I see here rivals in glory, and perhaps the masters of these illustrious Frenchmen.

If we fulfill the expectations of those respectable persons, our Maecenas, and the glory of Louisiana, the power of Europe, will be one submitted to our principles by the triumph gained by our arts and by the consideration of our internal prosperity.

In September, 1822, the *Gazette de la Louisiane* announced the opening of the new term of the College for October 1, and published the course of studies to be offered. These courses included moral instruction based upon scripture for every day and every class; pure mathematics and philosophy; Greek, Latin, English, French and Spanish languages; chronology, geography, and history, each professor to conduct his course in English and in French according to the needs of the pupils.

For the more advanced pupils, Lakanal will give courses in agriculture, navigation, and commerce. The method which he will use for his class in agriculture will be to study the methods of ancient and modern peoples, especially of the people of Holland who had to protect themselves against the invasion of the sea and of the rivers. In the course on navigation, he will stress the principles of Pilotage and will give six mathematical methods for resolving the two principal problems that this science offers: 1. To determine at a given moment the location of a vessel at sea; 2. To point out the direction that must be taken and the length of the passage which remains to be covered in order to arrive at the place of destination.

After exhorting the legislature and the friends of knowledge and of reason to back up the College of Orleans, the *Gazette* asks rhetorically: "Why send children to France, since M. Ferlus who directs the College of Sorèze was only a pupil of the Normal School of Paris of which Lakanal was president.[21] Also Ste. Barbe at Paris is only a celebrated secondary school of which M. Lakanal was one of the administrators for ten years."

The journal announces further that the President possesses and keeps at the disposition of the professors:

1. A cabinet of experimental physics composed of a good electrical machine with all its apparatus; a fine air-pump with a double-barrelled pump in copper; an air-gun; a telescope; an achromatic lens; a microscope; a magnet of great intensity; machines necessary for the development of the principles of static; the screw of Archimedes; the prisms for optics; a small galvanic apparatus; a treatise of mathematics executed in high-relief and in boxwood with a great elegance. The pieces composing this fine work render easily intelligible the principles of spherical trigonometry and conic sections.

2. An herbarium of eight thousand plants well dried and well preserved, and the collection of all the seeds necessary for the establishment of a botanical garden on land belonging to the college. This garden will be formed for the next fine season on the model of that of the plants at Paris.[22]

3. A large collection of objects of natural history, most of them rare and curious.

4. Around 200 fine geographical maps, of which those that are established on the largest scale serve as a complete treatise of ancient geography, modern and of the Middle Ages compared, according to a new plan by Lakanal, member of the Medical Society of New Orleans.

What was published in the article of the *Gazette* was no doubt copied verbatim from Lakanal's advertising propectus of the college.[23]

[21]Lakanal and Deleyre were appointed by the National Convention to represent that body in the École normale as inspectors.

[22]The reference is to the *Jardin des Plantes.*

[23]Associated with Lakanal as professors were Guillot, graduate of the University of Grenoble and former artillery officer in France, versed in mathematics and ancient literature, having a speaking knowledge of English and Italian; Chapelin, a lawyer at the bar in New Orleans, Irishman possessing a good knowledge of English literature, Greek and Latin, and speaking French and English; Sullivan,

The program of studies announced by Lakanal was very similar to that of the *Écoles Centrales* which he had fathered in France in the period of the Directory. The courses which he announced in agriculture, navigation and commerce had in view the practical training of youths for life in Louisiana. In combining the liberal arts, the sciences and technical studies Lakanal anticipated the trend that was to be followed in American education of the later nineteenth century.

For the execution of his plan, New Orleans was ideally suited. It was the largest port along the Gulf of Mexico, and hence the need for expert navigators and capable and enterprising merchants. The periodical overflows of the Mississippi and the resultant loss and devastation suggested the study of the Dutch methods of handling the encroachment of the waters. The practical needs of the region in addition to the cultural influences of the city gave a rare opportunity for a type of education that would be both liberal and practical.

By the time of Lakanal's arrival in New Orleans the College of Orleans had declined in enrollment from 100 students to 7. The new president had to turn his attention to increasing the number of students. By October, Lakanal was able to announce through the columns of the *Gazette:* "Letters from other parts of the State and even from Kentucky give reasonable hopes that the number will be augmented to sixty before the end of the year."[24] His expectations were more than realized, for before the end of the scholastic year the college had enrolled eighty, nearly half of whom were boarding students. Tuition from students together with the annual appropriation of $5,000 enabled Lakanal to administer the college with financial success.

Irishman, speaking Latin, English and French; M'Karaher, American, former proprietor and editor of the New Orleans Journal, *L'Amis des Lois,* speaking both English and French. From the qualifications of his faculty, it is to be inferred that the teaching of scientific and philosophical subjects would necessarily fall upon Lakanal himself.

[24]*Gazette de la Louisiane,* October 16, 1822. Note the words "even from Kentucky." This throws some light on Lakanal's stay in Kentucky. It must have been his personal influence which drew students from Kentucky. Kentucky was provided at this time with excellent facilities for education at Transylvania University at Lexington. This was just the moment of the greatest fame of that institution under the guidance of its brilliant president Holley. Students would not be drawn to New Orleans for lack of facilities in their own State.

During this same year he was able to put into effect only a part of his curriculum, as the students were not sufficiently advanced for the more technical subjects. After spending a year in preparing them, just as he was looking forward to fulfilling the whole scholastic program, in July, 1823, he suddenly resigned. "M. Lakanal has just resigned the presidency of the College," announced the *Gazette* (July 22).

In April, 1823, a committee appointed by the legislature had inspected the college and had made a favorable report. This report gives a fine insight into Lakanal's administration of the College. The inspecting committee was composed of members of both houses of the legislature. After investigating the College, the committee reported back to the legislature:

> The members of the joint committee, in conformity with the resolution by virtue of which they were named, after having assembled, were transported in a body to the College of Orleans in order to make an inspection of it, and to assure themselves of its present state. Upon their arrival, the person who fills the place of president welcomed them with all the marks of consideration due to the honorable body which they represented, and satisfied eagerly and precisely the inquiries that they made upon diverse objects which had to do with their mission.
>
> Immediately the pupils were brought in, who were examined on different branches of knowledge in the presence of the committee which believes it to be its duty to let you know that it was with the keenest pleasure that it observed the discipline and becoming behavior which reigned among them, and that it was a witness of the facility and correctness with which they answered the questions put to them, and translated and explained their authors. This examination dealt with the principal points which should form the basis of instruction in a truly national college, to wit: the French, Greek, Latin and English languages, arithmetic, the first elements of geometry, and algebra applied to geometry; the students are drilled in rendering Latin now into English, now into French.
>
> Our committee does not pretend to say, however, that the majority of the pupils have already arrived at a degree of advancement that time alone can procure; but the truth is that these children who entered the College less than a year ago, have made in this short space of time progress which does them no less honor than to their professors, since they are a proof of the application of the ones and the skill of the others.
>
> Your committee does not believe that it will be necessary to call to your attention that the number of boarding pupils, which was not more than seven when the President entered office in the College of Orleans, has steadily increased in spite of the prediction which was circulated then that the institution was bordering on its ruin, so that today the institution numbers 44 boarders and 36 day-pupils, making a total of 80 pupils, among which there are 2 boarders and 35 day-pupils who are admitted gratis. These last belong to

the class of society the least favored by fortune and which has the greatest need of the advantages which the wisdom and liberality of the institution concerned procure for the people.

Your joint committee also examined the different rooms set aside either for study or recreation, the dormitory, the refectory, and the laundry, and can not but conclude from the order, from the regularity which it observed everywhere, that the person charged with the direction and conducting of the College, watches over all its parts with the most active vigilance, and that he considers that no detail however trivial or minute can be beneath his attention, when this detail is connected with an institution from which the legislature of the State and the sane portion of society hope that the public will one day derive the greatest advantage.

Your committee desiring to make a report as complete as possible on the mission which was confided to it, examined the account of the receipts and disbursements of the College for the year which expired the 31st of last December. From this examination has come the conviction that the funds of the institution have been administered with the strictest economy, and that by means of the annual appropriation given by the State to the College and by means of the tuition paid by the pupils, after the expenses have been covered, there has remained at the end of the year a small surplus.

But there are debts owing by the institution which have been running several years, and which amount to the sum of $9,000.

Two-thirds of this sum is the balance owing since 1811 to the contractors who built the principal part of the college.

This balance bearing interest at the rate of 10 per cent per annum, renders more difficult the payment of the principal for an establishment which has no permanent revenue.

The remainder of this debt embraces several small accounts for objects furnished to the College and for balances owing to former teachers and professors. These last creditors from time to time demand payment, and if they are not satisfied in some manner or other, it is to be feared that they will soon involve the College in law suits and burdensome expenses. . . .

Before concluding this report, your committee believes that it is its duty to recommend that you declare that in the future the president of the College shall be a member of the board of administrators.

This report signed by the chairman of the committee, Elijah Clark, is entirely favorable to Lakanal, and there is no shadow of criticism unless it be in the suggestion that in the future the president shall be required to be a member of the board. There are a number of reasons which combined no doubt caused Lakanal's resignation after only 14 months of services. Possibly one of the causes was his relation to his board of administrators. Perhaps he assumed sole charge of the college and failed to consult his trustees in the various steps which he took. If so, it would have been better for him to have displayed more tact.

Upon the occasion of Lakanal's installation as President of the

College of Orleans, James Workman, in introducing him to the audience, stated that Lakanal had been in this country for 15 years and that he intended to become a citizen. Some years later in one of his letters to his friend in France, Geoffroy Saint-Hilaire, Lakanal states that he has not ceased to be French and that it was in order not to lose his title to being French that he refused to take an oath to the contrary, "demanded in order to preserve the presidency of the University of Louisiana." Thus we know that this refusal to take out citizenship papers had some influence on Lakanal's resignation.

It is very probable that the Board of Administrators had employed Lakanal without taking the people of the community into their confidence, for, from the very moment of his arrival in New Orleans, he became the subject of attack.[25] Within a week after his inaugural the *Gazette* published an item as follows: "There can be no dispute as to the outstanding scholarship of M. Lakanal, and that is exactly why he has under-handed detractors: how many pamphlets, how many biographies have not already been produced! These petty antics result in nothing except to prove that he who is the object of them is suited for his place; how many clear proofs must have shown the most incredulous that M. Lakanal has for detractors rather inferior people who because of this inferiority are always jealous of the success of others."

Throughout the year the battle was fought between the reactionary and the liberal elements of the community. The more liberal element sided with Lakanal. His enemies industriously exploited Lakanal's past history as a regicide, an apostate priest who had married, his religious position as a deist, and thus an anti-

[25]". . . The position of director of the College falling vacant, the trustees could think of no one more fitted to fill it than so illustrious a representative of learning and republicanism, than a refugee from the Bourbon restauration, and living within call on a farm on the banks of the Ohio. A *ci-devant* priest and professor of *belles-lettres* . . . a man known in all positions for brilliant intellect and indomitable energy, his qualifications for the position of director of the College of Orleans seemed indisputable to the trustees. To the good mothers of New Orleans, and to the vast majority of Creoles, however, anti-Christ alone was represented by the ex-priest and regicide; and the foul fiend would have been considered as good a director of youth. The trustees persisted in their choice; the citizens in their opposition."—Grace King, *New Orleans the Place and the People* (New York, 1907), p. 187.

Christian, and probably his membership in the Masons.[26] Everything became grist to their mill. When Lakanal, who was a member of the Medical Society of New Orleans, sought to aid in combating an epidemic of yellow fever in September and October of 1822, he offered the physicians an apparatus which had been invented by the French scientist Guyton de Morveaux. This instrument was supposed to disinfect the air, prevent contagion, and arrest the progress of the disease. This gesture of good will was twisted by his enemies into an insinuation that Lakanal had only scorn for the physicians of the city. This very criticism reflects that in their secret hearts his enemies recognized Lakanal's superiority.

For a time Lakanal remained silent, until a rumor circulated that the college was about to go under, and his enemies seized the opportunity to suggest a new president. This brought forth a public reply from Lakanal in the *Gazette* of October 16, 1822:

> It does not appear that the publications against the College have had any very fatal effects on its prosperity. It already reckons forty boarders who will be at their posts by the end of the month; and letters from other parts of the state and even from Kentucky give reasonable hopes that the number will be augmented to sixty before the close of the year. The latter number had hardly ever been exceeded in the most prosperous days of the establishment and it had sunk as low as 12 during the crisis but lately passed.

In response to the accusation that there were none in the College who could explain Laplace, Monge and Newton, he calls attention to a notice that had appeared the tenth of the past June in the newspaper *L'Amis des Lois,*[27] and states that his critics will find there

> a notice on my *Analytical Sketch of Human Learning at the Close of the Eighteenth Century.*[28] The great truths contained in the three works which the Censor of the College no doubt alludes to when naming Newton, Laplace, and Monge, are developed in mine: I mean the terrestrial system of Laplace, the descriptive geometry of Monge, the fluxions of Newton.

Lakanal had announced plans for a botanical garden. His enemies taunted him on this score: "What the Censor had said of the Botanical Garden, which is only a wished-for project, seems to be somewhat superficial." As a retort to the suggestion of another president: "I have not the honor of knowing the rival the Censor prefers to me—his very name was unknown to me; although the

[26]Lakanal became a Mason in 1807.

[27]The true title of the paper in spite of the grammatical incorrectness of *L'Amis.*

[28]It was never published.

members of the French Institute thought they knew all the learned men in America." Then he goes on to say: "For fifty years I have been exclusively occupied with public instruction although, for many other public functions, I acknowledge my superiors.

As late as April 30, 1823, in the columns of *L'Amis des Lois,* a defender of Lakanal who signed himself as *Verus,* challenged his critics on the ground that since the committee delegated by the Legislature to inspect the College of Orleans had made a report entirely favorable to its president, Lakanal should be judged by his acts and accomplishments since arriving in New Orleans rather than on his record of having voted the death of Louis XVI when he was fulfilling his duty as a Deputy to the *Convention Nationale* thirty years before.

Persistent opposition, however, seems to have disheartened Lakanal, and on July 22, 1823, the *Gazette* announced: "M. Lakanal has just resigned the presidency of the College." On the same day on which this announcement appeared, there appeared also in the same newspaper an article suggesting a certain Abbé for Lakanal's place:

> The Board of Administration is going, they say, to name in his place an *Abbé* strongly imbued with principles of monarchy and the absolute right of kings. The suitability of such a choice does not impress everybody; however, it must not be forgotten that the friends of the Throne and the Altar are on the eve of destroying the slightest vestige of democratic principles in Europe; that the Bourbons and the priests will soon operate as masters in France and in Spain; that this country was sold to the Americans by Jacobins, whose every act has been annulled today; so that there is thus nothing amiss in investing one of the faithful with a position which will enable him to shape the mind of Louisiana youth; a thing that might prove very useful when the House of Bourbon determines to seize again all of its former colonies. Certainly, Louisiana would be a gold mine both for the royal fisc and for the convents of monks. *Vive le roi, honneur à l'église!*

The article, although written in a satirical vein, permits us to know at least that there were efforts on the part of the ultra-royalists of New Orleans to get control of the College. But that their maneuvers did not succeed is witnessed by the fact that Lakanal's son-in-law, Lucien Charvet,[29] was elected to succeed him. This would seem to indicate the influence Lakanal still possessed at the moment of his resignation, and this action on the part of the Board of Administrators was in a manner a vindication of him.

The College of Orleans was an ill-starred venture with only one

[29]Cohen's *New Orleans Directory for 1855* lists Lucien Charvet as Att.-at-law, Chartres, C. Customhouse d. 102 Orleans.

bright moment in its history, the fourteen months when Lakanal was its president. The College did not prosper under Lucien Charvet, and three years later, in 1826, closed its doors forever.

Before Lakanal left New Orleans an incident occurred which must have caused him much satisfaction. In 1823 there was published in Paris a two-volume work, ornamented with beautiful engravings, descriptive of the *Muséum d'Histoire Naturelle,* published under the direction of the professors of that institution. On June 10, 1823, the professors addressed a copy of the work to Lakanal in the United States, each of them signing his name. The signatures were: Vauquelin, Thouin, Desfontaines, Geoffroy Saint-Hilaire, Latreille, Cuvier, Laugier, Cordier, Jussieu, Lamarck, Brongniart, Lacépède.[30] All of these names were famous in France a century ago, and the fame of several of them still persists not only in France but in other countries as well.

From a letter which Lakanal addressed years later[31] to the above-mentioned Geoffroy Saint-Hilaire, we learn that the volume in question contained an article on Lakanal by Saint-Hilaire, "During the ministry of Villèle[32] you caused to be inserted in the beautiful *Description du Muséum d'histoire Naturelle,* an article which moved me to tears. You did more, you addressed the work to me in my exile, after having elicited the signed approbation of all the honorable professors of your institution."

From New Orleans, Lakanal went to the French colony at Demopolis, Alabama, with the evident intention of occupying his grant and making his home in the well-known Vine and Olive Colony. But finding the colony disintegrating, he journeyed on to Mobile where he resided until his return to France in 1837. The exact moment of his departure from New Orleans is not known, but from a letter[33] which he wrote in 1830, we learn that he had then been in Mobile for the preceding six years. It is evident, therefore,

[30]*Exposé Sommaire des Travaux de Joseph Lakanal.* (Paris, 1838).

[31]Letter of October 28, 1838. Jouin, *Lakanal et David d' Angers.*

[32]The period of the reactionary ministry of Villèle was a rather dangerous moment for inserting an article of praise of a regicide. Lakanal recognizing this, hints that he is aware of the danger.

[33]Written from Mobile to Étienne Geoffroy Saint-Hilaire. Jouin, *Lakanal en Amérique.*

that he must have left New Orleans late in the year 1823, or early in 1824. There is no documentary evidence which would enable us to date his departure more exactly.

8

LAKANAL IN ALABAMA

BEGINNING IN THE LAST DECADE OF THE SEVENTEENTH CENTURY MANY Frenchmen came to America for many reasons. Among the more celebrated were Chateaubriand, who found here the materials for *Les Natchez;* Louis Phillipe, who later became King of the French; the Vicomte de Noailles; Chastellux, who wrote the first trustworthy record of life in the United States; Major L'Enfant, who drew up the plans for the city of Washington; and the Michaux, father and son, who founded the botanical gardens at Charleston.

In the decade 1790-1800, when the capital of the country was Philadelphia, that city became the Mecca for French visitors and refugees. Even prior to that Philadelphia was known to the French as the home of Franklin, and many celebrated Frenchmen had been elected to membership in the American Philosophical Society at Philadelphia, among them the naturalist Buffon, the chemist Lavoisier, Condorcet, the educational theorist, Lafayette, Barbe Marbois, who was later to act as Napoleon's agent in the sale of Louisiana to the United States, Cabanis, Volney, Talleyrand, Du Pont deNemours, and Destutt de Tracy.

From Philadelphia many of these refugees set out to establish colonies in various places. In 1816 the French Agricultural and Manufacturing Society was organized to set up a colony for the cultivation of the vine and olive.[1] Although they first planned to settle in the Ohio Valley, the colonists eventually accepted a grant of land on the Tombigbee River in Alabama and settled there in 1817. It was quite natural that Lakanal should decide to join the Demopolis colony when he looked about for a congenial place to live after leaving New Orleans.

[1]Gauis Whitfield, Jr., "The French Grant in Alabama," *Publications of the Alabama Historical Society,* IV, 321-355.

However, the colony had apparently failed before he reached Alabama. In spite of numerous severe trials and tribulations, the Demopolis colonists had been held together in a spirit of unity and hopefulness as long as their beloved Napoleon was alive. But when on May 5, 1821, Napoleon died on St. Helena, the colony began to disintegrate, and by 1830 had largely dissolved.

Lakanal recounts his arrival in Mobile in the following passage:

> After having long and honorably performed the duties of Rector of the University of the Beautiful and opulent Louisiana . . . I repaired to the vast territorial concession which had been conceded to me by the Congress of the United States in the French colony of the Tombecbée. This establishment, worthy of a prosperous fate, having dwindled bit by bit, through the fault of the colonists, I came to settle on the romantic shores of the Bay of Mobile, where in the midst of the golden mediocrity so much praised by Horace, I enjoy the esteem and friendship of my neighbors.

Lakanal must have arrived in Alabama toward the end of 1823 or very early in the year 1824. The land which he occupied lay at that time at a distance from the little town of Mobile, but with the growth of the town into a populous city, the southern boundary of the city has reached the spot where he lived. The court house records at Mobile reveal that in 1831 Lakanal purchased three tracts of land, and an additional one in 1835. Also that another tract was purchased in the name of his wife, Marie-Barbe François. On May 5, 1831, he bought at public outcry Lot 4 in Square 8 of Block No. 1 in the Mandeville Tract for a consideration of $187.50; on July 10, at public outcry, Lots 3 and 4 in Square 10 for a consideration of $148.50; on July 31, he purchased Lot 5, Square 10, "of the block and division of lots numbered one (1) of the third sale of real estate of John Forbes & Company," in the Mandeville Tract. The lot contained 3,100 acres and the purchase price was $50.75. During this same summer he purchased 15 *arpens* of land in Township 4 south, for a consideration of $330.[2]

It does not appear that Lakanal became a very extensive landholder, but in one of his letters he made mention of owning ten slaves, and in a later letter of owning twelve. This was about the

[2]Recorded in Deed Book K, pages 86, 81, 80, and 87 respectively. The author does not have at hand the details of the land purchased by Mrs. Lakanal.

number that would be required for the successful exploitation of a tract of 400 acres, the size of Clausel's plantation.[3]

General Count Bertrand Clausel lived in the same neighborhood, and it appears certain that Lakanal chose his home to be near Clausel. Both he and Clausel had come from Ariège, and were therefore known to each other. An uncle of Bertrand Clausel had been a fellow deputy of Lakanal in the National Convention. There is a tradition in Mobile that the two men were hostile to each other and not on speaking terms. This is belied by the fact that after Clausel had returned to France in 1825, he gave Lakanal power-of-attorney to sell his land. From a farm which had cost Clausel $1,200 Lakanal realized $1,500, which he forwarded to him in France. From this incident and from references to Clausel in several letters, it is apparent that the two men must certainly have been on good terms.[4]

Since the court house records at Mobile fail to reveal any purchase of land by Lakanal prior to 1831, the moment when he sold the "Clausel Plantation," it is to be inferred that in the meantime he may have occupied Clausel's land.[5]

[3]The French Revolution freed the slaves of the French colonies, but Napoleon decreed the revival of slavery for the West Indies. The French colonists at Demopolis did not own slaves, but Lakanal seems to have overcome his scruples in this respect. In doing so, he was in harmony with a revived French practice, and with the custom of this country.

[4]General Count Bertrand Clausel had served in the French Revolutionary armies and by 1797 had risen to the rank of General of Brigade. In 1815, Napoleon named him Peer of France and placed him at the head of the *corps d'observation* of the western Pyrenees. During the Battle of Waterloo which ended the One Hundred Days, Clausel commanded the Napoleonic legions south of the Loire and stubbornly refused to raise the white flag for a long time after it had become apparent that all hope of victory had vanished. With the return of Louis XVIII to Paris, Clausel was included among those condemned to death but escaped to the United States. He joined the Vine and Olive Colony in Alabama but left it in 1820 to remove to Mobile. He purchased a tract of land on the outskirts of this village and eked out a living by cart-peddling vegetables to the inhabitants of Mobile.

[5]Clausel's land lay in what was known as the Mandeville Tract. According to the deed recorded in Mobile, on June 23, 1831, $1,500 was paid to Joseph Lakanal and Victor Gammard (for B. Clausel) by one Thomas Yeatman of Nashville, Tennessee, through John Instone, for a piece of property 3 miles from Mobile, fronting the bay, known as Clausel Plantation; bounded on the north by the Mandeville Tract, south by Garrone's Plantation, east by the bay, and west unknown. This property lies just over the southern limits of the city today.

The principal source of our knowledge of Lakanal's life at Mobile is contained in fifteen letters which he wrote[6] to his friend of revolutionary days, Étienne Geoffroy Saint-Hilaire, the naturalist who was the master of the celebrated Cuvier.

At the moment in 1793 when the *Jardin du Roi* was reorganized under the leadership of Lakanal into the *Muséum d' histoire Naturelle,* Saint-Hilaire became a professor of zoology there. Five years later he accompanied Napoleon's army to Egypt as official zoologist; and subsequent to the founding of the Imperial University in 1808 he became professor of zoology in the Faculty of Sciences. He became a member and later officer of the Legion of Honor. He was a member of the Academy of Sciences and a Knight of the Empire. His scientific views were, in contrast to Cuvier's, more in harmony with those of Lamarck and Darwin.

Lakanal had been in this country more than nine years before he undertook a correspondence with his friend Saint-Hilaire. When he left Europe he seems to have desired to cut himself off from the past. So far as is known, he corresponded with only one person in France prior to writing to Saint-Hilaire. This was his friend Morand,[7] but there is no known letter extant from the correspondence between Morand and Lakanal.

Lakanal's first letter to Saint-Hilaire in 1825 had remained unanswered. It probably failed to reach its destination, since it was not preserved among Saint-Hilaire's letters from Lakanal. At any rate, on April 25, 1826, the exile addressed another letter to his friend of former times. In it he states that he had written the year before, but had received no response. He enumerates the things that he said in the previous letter. He had expressed gratitude for the autographed copy of the *Histoire du Muséum royal d'histoire naturelle,* and had thanked his friend for calling attention to the good said of him in this fine work, with the feeble service rendered.[8]

[6]The first is of the date April 25, 1826, and the last of the date October 28, 1839. Eight were written from Mobile, one from New Orleans, and six after Lakanal's return to France. Published in Jouin, *Lakanal en Amérique* and *Lakanal et David d'Angers.*

[7]Letter of Nov. 5, 1834, preserved among the Lakanal Papers in the Howard Memorial Library, New Orleans.

[8]See page 140 for an account of the incident.

In 1818 Saint-Hilaire had published a work entitled *Philosophie anatomique: des organes respiratoires,* and in 1822 a companion volume, *Philosophie anatomique: des monstruosités humaines.* According to Lakanal, this memorable work had been extolled in the journals of the United States, and he added that he would have forwarded copies of the book reviews to him had they not been mixed in with the fierce political discussions which accompanied the presidential campaign prior to the election of John Quincy Adams. Furthermore, he had stated in his earlier letter that several men versed in a knowledge of natural sciences had occupied themselves with translating the French scientist's work into English, one of whom was a member of the Royal Society of London. The translating, however, had been interrupted by an unusually severe epidemic of yellow fever.

Lakanal finally comes to the main object of his letter, and asks his friend to solicit the payment of his retirement pension. He states that the claim has been acknowledged to the amount of 1,500 francs, which the French government has paid him. His main contention is for the pension due him for his 18 years of service with the Doctrinaires.

Saint-Hilaire evidently did not succeed in having the pension restored, as on Nov. 20, 1831, Lakanal addressed a letter to General Clausel, who had become a marshal of France, to intercede with the government on his behalf. The absolutist government of Charles X had been succeeded by the more liberal rule of Louis-Philippe, and there was consequently a better prospect of getting favorable action. Upon the request of Marshal Clausel, the ministry reopened the case of Lakanal's pension. Fontanes, the head of the Imperial University, had in 1809 granted Lakanal a pension somewhat in excess of the amount due him as a professor, because of the services he had rendered to the cause of education during the revolutionary period; this excess together with the uncertainty of the status of Lakanal under the law of amnesty had no doubt operated to delay the restoration of the pension.[9] All who had served under

[9]Under the law of amnesty of 1820 certain categories of the exiles and refugees were permitted to return to France. An additional act of 1825 afforded restitution. The question was as to whether Lakanal, having served under Napoleon during the Hundred Days, was entitled to restitution of his pension and honors.

Napoleon in either a military or civil capacity during the Hundred Days had come under the displeasure of the restored Bourbons. Lakanal had in 1809 accepted the office of Inspector of Weights and Measures under Napoleon. During the period of the first Restoration (1814-15) he was not molested, and continued in the position not only through that period, but also during the period of Napoleon's return to power, the Hundred Days. When the Bourbons were restored to the throne a second time, Lakanal was deprived of his office because of his Napoleonic connections. Since he had served in no other capacity during the Hundred Days, it was finally decided that his pension should be restored to the 1809 figure of 3,000 francs, but that it should not be retroactive, and should date from April 1, 1832.[10]

In addressing Saint-Hilaire in a letter of 1832, Lakanal says:

> I wrote recently to Marshal Clausel, my friend of forty years. In the space of one year he addressed to me five letters from Algiers, Paris, d'Hauterive (Ariège) where he has his estates. I sold here a plantation that he occupied during the four years of his proscription under the Bourbons, and I sent him the amount (from the sale). I looked after his business free of charge, and I am certain that he will busy himself with mine. I addressed to him my affidavit of existence in order to claim my retirement pension fixed by virtue of the laws by the Council of the University; the news is entirely favorable, and what I claim is simply "le salaire de l'ouvrier à la fin de sa journée." Fifteen years of proscription; my elimination from the Institute; deprived of an obscure place in the government, and all the acts of harshness in explicit defiance of the *Charte,* should be in the eyes of a regenerated government motives for welcoming my just demand. I have not ceased to be French, and it was in order not to lose this fine title that I refused to take a contrary oath demanded to preserve the presidency of the University of Louisiana.

In a letter to Saint-Hilaire dated May 1, 1830, Lakanal says:

> You will learn, perhaps, with some interest that after my abdication from the presidency of the University of New Orleans in favor of my son-in-law Charvet, former pupil of the École Polytechnique, I acquired on the romantic shores of the Bay of Mobile, a fine and productive property. Since no matter what may happen, I shall never return to France,[11] I follow the American laws; in consequence, I have purchased ten strong and good slaves 'that I treat as unfortunate friends,' and whose moderate labor gives me, together

[10]Eugène Welvert, "Lakanal en Amérique," *Feuilles d'histoire, année* 1910, p. 366.

[11]Following this decision, Lakanal sent back to the *Muséum d'Histoire Naturelle* a key that he had received in 1793 and had carried off with him to America. When later Lakanal changed his mind and went back to France, the professors-administrators of the museum hastened to deliver to him another key on which they had had engraved these words: *"Le Muséum d'Histoire naturelle à Lakanal."*

with some funds deposited in the banks, a well-being very superior to the golden mediocrity of which Horace speaks. Seated upon the lowest step, *comme la plus stable en soi,* according to Montaigne, but surrounded by the friendliness of my neighbors, I wish that you at the summit of dignities and honors may enjoy the amount of happiness that my present situation affords me, and that all my efforts shall tend to maintain.

You alone can crown my wishes. I possess a good library, a nice cabinet of experimental physics. I would like to have a numerous collection of fresh seeds of the best and most beautiful species of garden plants, and of those which are usefully employed in medicine. I would annually spread their seeds abroad in this beautiful section of the country, and your name would be blessed here from age to age. The final article (*Titre IV*) of the law of organization of your superb establishment authorizes the sending to foreign parts of seeds from your garden.[12] I can send you seeds of plants and rare trees from a region that no French naturalist, so far as I know, has yet explored, or at least long inhabited in order to know well its productions.

I am sending you a barrel of sugar, the first made on my fine plantation. My neighbors have been making it for two years, and throughout the State of Alabama the fields of cane are spreading with a prodigious celerity. We shall soon rival Louisiana, and we are almost abandoning entirely the cultivation of cotton whose price has fallen from 32 francs to seven and six per pound.

At the close of the same letter Lakanal says:

I received six months after it was sent the box of seeds that M. Mirbel was kind enough to send me on your good recommendation. Ēriez Bros. of Le Havre had addressed this box to Fort Mobile "in Georgia." The fort has long ceased to exist, and Mobile is a large thriving city of Alabama, having three banks which pay on demand, three printing offices, two newspapers, and receives in its port annually more than 500 vessels from all the nations of the globe. I thanked M. Mirbel at the time for his obligingness, but was unable to derive any advantage from the package that he vouchsafed to send me. The seeds, entrusted to a soil suitably manured, did not come up. They must have been very old. The seeds which at the same time were sent to me by a *confrère* of the *Société d'Émulation de Rouen* throve very well. The person employed in the distribution of seeds caused me a great loss and plunged me into a big expense. A collection of leguminous plants would be precious for this country, and would have constituted a benefit for which all Alabama would have publicly testified its gratitude to your establishment, for I should have been very careful to distribute widely the seed that I harvested on my plantation.

I and all my neighbors would have been pleased to have the seeds of the finest species of garden plants. In exchange, I would have sent the seeds of trees and plants which are almost unknown in France. The richest planters of the region would have published in the newspapers a public testimony of thanks for the signal service that you would have rendered the country. I had talked so much about the package that I was awaiting: it had given birth to so many expectations, that to-day I receive for all my intentions only facetious jests.

[12]The reference is to the *Jardin des Plantes* at Paris.

With a parting word, Lakanal again insists that Geoffroy Saint-Hilaire send him a good collection of garden seeds with emphasis that they be fresh, as well as plants widely known for their curative properties, and concludes with a note of appreciation for the beauties which surround him: "Our lawns are bedecked with flowers of the most striking beauty. The gardens of Europe afford nothing like it."

In a letter of August 1, 1834, Lakanal, infected by the optimistic spirit of the moment at Mobile, exclaims: "At Mobile I find three banks paying out hard money (*piastres fortes*); I find 50 families having a carriage; I see the fair sex adorned with as much luxury as at Paris; the stores furnished with all that can be desired, and more richly displayed than at Paris. I see in winter from my gallery vessels loaded with all sorts of merchandise, and carrying back to the outside world the productions of our region, especially cotton. This year there were brought to Émile's Wharf at Mobile 150,000 bales, each of the weight of from 400 to 500 pounds."

In the same letter he announces that he has made a dictionary of the language of a tribe of Indians, the Chacta tribe,[13] of which several hundred individuals live peaceably at two hundred paces from his plantation. He says that they furnish him with excellent game. "I traverse their camp in going to Mobile, at a short league from my fine plantation."

The unpublished memoir of William H. Robertson (see page 189) says of these Indians:

> At this early period, and even for years afterward, and up to the time of the change of flag, a large number of Indians, from the Choctaw nation, were always encamped in the environs of Mobile; their camps not over more than one or two miles distance from the city itself; and these Indians supplied the people with game. I have known the finest of wild turkeys to sell tor twenty-five cents; and a fine, fat buck for a dollar; while ducks, in the winter time, brought proportionate prices.
>
> Beside the game, they also supplied the principal part of the wood burned in the city. The squaws, in this case, selling it at six cents a back-load.
>
> These Indians were a quiet, peaceable people, except upon occasions when the whiskey was too strong, and then they quarrelled among themselves. Such an incident occurred under my own observation, on one of the back streets. The Indians, somewhat intoxicated, were having an argument, whereupon one of them drew his knife and stabbed the other one under the

[13]*Choctaw* is the spelling commonly used in English.

ear. A squaw, seeing the fatal direction of the knife, grasped the sharp implement from the other Indian, and as the culprit was making his escape, she marked him on the arm with a severe gash, at the same time crying out the Death Yell, which of course, brought every Indian within hearing distance, to her side almost immediately. The squaw with a few words, pointed in the direction in which the culprit had escaped; and a hot pursuit was then started by some half dozen redskins, and in less than half an hour the guilty Indian was returned to the spot where the dying man lay. Both men were then taken to the outskirts of the town, placed on logs, side by side, and shot. One, to end his sufferings; the other for punishment.

Lakanal's keen interest in the United States is expressed:

I have traversed the States of the Federal Union during the seventeen years that I have resided in them. I have followed the Ohio from Pittsburg to its junction with the Mississippi, and have descended this old father of waters as far as New Orleans. I have gathered many productions of the regions that I have visited, principally from Philadelphia to Pittsburg, across the Allegheny ridges. I have collected many plants that I do not find in the *Genera plantarum* of Jussieu. But we are deprived of the most common plants of France. I have set up here a botanical garden. . . . I would have liked to try the plants which France possesses in abundance. The consignment which you were kind enough to send me did not succeed. . . . By one of the vessels to Le Havre which every year come and load our cotton for France, I will send you both the voluminous manuscript of my travels, and the various objects of natural history which I have collected: you will find among them the finest buffalo hide that our old hunters have ever seen; a rattle-snake skin with twenty-four rattles; a bone from the famous mammoth that I acquired at Big Bone while going from Vevay (Ohio)[14] to Cincinnati in the same State; and the flora of the environs of Mobile within a radius of three miles of this city: it is one of the most remarkable parts of the former Florida with reference to botany.

LAKANAL AND THE UNIVERSITY OF ALABAMA

During this period of his exile, Lakanal's attention was not entirely diverted from his former educational interests, as two other letters attest. One is the letter which appears elsewhere in this book notifying him of his election as President of the College of Orleans. The other is a letter-memorandum written by Lakanal from Mobile, and addressed to "J. G. Birney, Administrator of the University of Alabama."[15] The history of these two documents is an interesting one.

[14]Vevay, Indiana, originally a part of the Ohio Territory.

[15]Both of these documents were published for the first time in 1936 in John Charles Dawson's *A French Regicide in Alabama (1824-1837)*. The original of the document signed by Lakanal was written in French, but was inserted in the above book in translation into English. That translation is reproduced below. The original is reproduced in Appendix II.

The University of Alabama opened its doors to students for the first time in the Spring of 1831. The movement looking forward to the creation of a State University in Alabama had begun a decade previously, and after the opening of the University of Virginia in 1825 this movement was accelerated. By the middle of 1830 work on the buildings and grounds was almost completed, and the trustees undertook the task of securing a president and faculty. In a number of ways the University of Virginia served as a model for the University of Alabama, even to the manner in which the first faculty and president were secured.

Thomas Jefferson had employed F. W. Gilmer to procure members of the first faculty of the University of Virginia. In like manner the trustees of the University of Alabama obtained the services of James G. Birney, a prominent lawyer of Huntsville, Alabama, in seeking suitable men for the presidency and for the professorships.[16]

Dr. Alva Woods, a Baptist minister from Rhode Island who since 1828 had been president of Transylvania University at Lexington, Kentucky, was chosen as the first president, and began his duties in the summer of 1831.

Toward the close of the War Between the States when the Union forces invaded Tuscaloosa their commander, Brigadier-General John T. Croxton, came with orders to burn all the public buildings of the University. Through the efforts of slaves, directed by members of the faculty or their wives, two of the buildings—the president's mansion and the astronomical observatory—were saved from serious damage by the fire. During the excitement of the occasion some one had the forethought to attempt to save the University records, and did succeed in saving the records of the trustees. All other records of the institution were destroyed.

The trustees' records were tossed into the basement of the observatory where they escaped attention until 1888, when they were discovered by members of the faculty and removed to what is known to-day as the Round House. This miniature building had been erected as a shelter for the military officer of the day, and

[16]Records in manuscript of the Board of Trustees of the University of Alabama, University, Alabama.

was too insignificant, it is to be supposed, for the Union soldiers to go to the trouble of burning. The trustees' records remained in a vault in the Round House until Smith Hall was completed in 1911, when they were removed to that building, and a department of University archives was created with the late J. A. Anderson as curator.

Since the documents concerning Joseph Lakanal were connected with the choosing of a president and professor of languages, they had been filed and preserved among the trustees' records. This of itself is proof that Lakanal was considered for the first presidency and professorship of languages in the University of Alabama, and is proof also that these documents came into the hands of the trustees at some time between July and November of 1830, as one of them was addressed to "J. G. Birney Administrator of the University of Alabama." Birney's connection with the University began in July, 1830, and he was discharged from his task in November of that year, when a final payment was made to him for his services.

Respects to Mr. J. G. Birney, administrator of the University of Alabama, by his devoted servant J. Lakanal, member of the Medical Society of New Orleans and of the principal Academies of Europe.[17]

Note. J. Lakanal, after having resigned the presidency of the College of Orleans in favor of his son-in-law, Mr. Charvet, former pupil of the celebrated *École polytechnique* of Paris, retired six years ago[18] to his fine plantation on the Bay of Mobile, which he causes to prosper by the aid of 12 strong slaves which belong to him.[19]

. . . . he counts among the number of his friends whom he is in the habit of receiving into his home all the citizens of the region distinguished for their uprightness and their intelligence. The following, he is sure, will give him an honorable recommendation:

LAWYERS: Messrs. Acre, Durand, Aisckot, Garow, Chambodouin, Elliot, etc.

DOCTORS: Messrs. Gannard, Cheusse, Corez, etc.

MERCHANTS: Messrs. M'Kloskey, Durand, Robertson, Dunier, Armstrong.

Judge Hull, General Avrit, (Everett) Colonel Storm, my friend Yertas, and without exception all good men.

Lakanal taught for 20 years belles-lettres, philosophy, and mathematics in the University of France.

[17]See Appendix II for the original French.

[18]This fixes date of Lakanal's arrival in Alabama as 1824.

[19]Manuscript defective.

He has a good knowledge of the ancient languages and speaks Latin with ease. He knows the French language he ventures to say, thoroughly, having been for 18 years one of the editors of the New French Dictionary in 2 volumes in-4 adopted by the Institute and the Legislative Corps.[20]

Possessing a numerous and good library, and devoting himself almost exclusively to study for the past 55 years, he dares believe that he combines nearly all of our positive knowledge of the sciences, letters and beaux arts. A large work in which the branches of knowledge are analyzed under the title of "Survey of Human Knowledge at the End of the 18th Century," has been the fruit of 30 years of toil, and was adopted by the Institute of France after five sittings of deliberations.

Mr. Lakanal, in the United States for the past fifteen years, not having made consistent study of the English language, speaks and understands it imperfectly, although he has composed a little dictionary and a little grammar for his use in this language.

Salve mi Maecenas; peropto ut quod instituisti, superis bene fortunantibus, feliciter absolvas, et bonis avibus coepta res, melioribus exeat.

tui deditissimus

J. LAKANAL.

There are at least four reasons why Lakanal may have been considered unsuitable for the presidency of the University of Alabama. One is that he confesses his imperfect knowledge of spoken English. A second is that he was not a citizen of the United States. Another is that it used to be thought in America that college presidents should be ministers of the gospel. A fourth is that his mention of having twelve slaves may have been offensive to James G. Birney, who so strongly opposed slavery that he became a candidate for the presidency of the United States in 1840 on the Abolition ticket.[21]

LAKANAL IN SOUTH CAROLINA

During his sojourn in this country, Lakanal made three trips to South Carolina, two from Kentucky and one from Alabama. It is probable that his first journey was made in 1817 when he was engaged in the Napoleonic conspiracy. In a letter to Joseph Bona-

[20]Evidently the 1835 edition of the Dictionary of the French Academy.

[21]It may be of interest to note that prior to the appearance of William Lloyd Garrison's *Liberator* on the streets of Boston on January 1, 1831, there had for a decade existed in the South abolition journals which avowed the extinction of slavery as one of their objects, if not their chief one. In Tennessee *The Emancipator* was founded in 1819; in Kentucky in 1822 *The Abolition Intelligencer;* in Tennessee and Maryland 1821, *The Genius of Universal Emancipation;* in Louisiana in 1828 *The Liberalist.*

parte (1817) he speaks of a long and tiresome journey that he has to undertake, and in another letter he refers to the excessive heat of July, 1817, in South Carolina. In this same letter (1837) he mentions his second journey as of 1821. He also states that he took with him on his third journey three of his slaves. Since he acquired slaves while residing at Mobile, his third journey must have been at some time between 1824 and 1836. The lists of letters uncalled for at the Mobile post-office show that Lakanal's letters were advertised as uncalled for during the month of January, 1829.[22] The only other time his letters were advertised was in the year 1837, when he had left for New Orleans prior to returning to France. Thus it seems safe to conjecture that the third journey to South Carolina was made from Mobile in 1828-29.

In a long letter to Saint-Hilaire (undated) Lakanal says:

One of the three ladies to whom you have done me the honor of introducing me has formed such a favorable idea of South Carolina from erroneous narratives that I believe I should submit to you the result of my numerous explorations in this little known part of the United States. Facts speak louder than arguments; now here are the facts. With a considerable fortune, entire knowledge of the language spoken in the country,[23] an inalterable state of health, an extreme desire to know thoroughly, and to describe in a lengthy work the United States, which we do not know in France, I traversed in every direction and "slowly" the various parts of South Carolina, as well as the other states of the Federal Union.

I can understand how a young native Carolinian is passionately attached to a country which in the midst of riches offers many amusements. First of all, the inhabitants of South Carolina are conspicuous for elegant manners, for their politeness, and for their hospitality toward strangers. They are very fastidious in the matter of honor. Horse races are a source of great amusement. The dance is an exercise in which the youth excel. The taste for music is extremely keen, especially among the young ladies. But when it comes to appraising a country, the philosophical observer does not stop at the surface of things. Let us judge them without passion, but also without flattery. And first, the soil is generally bad. It is composed 1. of pine barrens, land sterile, sandy and of little value; 2. of savannahs yielding only rude grasses which all the animals reject; 3. morasses or swamps along the rivers. There are left then but a few good elevated lands. In certain spots I had three of my slaves whom I had taken with me on my third journey to dig down into the ground, and I found sand to the depth of twenty foot. The

[22]He probably left Mobile in November or December of 1828, and returned at beginning of February, 1829.

[23]He evidently means the French of South Carolina, for in his letter to Jas. G. Birney he had confessed that he did not have a good speaking knowledge of English, or it may be that Lakanal is exaggerating his knowledge of English.

rivers of this country are subject to prodigious floods. The Pedee, the Santee and the Savannah rise sometimes as high as the Nile, that is to say, 33 feet. This country is subject to terrible hurricanes: in that of 15 September, 1752, the tide rose 6 feet in ten minutes, and if the wind had not taken a southwesterly direction, Charleston would have been destroyed in the space of an hour.

The temperature is excessively variable. I saw in 1821, second journey that I made into this country, the thermometer vary by 46 degrees in 24 hours, difference greater than in the tropics. The heat and the cold are extreme sometimes. In July, 1817, the heat was so excessive from the 18th to the 24th that three persons died in the streets of Charleston, and the 15th of January 1816, the thermometer fell at sunrise at Columbia to 10 degrees below freezing.

South Carolina has been ravaged several times by furious tornadoes. That of 1764 broke the masts of vessels and submerged a fleet of loaded boats near Charleston. Hail ravages this country often. In 1797 there was a fall of hailstones, which measured three inches in circumference, along the banks of the Cooper river. Charleston is subject to the most violent earthquakes: witness those of the 16th of October, 1811, and January 23, 1812. In the country districts the sheep are often devoured by wolves, and the hogs by bears, which find a sure retreat behind the marshes. In the lakes and rivers there is an abundance of alligators and "your" *trionyx ferox.*

All of Carolina, and particularly the most southern part, is subject to endemic diseases resulting from the inundations of the rivers, stagnant waters from whence are exhaled deleterious miasmas, and which produce intermittent bilious fevers. Yellow fever often rages; tetanus is common; grippe (influenza) is a serious epidemic.

In South Carolina marriage is legal without the concurrence of the civil authority, which is a strange anomaly; and yet the ministers of the various creeds are disqualified from filling civil office in the state.[24]

I have found abundant in this country the *gleditsia triacanthos* (honey-locust), the *acer saccharinum* (sugar-maple) and the *dirca palustris* (leather-wood). I have analyzed the waters from the mineral spring of Pacolet, and I have found that they contain sulphur and iron in solution.

You can imagine that public education particularly attracted my attention. Considerable funds have been granted by the legislature to the two colleges of Columbia and Beaufort. The college at Columbia has a library of eleven thousand volumes and a fine physics cabinet. The president's salary is $3,000 (15,000 francs) and that of the professors to the number of four, is $1,500 (7,500 francs).

Charleston has a college directed by five curators. The system of education of our French colleges is in use there. This city has societies of agri-

[24]Common law marriage is still recognized in South Carolina. As for the clergy being disqualified from holding civil office, that goes back to colonial times when the Anglican Church exercised both political and religious control of the colony. "Far from accepting the leadership of the clergy, the laity kept the strictest control over all matters of church policy . . . the clergy had no voice in the assembly where laws affecting them and the Church were passed without their consent or even knowledge."—Frederick P. Bowes: *The Culture of Early Charleston,* (Chapel Hill, 1942).

culture and benevolence. The father of our Michaux had formed at 10 miles from Charleston, a botanical garden of which the Society of Agriculture takes care. The public library is composed of 12,000 volumes. But the primary schools, whose purpose it is to introduce into society the coming generation to replenish us, are entirely neglected. It is in Massachusetts, and principally at Boston, the capital, that they are an object of the paternal solicitude of the government. A law of the month of June, 1789, of which my confrère M. Cousin called the existence into question[25] and which I placed textually under his eyes compels the inhabitants of each township or canton to support a primary school, under penalty of a fine in proportion to the length of the negligence.

I have read in my Academy several treatises on the United States which are unknown in France.[26] These treatises were received with an extreme benevolence. However, I shall not continue these readings because I have treated with a publisher. My work will have three large volumes in-8. All of those who up to this time have written of the United States, know them only in the most superficial manner. I lived in them for twenty-two years, traversed them in all directions, and my work will appear to be a fiction. But all my assertions will be supported by convincing documents.

MOBILE AND LOUIS-PHILIPPE

The writer, in quest of information concerning Lakanal at Mobile, has succeeded in finding but one mention of him in connection with the life of the city. In the issue of October 23, 1830, the *Commercial Register for the Country* published an account of a dinner held in Mobile celebrating the enthronement of Louis-Philippe as King of the French.

[25]The reference is to Victor Cousin, Peer of France, member of the Superior Council of Public Instruction, Director of the *École Normale,* and Minister of Public Education. In a letter preserved among the Lakanal Papers in the Howard Memorial Library (now part of Tulane University) in New Orleans is the following letter from Cousin to Lakanal of the date of November 17, 1837, written presumably shortly before Lakanal's letter on South Carolina:

"University of France
Ministry of Public Instruction
Sir and very honored confrère:

A thousand thanks for your good communication. I am keenly interested in the destiny of America, and I am following with a feverish curiosity the progress of education of the people. All that relates to this great subject is welcomed by me with a sincere gratitude. I am dreaming of a work on the *Éducation du peuple dans la démocratie.* You furnish me with the best page of my book. Do you know that I am your successor? Yes, Monsieur, at the *École Normale* of which I am to-day the Director, and of which you formerly laid the first foundation. It is one more tie between us.

Goodbye, Monsieur,
your devoted confrère and servant,
(SIGNED) V. COUSIN
at the Sorbonne.

[26]The Academy of Moral and Political Sciences.

The Bourbon Charles X had been dethroned in the Revolution of July, 1830, and the choice of the Orleanist Louis-Philippe was hailed in this country as well as in France as a step toward liberalism.

On Saturday last, said the *Register,* a dinner was given at the City Hotel by our French and American citizens in commemoration of the recent triumph of constitutional liberty in France. Basil Meslier, Esq., presided, assisted by his Honor the Mayor A. Batre and A. W. Gordon, Esqs., as vice presidents; J. Hurtell, J. Fourcade and A. Armstrong, Esqs., as managers.

At four o'clock about one hundred gentlemen sat down to a sumptuous repast. A number of strangers, some from New Orleans, honored the company as guests. Mirth, sentiment and song enlivened by an excellent band gilded the hours, and the day passed off amid the cordial greetings and congratulations of friends, and the most enthuiastic demonstrations of devotion to those principles which have rendered the United States free, prosperous and powerful, and which have redeemed our ancient ally from the thralldom of despotism.

A patriotic Ode, in French, written for the occasion, by our highly respected fellow-citizen, S. Chaudron, Esq., was listened to with the most gratified attention, and the health of the venerable author drunk in full bumpers. A song from the same gentleman, satirizing in a happy strain of ridicule, the vices and follies of all the kings, English as well as French, who have borne the name of Charles, was sung by himself in a style of comic humor that would have provoked a smile from Melpomene herself.

Following a patriotic address by the chairman Basil Meslier, 15 set toasts and a number of voluntary ones were offered by the various guests. Among the voluntary toasts was one offered by Lakanal: "The illustrious citizen of the two worlds, General Lafayette."

The Revolution of July and the advent of Louis-Philippe to the throne of France brought a complete change of outlook for Lakanal. He was now free to return to France, and his first impulse was to do so, but some men of influence in America pointed out to him that the change of administration in France would no doubt bring about great changes in the personnel of the French diplomatic and consular corps in America, and presumably advised him to apply for a place in one of these services. At any rate, on November 25, 1830, he wrote a letter to Saint-Hilaire in which he said:

It was in my sweet retreat that I learned through the newspapers received from New York of the admirable Revolution of the last days of July. My first thought was to see again that beautiful France which has been delivered through prodigies of valor from the most inept, the most cowardly, the most odious government that ever weighed upon a civilized people. . . . Eminent persons with whom General Lafayette long since put me into touch have observed to me that the furibund conduct of the majority of the diplomatic and consular agents appointed by the government of Villèle and Polignac, should perforce bring about their immediate dismissal, and that in principle individuals placed in posts of confidence by the professors of absolution and the secret agents of the Congregation[27] could not serve a government truly liberal. Struck by these observations, whose accuracy I appreciate, in casting my eyes around me, I addressed myself to the minister of foreign affairs[28] to ask that I be employed in the diplomatic or consular career in America. Having resided here for fully fifteen years, knowing the laws, the manners, the customs of the country and especially the language, without which I hold that there is no sureness, even with a good interpreter, I can still be useful here to my dear country while making an honorable exchange of a useful work for a just salary.

I invoke your support and the august patronage of your illustrious confrères in backing up either by word of mouth or in writing my just request to the minister. I possess the gifts necessary for fulfilling honorably the post that I am soliciting, and I believe it superfluous to prove that I will cooperate with a government which is friendly to liberty and enlightenment. I hope that the illustrious professors of the metropolis, of the headquarters of natural history in Europe, will not refuse to oblige, in this circumstance, above all, a former friend of their fine institution who for nearly forty years has devoted to all of them a *culte de Dulie.*

Whether or not Saint-Hilaire and his colleagues supported Lakanal in his desire for a diplomatic or consular post in this country is unknown, but it is certain that the Minister of Foreign Affairs did not exert himself greatly in Lakanal's behalf, and very probably did not even answer his letter.

LAMARTINE

Although Lakanal had declared his intention of never returning to France, the change of government in his native land turned his mind in the direction of going back home. In several letters to Saint-Hilaire he begins to speak of his intention. When he seriously began to study the question of whether or not to leave the United States for France, he must have puzzled over it long and arduously. He must have weighed the virtues and defects of the two countries on many occasions in his own thinking. Mobile and its warm sunshine appealed to his constitution; its sub-tropical flora and fauna had a great attraction for a devoted naturalist. He had made many friends among the best people of the town and among the French group at Spring Hill. He must have meditated over the future of a young and vigorous country such as the United

[27]The influence of the Congregation in political matters during the reigns of Louis XVIII and Charles X is portrayed in Stendhal's famous novel, *Le Rouge et le Noir.*

[28]De Broglie.

States presented. On the other hand, France had the appeal of family associations and as the scene of his earlier triumphs. It was his native land. How should he decide? It is refreshing to contrast Lakanal's quandary with that of his younger contemporary, the great French romantic poet Alphonse de Lamartine, who some years later was apparently to be considering the possibility of leaving France for the United States, if we may be permitted to judge so from a letter written by Lamartine which has been preserved among the papers of William H. Robertson, from whose unpublished memoirs excerpts have been included in this book.[29] In this letter Lamartine says:

Dear Sir: I need not tell you how much I was delighted by the promptness of your answer and by your kind assertions in my behalf. In dining yesterday with Mr. de Girardin, I was fortunate enough to meet Mr. Soulé, your Minister to Spain; the conversation at table was about yourself, about America and France;—your letter was subsequently handed to me by Mr. Soulé. A trip to the United States would, at the present moment, be to me a cause of satisfaction and of glory. Never did an individual, bowed down by the loss of that character which his country had hitherto sustained stand more in need than I do of reposing myself and of brightening my hopes in the contemplation of the dignified, bold and rational liberty which your great nation manifests to the world. Such a spectacle would not be less gratifying to my heart than to my mind. Your fellow-citizens have been kind enough to place too high an estimate, I fear, on the slight services which it was my endeavor to render to the cause of democracy as well as to that of civilization,—which I consider to be inseparable. I am aware that I would be indebted to you for the reception and hospitality which I would be so happy to enjoy. . . . Unfortunately, however, circumstances of a private nature and the difficulty in procuring means of existence, arising from a neglect of my personal affairs, during twenty-five year's devotion to public interests, are now weighing heavily upon me and condemn me to a life of constant labor and exertion, which does not leave me a single week's repose. I must first think of my creditors before thinking of myself. . . . So long as I shall not have repaid, by my pen, the considerable sums which I owe them, I shall consider myself as bound down to the spot I now inhabit. I cannot think of absenting myself; for my presence here is the only pledge that they will be paid. Should my efforts, however, be crowned with success in the course of two or three years, I assure you that I shall avail myself of the first moment of liberty to visit at leisure the men and things, beyond the Atlantic, that reflect the most honor upon our miserable globe. The moral distance between the two hemispheres, is unfortunately, not less than the geographical one. I leave Paris to-morrow to return to the country and to my labors. I shall always be happy to

[29]The French original was not preserved, but a translation into English was made which is here reproduced.

seize every occasion which can recall the sentiments of friendship which I so fully reciprocate for you. Receive, Sir, the assurance of my high and cordial esteem.

A. DE LAMARTINE

Rue de la Ville L'Évèque, 31, Paris.

However, it was even after the change of government which would have permitted his return to France in safety that Lakanal purchased land at Mobile in 1831, and again as late as 1835. This does not have the appearance of a serious intention to return to France. Whatever ideas he may have had in this direction were weakened by the knowledge that the *Académie des Sciences Morales et Politiques,* to which he had belonged and which had been dissolved by Napoleon in 1803, had in 1832 been restored, and all the former members still living with the exception of him had been restored to membership.[30] From his letters we learn that Lakanal considered this oversight an affront, and that he resolved that if he could not go back to France through the front door, he would never return through the back.

There was nothing intentional in leaving Lakanal out of the list restored. He had been absent many years and had communicated with none of his friends except Saint-Hilaire and Morand. Most of those connected with the Institute had forgotten his existence, and no doubt thought that he was dead. In fact, a rumor reached Paris of his death. On March 12, 1836, the *Journal des Débats* contained the following brief announcement: "On annonce la mort de M. Lakanal, qui, proscrit en 1815, vivait retiré aux États-unis. Il était membre de l'Académie des sciences morales et politiques."

The statement that he was a member of Academy of Moral and Political Sciences was correct, even if his death notice was premature. Upon the death of Garat in December, 1833, the Minister Guizot wrote to the Academy that there was no need to elect a successor to Garat: Lakanal would replace him *de plein droit.* In the sitting of the Academy of March 22, 1834, Lakanal was restored to full membership. No doubt Geoffroy Saint-Hilaire had called Guizot's attention to him. In a letter of the following August 1,

[30]Those who had been restored were: Destutt de Tracy, Dacier, Garat, Lacuée, Roederer, Daunou, Merlin de Douai, Sieyès, Talleyrand, Pastoret, and Reinhard.

Lakanal writes to Saint-Hilaire: "Thanks especially to your good offices, I shall re-enter France through the door of honor."

Years later, in 1849, when Isadore Geoffroy Saint-Hilaire, a son of Lakanal's life-long friend, came to write a biographical sketch of Lakanal, he said:

> We have under our eyes the extract from the *procès-verbal* of the sitting (of the Academy) of March 22, 1834, which was sent to Lakanal in America. The illustrious old man added at the bottom in his own hand these touching lines:
>
> Nescio qua natale solum dulcedine euntos
> Ducit, et immemores no sinit esse suit.
>
> Ovid., lib. II, *De ponto.*
>
> This delicious and profound emotion, I experienced it on returning to my dear country after 22 years at two thousand leagues from our beautiful France. This unexpected happiness I am proud to owe to a man as illustrious as my very dear confrère M. Geoffroy Saint-Hilaire. My gratitude toward him will be imperishable.

END OF EXILE

Even though there were no longer any difficulties in the way of his returning to France, Lakanal still hesitated, and it is possible that he would have continued to the end of his life at Mobile had it not been for the death of his wife, Marie-Barbe François, who died on May 10, 1836, and who was buried in the little cemetery of Ganon Bend.[31]

Within a month after the death of his wife we find Lakanal applying for a passport. He must have left Mobile by the end of 1836, for the post-office at Mobile from January through April of 1837 advertised his mail as uncalled for. His daughter Alexandrine had married Lucien Charvet, and after his death had married Henri Germain, *chancelier* of the French Consulate in New Orleans. It is probable that he must have spent the time between his departure from Mobile and his sailing for France with his family in New Orleans. In a letter which he wrote to Saint-Hilaire from New Orleans of the date of April 4, 1837, he said: "M. de l'Hoste who will

[31]Evidently what is known to-day as Garrow's Bend. For a time the writer considered that the word "Ganon" must have been a misprint, but he has discovered that there was a Wm. Ganon who was appointed Justice of the Peace at Mobile on Oct. 20, 1830; so it may very well be that what is now Garrow's Bend was called in the earlier nineteenth century Ganon Bend. Wm. Ganon is listed in the "Civil Register of State and County officials," Vol. I (1819-1832), a. 217, Dept. Archives and History, Montgomery, Ala.

present you my letter has seen the passport that I acquired nearly ten months ago at the Consulate in New Orleans for returning to France. The powerful reasons which keep me here momentarily have been exposed in a letter which I addressed to the perpetual secretary of my class, and all the details which that letter contain have been declared authentic by the affidavit of the French Consul which is attached to it."

In a letter addressed to Pierre Soulé, a celebrated lawyer in New Orleans, Lakanal in soliciting his influence toward helping his son-in-law secure a position in a bank, says as follows:[32]

"There exists near you one of the best creatures in the world: it is the god-daughter of M. Morand, it is my daughter, Mme. Germain; her husband is *Chancelier* of the French Consulate in New Orleans.[33] M. Germain is the head of a somewhat numerous family, and his place has no future. . . ." Lakanal goes on to ask that Soulé use his good offices to help his son-in-law get a place in the bank where Soulé is to act as legal adviser.[34]

In 1919 when Miss Grace King was engaged in writing a book on New Orleans, she addressed a letter of inquiry concerning the descendants of Lakanal to Dr. Y. R. Le Monnier, of New Orleans. In replying, Dr. Le Monnier said:[35]

> Lakanal to my knowledge had a daughter Alexandrine, but know not if there were other children. She married Lucien Charvet, Sr., a school teacher of note. They lived in Baton Rouge where, I suppose, her two children, Alexandrine and Lucien, were born; Lucien, I know, was and I think, his older brother. I know very little of this one who went to Paris, France, and

[32]Letter in manuscript in the Lakanal Papers, Howard Memorial Library, New Orleans, dated Nov. 5, 1834, from Mobile.

[33]Cohen's New Orleans Directory for 1855 lists Henry Germain Chancellor of French Consul. 102 Royal, d. Orleans n. Burgundy.

[34]Pierre Soulé (1801-1870), like Lakanal, was born in the Pyrenees region of southern France. His father was a brilliant Napoleonic officer. Destined for the church, Pierre, like Lakanal, was educated in the Collège de l'Esquille at Toulouse. Turning aside from a priestly career, like Lakanal, he entered politics and became an anti-Bourbon conspirator at Bordeaux and took his course in law at Paris. Becoming a full-fledged lawyer by 1822, he soon joined the republican movement against Charles X, publishing with others the journal, *Le Nain* and convicted in 1825, escaped to England, finally landing at Baltimore, from where he made his way to New Orleans. He had a career there as criminal lawyer, orator, financier, senator for an unexpired term of three months. Later he became U. S. Minister.

[35]Manuscript letter. Howard Memorial Library, New Orleans; Lakanal Papers.

I believe, died there. He was in politics, but not a success. Lucien lived in New Orleans, was a lawyer of reputation in Pierre Soulé's last years of practice, his partner: this one died insane in his fine house, corner Esplanade and Rocheblave, where the girls' high school is to-day. Before our war of the sixties, Lucien of remarkable memory and superior instruction, was one of the Public School Directors, and examined the applicants for teachers. He went through the war, first as a lieutenant in the Orleans Guard Battalion, then as a private in the Orleans Light Horse. We returned together after the war, walking from Greensboro, N. C., to Mobile, Alabama, and from here by boat to New Orleans. On January 7, 1866, he married my oldest daughter Amire, with whom he had only one child, Adèle Alexandrine, who died at the age of 20 years and five months, on May 29, 1887. Her mother had died on June 10, 1882, aet. 42 yrs. 11 mos., and her father on Nov. 20, 1878, aet. 52 yrs. After the death of Lucien Charvet, Sr., his widow married Henri Germain, a Frenchman, vice-consul of France. During our war he returned to France where they died. Of this marriage two children were born, Émile and Henri. Henri died here a bachelor before the war; Émile married a Mr. Roubieaux. They had only one child, a girl. They were all dead, no issue left. Unless Alexandrine married in France, and left descendants, the Lakanal family is extinguished.

From the above, it is apparent that there are no surviving descendants of Lakanal in America.

Lakanal must have sailed for France in the month of August, for he landed at Bordeaux in September, 1837, and made his way directly to Paris.

9

DEAN OF THE FRENCH INSTITUTE

OF LAKANAL'S RETURN VOYAGE TO FRANCE NOTHING IS KNOWN FURTHER than a few hints contained in letters written soon after his arrival in his home land. The voyage was long and perilous, the captain ignorant, the voyage and change of climate brought on a grave malady, presumably malaria, and one of his fellow passengers defrauded him of 30,000 francs. Upon landing at Bordeaux he made his way directly to Paris. Mignet describes him as he appeared after his long exile:

> One day I saw arrive at my house, wearing the old uniform of the Institute such as they used to wear under the Directory, a man whose stature was still erect, whose hair was abundant and black, whose face was grave, whose glance was steady, whose mouth was severe, whose manners were confident and elegant, whose speech was witty and sententious, and who seemed to belong to another time. It was M. Lakanal. This energetic old man, then aged seventy-five years, appeared to be not over sixty. A firm intelligence, temperate habits, a robust constitution which had resisted the raw or enervating solitudes of Kentucky and Alabama, as well as the convulsive shocks of the Revolution, the activity which he had kept up had preserved the health of his body and the vigor of his soul. He used to say, with as much truth as wit, "My baptismal certificate is old, but not I; and when people attribute to me a great age, I answer as did Moncrif to Louis XVI: *On me le donne, mais je ne le prends pas.*" So little did he accept it, that he married and had a son at seventy-seven years of age, and celebrated the eightieth anniversary of his birth by setting out on foot, July 14, 1842, from the *Rue Royale de Saint-Antoine,* to go botanizing on the hillsides of Montmorency, as had done his master J. J. Rousseau and his friend Bernardin de Saint-Pierre.

That he had trouble in clearing the customs-house is brought out in a letter which Lakanal wrote soon after arriving in Paris:

> It has been only in the past few days that I have received from the customs-house a part of my effects. The labyrinth of the laws in this administration and the abject ignorance of my captain furnish me these tribulations. A little later Lakanal wrote his friend Saint-Hilaire: I have not been able to come to see you in order to ask you to present me to your honorable family. I have experienced a thousand tribulations since I have been in Paris. An industrialist who came over the Atlantic with me, and who belongs to one of the most numerous and most respectable families of France, had defrauded me of a deposit of 30,000 francs in Spanish doubloons. Thanks to the com-

pany of which M. Dumoustier, brother-in-law of Marshal Clauzel is the principal member, I am sure to recover my deposit. I have an interview tomorrow with those gentlemen. So, my illustrious friend, pity me. I shall not enjoy the extreme pleasure of seeing you, but certainly next week will not wholly pass without my presenting myself at your house.

Let it be recalled that Lakanal left France in 1816 with thirty thousand francs, and after twenty-one years has returned home with exactly the same sum with which he apparently had set out. Also, it seems evident that he recovered his money of which he had been defrauded, for he acquired a country place and spent 6,230 francs in repairs and embellishments. In a letter of Dec. 7, to Saint-Hilaire, he says:

I am living alone at Labillardière with two servants whom I would exchange for one good one. I have tried to embellish my peaceable retreat. I have spent 6,230 francs, and I still lack many necessary things. I am working laboriously at a big work that I hope to publish this winter. I have read fragments of it to my class which received them with an extreme benevolence, but the public may reserve for them a less friendly reception and apply to the totality of the work, 3 volumes in-8, the anathema pronounced by the poet Callimachus: *mega biblion, mega kakon*: the bigger the book the bigger the fool. However that may be, I shall find a way, by no means forced, of paying a just tribute of gratitude to the men who did not abandon me in exile. Judge if you can be forgotten!

However eagerly Lakanal may have hastened from Bordeaux in order to see once more his beloved Paris, he was doomed to certain momentary disappointments. His best friend Étienne Geoffroy Saint-Hilaire, was absent on an expedition into western Normandy in the interest of natural history. As soon as he was informed of Lakanal's arrival, Saint-Hilaire hastened to write:

Bernay, September 16, 1837.

Oh happy day for me! You are at Paris! Honorable friend, you who were my benefactor at the dawn of my life, you have freely returned to me in the winter of my years! My wife and daughter had gone out and my son was at the criminal court as a member of the jury when you appeared in that garden which you founded with the title of our restorer. Your co-associates are 1. Guy de Brosse; 2. Fagon; 3. Buffon; 4. . . . (Lakanal); 5. Cuvier; 6. Thiers; 7. . . . (Saint-Hilaire), etc. I beg to M. Lhotte[1] that he send your address to me at Paris in order that on my return from Normandy, where I am at present, I may fly into your arms! Whatever haste I may make, it can only be towards the end of the week. At least I am sure of being at my Sunday *soirée*, a week from to-day. And how precious it will be for me to be able to introduce you to my friends gathered together on that day. Last Sunday, my daughter wrote me, at mention of your name and the news of your arrival one of them clapped his hands. It was David, our great sculptor,

[1]Does he mean M. l'Hoste, the Louisiana poet to whom Lakanal had given a letter of introduction to Saint-Hilaire just before he left to return to France?

our confrère in the Institute, the grandson-in-law of La Revellière-Lepaux[2] He has been pleased to create as his Pantheon of great men three hundred medallions with beautiful illustrations of their times, and in which he desires to place yours.

A few days after his arrival Lakanal learned that one of his former colleagues of the Convention was living in Paris. He hastened to his house and asked to see him. "M. le Comte has gone out," was the reply. Lakanal was astonished to encounter a noble Count where he expected to meet again an austere Republican. Afterwards he often met his former colleague and always scrupulously addressed him with the title that had so shocked him at first. Saint-Hilaire recounts a visit which the English Lord Brougham made one day to the ex-Conventionnel. "Your lordship," said Lakanal to Lord Brougham, who responded with "Dear Citizen."

Lakanal expressed a desire to see once more the modest pavillion where he had lived in 1793 in close proximity to his friends of the Museum. Saint-Hilaire accompanied him and aided in the search for his former dwelling. "But how difficult it was to discover it," says Saint-Hilaire, "in the midst of all the new buildings which surrounded it." In the twenty-one years of his absence Paris had changed, and most of the men he used to know were either scattered or dead. He was fortunate however in the friendship of the Saint-Hilaire family and in a few new friendships which he was able to make, notably his physician, Dr. Lélut, head physician of the Salpétrière and of LaRoquette prison, and the celebrated sculptor David d'Angers.

When in 1879 E. Nigoul who wrote a life of Lakanal under the pen name of "Marcus" paid a visit to a great-nephew of Lakanal, the nephew said in speaking of a call he had made on his great-uncle directly after his return from America:

> As in the course of conversation I learned that he was working regularly every day until one and two o'clock in the morning, I expressed fears for his health, for he was going on 80 years of age, he replied: I did not come back to France to break eggs and plant cabbages, but to work. Even at 80 my uncle was a rugged man, alert, jovial, young, with only one tooth missing, which had been pulled after his return from America, and not a single white hair.[3]

[2]One of the five Directors of the government of the Directory, and also President of the Directory.

[3]The tooth was preserved and kept as a memento by Lakanal's widow.

Lakanal did not remain long alone at Labillardière. In 1838 he took a mistress, Rosalie-Céleste-Bienaimée Lepelletier, a young woman thirty-two years of age, by whom he had a son in 1839. On December 21, 1842, at four o'clock in the afternoon, in the presence of four friends as witnesses, Lakanal made an honest woman of Rosalie-Céleste-Bienaimée by marrying her in the mayor's office of the 8th Arrondissement of Paris. The witnesses were Hortensius de Saint-Albin, Deputy from La Sarthe; Lakanal's physician Dr. Lélut; Marchand, *Juge de paix;* and Séneuse, *rédacteur* in the Ministry of Foreign Affairs. Mention of the witnesses is worth while as it affords the names and positions of several of Lakanal's friends which would otherwise be unknown. Rosalie-Céleste-Bienaimée was at this time thirty-six years of age. She outlived her husband many years, dying at the age of seventy-three in the year 1880.

DAVID D'ANGERS

One of the most charming incidents in the life of Lakanal was his friendship with David d'Angers. As has already been stated, David had made his life's chief work as an artist the portraying of the survivors of the French Revolution. As an intimate of the Saint-Hilaire family he had no doubt heard much of Lakanal, and especially in the months when the family were eagerly awaiting the exile's return. His curiosity aroused and being already predisposed, it is no wonder that he readily formed a great affection for this old man who had played such a prominent part in the Revolution and whose exile had invested him with a sort of romantic halo. "Scarcely had they seen each other," says Henry Jouin, "when the two men felt themselves drawn to each other in a lively bond of sympathy. It does not appear that during the seven years lived in a genuine intimacy the least difference ever separated them."[4]

There are extant some fifteen letters written by Lakanal to David d'Angers, the first of which reads:

> Pity me!—You came and I did not see you; it is an unlucky day for me. The Frenchman who by his genius has placed himself at the head of the masters of the admirable art of sculpture, and who unites with this fine talent the soul of a courageous and enlightened friend of the liberty of his

[4]Henry Jouin: *Lakanal et David d'Angers,* p. 2.

country, deserves and obtains all my homage, and this adorable Liberty, you understand her as I do; she is a courageous and beneficent divinity, not an unbridled bacchante. I have served her in public offices, in a long exile; I shall serve her until death, and my name will never appear in the voluminous Dictionary of the Weathervanes. I love the fine arts with passion. You are my man . . . the desire, I will say, the need of seeing for the tenth time your beautiful *Philopoemen*[5] has made me triumph over the repugnance I experience in finding myself so close to the powers that be, for, scrupulous observer of the laws of the country in which I live, the antichambers of the gods of the earth, their gilded salons, are for me reservoirs of the air pump when the air has been pumped out. I never appear there, in order not to smother. I feel myself attracted to you, my honorable confrère, by your admirable talent, by our common friend the excellent M. Geoffroy Saint-Hilaire, and by the memory of the courageous and upright La Revellière, who *alone* among us, members of the Institute of that day, refused to take the oath *ordered* by Bonaparte, and because it was at the University of Angers[6] that I received the Doctor of Letters, to teach at La Flèche. I request that you permit me to cultivate your friendship. . . . I have infinitely to congratulate myself on my confrères of my Class,[7] in the number of whom I find again several of my former colleagues of the Convention and of the Council of Five Hundred, but I have had difficulty in recognizing them. Ye gods, how quickly people grow old in monarchies. Nor have they recognized me either. . . . I am almost such as I was twenty-two years ago at the time of my departure from France; fresh proof in support of the system of Montesquieu on the influence of governments for men as well as for things. You conceive of it better than anyone, since in your admirable conceptions you transport yourself in thought to beautiful Greece in the *beaux jours* of its glory. I shall not die, I hope, without visiting that classical land and without reading the works of Plato on Cape Sunnium. . . .

On November 17, 1839, the city of Angers solemnly inaugurated the *Musée David.* The artist, however, declined to be present at his own triumph. The celebration brought forth the following words which form the opening paragraph of a letter which Lakanal wrote to David:

"On reading in the newspapers the details of the ovation which you have just received in your natal city, I felt happiness surging up in my soul! How much such disinterested, such solemn testimonies, should compensate you for your jealous adversaries. . ."

David had looked forward to Lakanal's return as an opportunity of adding one more medallion to his Pantheon, but as he came to know and to appreciate the ex-Conventionnel, he felt that a medallion was an insufficient testimony of his esteem for the octogenarian

[5]David's *Philopoemen* found its niche in the gallery of the Louvre museum.
[6]Angers was David's native town.
[7]Class of Moral and Political Sciences of the French Institute.

champion of education and democracy. He resolved, therefore, to sculpture a bust of Lakanal, a project which was put into execution in 1839-40. When it was finished Lakanal visited David's studio in order to see it. Upon returning home, he wrote the following lines to David:

Illustrious Citizen: Your genius prepares immortality. It has pleased you to make a prodigious use of it in my favor. I make a note of the extreme reluctance that I have always shown to you for receiving this immense and unmerited benefit. Yesterday on seeing your fine work, I was astonished at your sublime talent and humiliated at my feeble merit. I recalled involuntarily the history of that celebrated artist who having hesitated as to whether to make of a block of marble a wash basin or a god, decided in favor of the latter. That device: *"A l'Immortel"* is a concession of one of your rights, but one can be generous with impunity when one swims in abundance. I would have preferred the inscription much more glorious to my eyes and much more dear to my heart: *"A Lakanal, David, son ami."* I would have shown that with pride. I shall be careful to conceal the other. That Convention, truly national, composed in the majority of men of bronze, lions of the desert, and which ordered victory and made itself obeyed will arrive at immortality. Feeble soldier in its train, my sole title to this honor will have been never to have taken a step backward nor to one side on the road that leads to liberty, to true glory, to the real independence of the country. This sentiment would be the most powerful that I experience if it did not yield to my respectful devotion for your person.

August 8, 1840.

Recalling that Lakanal had championed and had caused the Convention to decree the erection of a column in the Pantheon on which were to be inscribed the names of the citizens who had perished in the massacre of August 10, 1792, on August 10, 1840, David addressed the following letter to Lakanal:

LAKANAL.

"Paris, August 10, 1840.

"My dear and illustrious colleague:

When I knew you only by renown, I admired you. At present, now that I have the invaluable good fortune to know you personally, I love you. Permit then a man who admires you and who loves you to offer you this feeble testimony of his keen and profound sympathy for you.

"This bust will recall to you sometimes the author who is so happy at having been one of the first to write on marble his sentiments of keep acknowledgment for one of the members of that sublime Convention, to which the future will rear monuments of admiration and veneration.

DAVID

The marble bust of Lakanal which David made was placed in a hall of the Institute. The medallion was preserved in the David

Museum at Angers, and the portrait of him painted by Mlle. Berriat-Saint-Prix[8] was placed eventually in the Lycée Lakanal at Paris.

Lakanal's friend Dr. Lélut was inspired to compose the following inscription in verse to accompany the bust:

> Ferme comme ce marbre, où revit son courage,
> Tout ce qu'll révérait au matin de son âge,
> Tout ce qu'il défendit au mépris de la mort,
> Savoir, vertu, patrie, et toi liberté sainte,
> Son coeur, pour vous, des ans n'a pas subi l'atteinte,
> Et sa voix, sans faiblir, vous défendrait encore.[9]

EXPOSÉ SOMMAIRE

In 1838 Lakanal published a book of 225 pages entitled *Exposé sommaire des travaux de Joseph Lakanal pour sauver, durant la Révolution, les sciences, les lettres et ceux qui les honoraient par leurs travaux.* This summary exposition of his labors to save during the Revolution the sciences, the letters, and those who honored them was a work of self-defense. Lakanal had been absent from France for twenty-one years, and had been forgotten by all save a few. In this book he sought to bring himself advantageously to the mind of the French public of the reign of Louis-Philippe. When Lakanal fled France in 1816 he carried with him his cherished papers including his correspondence with many of the men prominent in the French Revolution. Since he had been back in France for so short a time when he published his book, it is very likely that he had compiled and edited its contents while he was still living at Mobile. The book contains explanatory pages and copies of documents and letters, the intent of which is to justify its author and to present him in a favorable light. Certainly there can be no complaint of that; but twentieth-century scholarship has criticized Lakanal severely, and largely as a result of this book. Guillaume, who edited the *Procès-verbaux* of the Committee of Public Instruction of the National Con-

[8]The daughter of the Jurisconsult Berriat-Saint-Prix, a fellow member of Lakanal in the Academy of Moral and Political Sciences and a friend of the family. The daughter was Mme. Lakanal's best friend.

[9]Firm as this marble where relieves his courage, all that he revered in the morning of his age, all that he defended with scorn of death, knowledge, virtue, and thou sacred Liberty, his heart for you has not undergone the attack of the years, and his voice without weakening would defend you still.

vention, took particular pains to check Lakanal's book against the records and found numerous discrepancies, omissions, and changes of text. As a result, Guillaume became a rather unsympathetic critic of Lakanal. A few illustrations will serve to show the nature of Lakanal's defects. In his book he published the list of forty-eight names suggested by himself as the *tiers-électeur* for the newly created *Institut de France,* but failed to show that only 24 of the men of his choice were elected. In publishing his report on Rousseau he failed to state that the preliminary essay of that report had been composed by Garat. In several places he changed words and phrases in texts in order to relieve them of the harsh language which had been customary during the Revolution; in others he sought to make the contents more palatable to readers under the more liberal government of Louis-Philippe. No doubt some of his errors were due to faulty memory. It must be kept in mind that he dealt with events that had happened a half century previously, that he was a very old man, and like the aged, his memory was more or less distorted; and then too he had been expatriated for more than two decades and thus the continuity of his memory and experience was broken. Notwithstanding the errors that have been discovered, Lakanal's book is essentially correct in its portrayal of his public career. The *Exposé sommaire* was followed in 1840 by a pamphlet of eight pages entitled *Suum cuique,* a defense of Lakanal's part in the founding of the Institute. This pamphlet brought on a small controversy, which led Lakanal in the same year to publish another pamphlet: *Première réponse à la Note sur la création de l'Institut.*

LAKANAL THE ACADEMICIAN

Lakanal's restoration to membership in the Academy of Moral and Political Sciences gave him very great satisfaction, and in the interim between his restoration in 1834 and his departure from Mobile in 1837 he was in correspondence with the Academy, and submitted to it papers outlining his experiences and containing his observations of American civilization. Mignet in his biographical sketch of Lakanal which he read before the assembled members of the Academy of Moral and Political Sciences on May 2, 1857, said:

While awaiting until he should come back to his country, M. Lakanal addressed to you a curious memoir, filled with shrewd observations and original sallies concerning the country that he had lived in for twenty years. In it he did not show himself, it must be said, smitten with American democracy. He depicted with a spirit perhaps somewhat melancholy that civilization which he found at the same time crude and degenerate, where, according to him, the greedinesses of corruption were joined to the violences of barbarism, and where, in a restless movement and with a boundless pride, the enterprising and bold man often put himself above the rules, never let himself be stopped by reverses, and applied himself much more to conquering nature with which he was at grips than to the perfecting of society. Seeing the Americans too much addicted to the pursuit of material interests which had then such a great attraction for them, and too negligent of the things of the intelligence which had always held such a high worth for him, he said with a barb of wit and bitterness, which would be both untimely and unjust today: "Je ne tardai pas à m'apercevoir que les seules lettres qui eussent auprès d'eux une valeur réelle étaient les lettres de change; which may be paraphrased in English, preserving the spirit if not the *letter*: I was not long in perceiving that the only bills which had any real value to them were dollar bills.

Following the reception of the news of his restoration to membership in the Academy of Moral and Political Sciences, Lakanal, on August 1, 1834, wrote to Saint-Hilaire: "I am bringing to France the materials of two large volumes, fruit of nineteen years sojourn in the United States, which I have traversed in all directions, and which I think I know thoroughly, both the physical state of the country and the customs and spirit of the inhabitants. I gave in my response to the Academy . . . the analysis of my work. After having appraised and often refuted the French writers who have treated of the physical state and of the customs and spirit of the United States,—La Rochefoucauld, Chastellux, Lezai-Marnezia, Volney, Talleyrand, Michaux, H. Hamilton, I gave the history of the French colonies established in the United States: Gallipolis, Champ d'Asile, Tombeckbée." Other chapters, he goes on to say, will deal with the flora of Kentucky, Louisiana and Alabama; the state of the sciences, letters and arts in the United States; upon the fate in store for the French who come to establish themselves in the United States, whether for the purpose of devoting themselves to agriculture or to follow the career of commerce; a chapter in which he will try to forecast the immediate and future destinies of the Federal Union; upon the finances of the American Government; upon the Choctaw Indians of Alabama, a small tribe of which lived near Lakanal at Mobile.

In the same letter Lakanal says further:

> The United States which I have traversed in all directions during nineteen years of sojourn are not known in France, because those who have spoken or written about them have only passed through or have seen only the cities where only foreigners are found. The true Anglo-Americans are on the plantations, in the interior, and I myself have been a planter among them in Kentucky.

Four years later, after his return to France, Lakanal wrote on April 1, 1838:

> Our romancers, in order to whet the curiosity of the public, have paraded their wit respecting the United States. Their method is easy to seize. They have rehashed in the libraries what has been written about them, then they have gone to New York, to Philadelphia, in order to give an exotic character to a purely indigenous work. A bit of trickery is to give as if gathered together on the spot details about places they have not visited.

Lakanal's statement sounds very modern.

When "Marcus" in 1879 discovered the widow of Lakanal, who was at that time seventy-two years of age, among the several reminiscences which he recorded, was the following:

> You know that on his return from America at his first meeting with the Institute, they asked him for an account of his trials in exile and his impressions of America, and that he spoke two hours in the general silence without his voice weakening an instant. Mm. Lélut and Geoffroy Saint-Hilaire told me this detail.

Mignet says that Lakanal quitted the United States without regret. That may have been true when he first arrived back in France, but in the course of time he seems to have longed to return to America. In one of his letters to David d'Angers he says: "I turn up my nose at the Carlists, who however, have enriched me by sending me to the United States, where years of domicile have not aged me by a day, because one does not grow old in the land of Liberty. I shall probably return there, for it is there that a man enjoys the plenitude of his being . . . I am almost just as I was 22 years ago at the time of my departure from France: new proof in support of the system of Montesquieu on the influence of governments for men as well as for things."

In a letter to David in 1844 Lakanal said:

> Upon my return from the United States, where I would like to be again,

because one breathes there the pure air of sacred Liberty, I was seized with a grave malady, result of the change of climate in an advanced age, and of a long and perilous voyage. A doctor who was recommended to me by two old companions of the Revolution saved my life. As the price of his good offices he only desired to have a portrait made of me by a painter friend of his from the medallion with which you were kind enough to gratify me.

From this letter we not only learn more about Lakanal's attitude toward America, but we learn the circumstances under which he no doubt became acquainted with Dr. Lélut who remained his good friend until his death in 1845. We can surmise that the malady of which he speaks must have been malaria. Also Lélut's painter friend must have been Mlle Berriat-Saint-Prix who painted Lakanal's portrait when he was seventy-eight years of age. A reproduction of this portrait, which forms the frontispiece of this book, shows that Lakanal had an abundance of black hair, a very remarkable circumstance for a man of his age. The portrait also shows him dressed in the costume of member of the Institute of the period of the Directory.

Lakanal devoted himself wholeheartedly to the various interests of the Institute, and towards the end of the year 1843 he received a striking testimony of the respectful esteem of his colleagues of the Academy of Moral and Political Sciences. He was elected almost unanimously Vice President for 1844 and President for 1845. He was deeply touched, but declined the honor, saying:

At eighty-two years of age when one seeks show or display one loses in dignity what he gains in ridiculousness. La Rochefoucauld said: "There are few people who know how to be old." I have thought on this maxim and I have not lost my time, since through the practice of the rules of conduct that I have drawn from this meditation, I find myself contented with my lot . . . I promised myself on returning to France to neither seek nor accept any place, any distinction, fully satisfied to have been recalled to the Institute. That is what I wrote to the Academy six years ago when I did it the homage of the *Exposé sommaire* of my labors in the Convention and in the Council of Five Hundred; that is what has made me obstinately refuse the presidency of the section to which I have the honor to belong. I am decidedly devoted to the worship of that Tenth Muse, to which Numa caused altars to be erected, and who presided over the art of listening and of remaining silent.

Ne parler jamais qu'à propos
Est un rare et grand avantage,
Le silence est l'esprit des sots
Et l'une des vertus du sage."

At every age a man must have an occupation, even the opulent man, for when fortune exempts him from work nature overwhelms him with time.

I have therefore imposed upon myself the duty of following with persevering zeal the Academy in its tasks, and especially in the conscientious examination of the memoirs sent to the contest for the prizes. It is thus that I force myself, *pro captu mediocritatis meae,* to pay my academic debt and to merit the benevolence of my illustrious *confrères,* all of whom I revere and cherish without any exception. I beg them to accept my respectful thanks for the honor that they have just done me, and from which I regret that I can not profit, but the memory of which will embellish what remains to me to traverse of my long and stormy career.

LAKANAL'S TWO BOOKS

Even though he had promised himself on returning to France that he would accept no public office, no sooner had he arrived in his old surroundings than a final flickering flame of ambition arose in his heart and he longed to throw himself once more into the political arena. "Stormy Liberty is preferable to a tranquil slavery . . . I will go to Ariège. I was invested twice with the confidence of that Department. Who knows? I have the plenitude of my physical and moral faculties, and the tribune has not lost my memory."

The little flareup of ambition was shortlived, and Lakanal settled the course of his declining years by devoting himself to the various occupations of the Institute of which by virtue of his age he was the dean, and by redoubling his efforts to complete two works which he had conceived if not partially completed during his American exile. These two books were *Souvenirs sur la Convention* and *Vingt-deux ans de Séjour aux États-Unis.* That he spent a great deal of his time on the preparation of these books and that he nearly if not entirely finished them before his death is borne out not only by Lakanal in various of his letters, but also by the testimony of several of his closest friends. But at the time of his death the manuscripts disappeared and it was thought that they had been stolen for political reasons for fear of the disclosures he might have made concerning certain survivors of the Convention.

In the later nineteenth and earlier twentieth centuries exhaustive search was made in France for the manuscripts, but without success. Also an investigation was made in New Orleans. The writer of this book is of the opinion that the manuscripts were not stolen, but were destroyed by Lakanal himself as he approached his death.

In studying the life of Lakanal the writer has observed a certain sacrificial tendency in the man. This was evident when he refused to endorse the dictatorship of Bonaparte, thus condemning himself to obscurity. Again it was evident when, having accumulated 30,000 francs and being on the verge of flight, he offered to give the money, his only capital, to help save Paris from occupation by the allies after Waterloo. Not only was he ready to sacrifice his money, but his liberty and his very life, for without the money he would have been unable to escape from France. A third example is the suddeness and readiness with which he resigned the presidency of the College of Orleans. Although his administration had been a success, he readily yielded to the opposition without thought of his own personal welfare. It is very likely that this same spirit of self-immolation took possession of him when he saw his end approaching, and that he himself did away with his two books.

The remarkable vigor of the octogenarian Lakanal is well illustrated by Mme. Lakanal on the occasion of "Marcus's" visit to her in 1879. As has been stated, Berriat-Saint-Prix and his daughter were on the best of terms with the Lakanal family. Member of the Faculty of Law, the jurisconsult Berriat retained the manners and costume of a former generation, and, says Jouin, "He was seen everywhere with an enormous portfolio under his arm, *en perruque,* in short breeches and silk stockings. A survival from the times of Louis XV.[10] What does that matter? Berriat is an authority. His speech, his writings render the study of law agreeable." One day while visiting the Lakanals at their Paris abode, No. 10 Rue Royale Saint-Antoine, the hosts and the guest decided to visit the Column of July. "Marcus" relates:

> M. Berriat, said Mme. Lakanal, was always astonished and somewhat anxious at the juvenile behavior of M. Lakanal. I even remember a clever *mot* of his on the subject. One day while we were climbing, all three of us, M. Berriat, M. Lakanal and I, to the Column of the Bastille, M. Berriat, who was very corpulent and somewhat obese, and as always with his wig, his short breeches and his silk stockings, climbed slowly, stopping to rest from time to time on his big portfolio placed upon a step. He was in his seventies. M. Lakanal climbed boldly without stopping the steep stairway. "Madame,"

[10]And Louis XVI.

said to me while puffing and blowing, M. Berriat when half way up the ascent; "let us let this young man go on." The young man was eighty years old. He never stopped until he got to the foot of Genius of Liberty. M. Lakanal had a particular affection for the Column of the Bastille. You understand, he was born on the 14th day of July. . . .

DEATH OF GEOFFROY SAINT-HILAIRE

In 1844 Lakanal underwent a great sorrow. His oldest and best friend, Étienne Geoffroy Saint-Hilaire died on June 19. David begged Lakanal to speak at the obsequies. He consented, but did not prepare a speech, preferring to speak extemporaneously. In a note written a few days later to David, he said:

> Illustrious Friend: In putting foot on the soil of France seven years ago, I had promised myself never to appear in a public ceremony. One man alone could make me violate my engagement. You know who that man is. I spoke from simple notes, and I refused to several journalists communication of what I said. You will do with it what you wish. I observe only that I have had disputes with the irascible Bastide of the *National.*

That Lakanal did not furnish the text of his address to David is evident from the following letter written on July 15, 1844:

> Illustrious and very dear Confrère:
>
> On the eve of his departure to go back and resume in the Departments his duties of *Inspecteur des Études,* M. Isidore Geoffroy came and asked me for the discourse which I had pronounced over the tomb of his father. I replied that I had spoken only from notes, and that was the truth. He insisted. I promised to draw up what I had said and to place it in your hands, expressing the extreme desire that this manuscript should not be published. Most decidedly I wish to entertain no more the public with my worthless person. After having been beaten by so many storms it should be permitted me to put in at the Cape. Resolutely have I adopted the maxim of Descartes which he had borrowed from Ovid: "To live in seclusion is to live happy." Ovid had said: "Benè qui latuit benè vixit." I have kept the promise that I had given to M. Isidore, and in your absence I handed my manuscript to Madame David. . . . I had promised myself on returning to France never to appear in any public ceremony. You alone in the world could make me break my promise. I resume my silence forever.

In his biographical sketch of Lakanal published in 1849, Isidore Geoffroy Saint-Hilaire gave only the last words of the discourse of Lakanal at the tomb of his father on June 22, 1844:

"Goodbye, until we shall meet again in a better life, far from this vale of tears,

> "Et dans un autre monde où l'équité préside,
> "Où, dans le sein de Dieu, l'éternité réside."

The above words constitute the last public utterance of Lakanal.

In the winter of 1843 Lakanal was assailed by a persistent cold, and the following winter brought a return of the malady. Towards the end of 1844 he caught cold on leaving the Institute. A few days later he was compelled to take to his bed, and from that moment his strength declined rapidly. Of his final sickness and death his friend and biographer Isidore Geoffroy says:

> One of his dearest colleagues at the Academy, a friend that he loved as a son, M. Dr. Lélut, surrounded him in vain with the most enlightened and the most tender cares. Death approached from day to day. The patient as well as the doctor soon knew the gravity of the illness, and his firmness did not belie him for a single moment. "Your cares can not save me," he said one day to Dr. Lélut, "there is no more oil in the lamp!" And to another of his colleagues: "I am going to appear before God with my heart pure, with my hands clean" .... February 13, 1845, several symptoms of the approaching end were manifest: the speech of the sick man, slow, feeble, seemed almost extinguished. It was at this very moment that taking the hand of M. Lélut and holding it close to him: "My friend," said he, "I have nothing more to do in life. Nothing remains for me but to leave it. . . . I am going, he added smiling, I am going, as Rabelais said, to seek the answer to a great riddle. Saint Augustine said: *Deus, ens de quo valde dicitur, parum concipitur.* I know nothing more than he upon this point. . . . I believe in Providence. What is it? I don't know, but I shall present myself with confidence before it. I have no regret for anything I have done, and I shall face without fear the moment of accounting." Such were the last words of Lakanal! that very evening a terrible crisis had commenced! On the 14th in the afternoon he appeared to rally, and expressed a desire to see once more his friends on the earth that he was about to leave. He asked that they send for M. David (d'Angers); he also asked for the one who writes these lines. . . . Those were his last wishes, and they were too late. An hour afterwards we both arrived at the bedside of Lakanal. . . . He had just expired!

Lakanal died in the midst of public indifference and ingratitude. When the benefactor of the sciences and letters was borne to his final resting place, the official delegation of the Academy of Moral and Political Sciences was joined by only three members of the other classes of the Institute: twenty persons in all.

At the graveside in the Cemetery of Père-Lachaise his fellow members of the Institute, Rémusat, Lélut and Blanqui, together with Carnot, a Deputy, spoke of the deceased in simple and touching language. In the words of Rémusat:

> This grave and calm old man through whose gentle manners the interior energy could be perceived will remain present to our memories. His manners were simple, his character stoical, his convictions unshakable. Invariably faithful to the thoughts and to the memories of his youth, his in-

flexible spirit had resisted all ordeals. His past was to be read in some sort on his severe brow. But his old age was serene. He loved to his last day his friends, letters, and when the end approached he viewed death without fear and without regret.

A modest monument was erected to Lakanal in the Cemetery Père-Lachaise (Donon Road), and as previously stated, an imposing statue was in 1882 erected to his memory at Foix in his native Ariège, a statue which had the distinction of being the first ever to be erected to the memory of a Deputy to the National Convention.[11]

In 1845 the government of Louis-Philippe awarded Lakanal's widow a pension of 1,200 francs. In 1857 this was reduced by one-third, but ten years later was raised again to the original figure. In 1880 the amount of the pension was 1,800 francs. Mme. Lakanal died in 1881. The son, Joseph-Hippolyte Lakanal, was brought up at the expense of the State in a Lycée in Paris. He died in 1882.

[11]Lakanal died at No. 10, rue de Biragué, just off the Place des Vosges. This street enters Place des Vosges, formerly Place Royale. It runs from the rue Saint-Antoine to Place des Vosges.

Rue Lakanal, named for Lakanal, is located in the fifteenth Arondissement of Paris, not far from Avenue Émile Zola, and begins at the Place du Commerce and ends at the Rue Croix-Nivert.

APPENDIX I.

Thirty letters from the correspondence of Lakanal have been preserved among the Lakanal Papers in the Howard Memorial Library of New Orleans, now connected with Tulane University. Several of them have been published in recent years, but most of them are as yet unpublished.

1. Addressed to Lakanal 20 frimaire An III concerning the National Institute of Music. Signed by Lesueur, Gossec, Méhul, Sarrette, Devienne, Chérubini.

2. Addressed to Lakanal "Citoyen Président", 23 brumaire l'An III, concerning the composition of elementary books. Signed by Lagrange.

3. Addressed to Lakanal, 3 pluviôse, l'An III, offering a copy of *Études de la Nature*. Signed by (Bernardin) de Saint-Pierre.

4. Addressed to Lakanal 8 pluviôse, l'An III, soliciting his influence in behalf of Citoyen Gorgu. Signed by Marie Joseph Chénier.

5. Addressed to Lakanal 19 ventôse, An 3, soliciting Lakanal's aid in procuring a place for a citizen Soissy, son-in-law of the petitioner. Signed by Corancer, Bureau du Journal de Paris.

6. Addressed to Lakanal 9 brumaire, l'An III, concerning the composition of a book to be called *Élémens de Morale républicaine*. Signed by (Bernardin) de Saint-Pierre.

7. Addressed to Lakanal 15 nivôse, l'An III, thanking him for his kindness and his using his influence with the National Convention: "vos bons offices m'ont procuré la faveur que la Convention vient de m'accorder au sujet de mon instruction pour les bergers, etc." Signed by Daubenton, collaborator of Buffon.

8. Addressed to Lakanal le 3éme jour complémentaire de l'An III, soliciting his aid in securing a place as professor of music in the Conservatoire National. Signed by Aridzeri.

9. Addressed to Lakanal, no date, concerning the Observatory. Signed by Cassini, member of the Academy of Sciences and Director of the Observatory.

10. Addressed to Lakanal 12 frimaire An IV, acknowledging a letter that Lakanal had written previously giving details of the Institut National. The writer recalls the services that Lakanal had rendered in the establishing of Primary Schools, Secondary Schools (Écoles centrales), and the Normal School. Signed by Laplace.

11. Addressed to Lakanal Nov. 1837, by the Minister of Public Instruction, Victor Cousin, in which Cousin thanks Lakanal for information on America, stating that he looks forward to publishing a book on *Éducation du peuple dans la Démocratie,* and stating that Lakanal has furnished him with the best page of the book. Also reminding him that he (Cousin) is his (Lakanal's) successor as Director of the École Normale. Signed by V. Cousin (à la Sorbonne).

12. Addressed to Lakanal 20 nivôse l'An III, requesting that a sufficient quantity of wood be furnished to heat the hot houses of the Museum of Natural History, since the supply on hand has been depleted by the borrowings

of the students of the École Normale, whose sessions were held in the amphitheater of the Museum. Signed by Jussieu, Director of the Museum.

13. Addressed to Lakanal from Nice, 14 brumaire, l'An III, acknowledging a letter from Lakanal in which he indicated that the Committee of Public Instruction had chosen Volney to be associate with the Committee in its works. Signed by Volney.

14. Addressed to Lakanal, no date, thanking him for a recommendation. Signed by Lanjuinais.

15. Addressed to Lakanal from the Collège de France, 24 germinal, in behalf of the Bureau de Longitudes. In this letter the writer calls Lakanal "notre créateur" and wishes to pay him the homage "de ses créatures." Signed by Lalande.

16. Addressed to Lakanal 17 Floréal, extending an invitation to dine. Signed by Garat (who was Minister of Education).

17. Addressed to Lakanal 22 May, l'An II, thanking him for ten copies of decrees passed the day before. Signed by Lavoisier.

18. Addressed to Lakanal 5, lundi, inviting him to dine at a restaurant. Signed by Sieyès.

19. Addressed to Lakanal 30 July, l'An 2, stating that he is sending a little "opuscule en question qui m'a valu plus d'injures qu'il ne contient de lignes." Signed by Chamfort.

20. Addressed to Lakanal 13 août 1793 l'An II, introducing Citoyen Dumoulin who desires an interpretation of a Decree rendered the previous November. Signed by Cambacérès.

21. Addressed to Lakanal 4 ventôse, From Montalais, France, thanking him for his generous interest and characterizing him as an "être instruit, sensible et honnête." Signed (B. G.) Sage.

22. Addressed to Lakanal 24 germinal An IV, from Ellonay, France, thanking him for the loan of 20,000 *livres,* and adding: "J'ai lu avec bien de l'intérêt votre adresse pleine de chaleur à vos frères de l'Ariège et votre raport (*Sic*) plein de vision au conseil des Cinquante." Signed (Bernardin) de Saint-Pierre.

23. Addressed to Lakanal 21 pluviôse, l'An III. Lacépède has just been named to the chair of Zoology of the Museum of Natural History. He writes Lakanal a letter of thanks. Signed by Lacépède.

24. Addressed to Lakanal 5 juin 1739, l'An II, The letter states that the Académie des Sciences desires to send instructions and funds to Citizen Méchain who is engaged in Spain in making astronomical and trigonometrical observations relative to the degree of terrestrial Meridian. In the course of this letter the writer, Lavoisier, says: "Les sciences ne sont point en guerre, etc." Signed by Lavoisier.

25. Addressed to Lakanal 25 brumaire, thanking him and regretting his absence from home on the occasion of a personal visit from Lakanal, the intent of which was to reply to a question that the writer had previously put to Lakanal. Signed by Morellet.

26. Addressed to Lakanal 1er September 1793, concerning a decree of the Convention Nationale of August 14, 1793, In the course of this letter the writer says: "Il est désolant de voir que les sciences et les arts qui faisaient en France des progrès si rapides et qui pouvaient contribuer d'une manière si efficace à la gloire et à la prospérité de la République soyent sacri-

fiés à des opinions exagérées sur le danger desquelles on s'éclairera trop tard." Signed by Lavoisier.

27. Addressed to Lakanal 29 août 1793, l'An II, begging him to expedite the sending of fifty barrels to the Château de Chantilly in which to collect a cabinet of natural history (to be sent to the Museum of Natural History in Paris). Signed by Daubenton.

28. Addressed to Citizens Lakanal and de Leyre, Représentants du peuple près de l'École Normale, 6 ventôse, l'An III, discussing the preparation of an arithmetic and a geometry for use in the Primary Schools. Signed by Legendre.

29. Addressed to Lakanal 16 mai, l'An II, thanking him for a letter and inviting him to a "petit banquet fraternal" in his own home where he wishes Lakanal to meet Citizen Ginguéné (author of *Histoire littéraire de l'Italie*). Signed by Th. Grouvelle. (Grouvelle was at the time Secretary of the Conseil exécutif, later minister to Copenhagen).

30. The person addressed by Lakanal in this letter is not named, but internal evidence indicates that it was written to the celebrated New Orleans lawyer, Pierre Soulé:

Mobile du 5 Nov. 1834.

Monsieur et honorable compatriote:

Depuis notre très et trop courte entrevue, dans ma robinçonnière des nouvelles de notre ami commun, Mr. Morand, votre ancien professor de droit, et qui vous a, m'avez vous dit, bien souvent parlé de moi; voilà tantôt 50 ans que nous sommes étroitement unis, lui et moi, l'amitié aime les vieux baptistères. Notre ami me presse fort de me rendre auprès de mes confrères de l'Institut, et il m'allèche par l'assurance que je serai vu d'eux avec une vive satisfaction; je le crois un peu, mais pas jusqu'à laisser tomber lourdement le fromage[1]; du reste je suis très décidé à rentrer dans notre ancienne et chère patrie, et de revoir ces Pyrennées, témoins des plaisirs si purs et si vrais de mon enfance et de la vôtre; oui, nous nous y trouverons ensemble, et je seconderai de tous mes efforts, le projet que vous m'a communiqué: il est tout à fait covenant, qu'après avoir illustré le premier Barreau des Étas-Unis, vous veniez briller à la tribune de nos assemblées nationales; les braves arriégeois se ressouviendront, je m'en assure, qu'ils m'y ont envoyé, il y a 40 ans, et j'ai la conscience d'avoir justifié leur choix; je leur demanderai de porter sur vous, tout l'intérêt qu'ils auront conservé pour moi. Ma famille établie depuis deux siècles, dans la vallée de la Barguillère, qui s'étend jusqu'à Foix, y ont toujours exercé une sorte de magistrature patriarcale et la famille des Portal, mes proches parens, s'y perpétue dans les fonctions de juge de paix. Mon oncle Font, évêque constitutionnel de Pamiers, et quit fut membre de l'assemblée législative qui précéda la Convention, a laissé, dans notre pays, la réputation d'un autre François de Paule. J'ai conservé une partie de mon patrimoine, ainsi j'espère pouvoir, un jour, m'écrier, avec le Mélibée de Virgile:

"Post aliquot mea regna videns, mirabor aristas."

Je suis sûr que le brave Mr. Morand sera des nôtres. Je passerai chez lui et l'emmènerai chez moi; sa famille est établie près de Moulins, chef-lieu du Département de l'Allier où j'ai professé la philosophie chez les Doctrinaires. C'est dans le sein de cette savante congrégation séculaire que vous

[1]Allusion to the popular fable of La Fontaine.

avez fait vos études. Durant les 30 années que j'ai rempli de hautes fonctions en France, Mr. Morand ne m'a jamais quitté. Il a parcouru avec moi les départements du Centre lorsque, Représentant, j'ai organisé les écoles centrales: il m'a suivi dans la malheureuse Vendée où, avec des pouvoirs illimités, je n'ai pu opérer aucun bien; il est venu avec moi à Mayence quand j'ai été chargé d'organiser les Départements de la Rive gauche du Rhin. Enfin Mr. Morand a toujours été, et sera toujours, en France, mon "fidus Achates." Sa présence fera grand bien à votre cause. Durant son très long professorat, il a eu des rapports avec tous les légistes de nos contrées, et j'ai toujours vu que, dans les assemblées délibérantes, c'est vous autres MM (for *Messieurs*) qui déterminez les élections. Vous avez seuls la connaissance des lois, et ce qui vaut bien autant, dans une grande assemblée libre et peu tolérante, vous avez l'audace de la tribune.

Vous attendez-vous à recevoir, incessament, de ce M. Morand, une lettre dans laquelle il prendra l'attitude d'un chalereux solliciteur auprés de vous? Il viendra bientôt appuyer, de toute son influence, sur votre esprit une demande au succès de laquelle j'attache le plus vif et le plus tendre intérêt. Il existe, auprès de vous, une des meillures créatures qui soient au monde, c'est la filleule de Mr. Morand, c'est ma fille, Mme Germain. Son mari est chancelier du Consulat de France à la Nlle. Orléans. Mr. Germain est le chef d'une assez nombreuse famille, et sa place n'a aucun avenir, parce qu'il a plu à Mr. de Broglie de faire statuer, par le Roi, que les *capacités* seraient hériditaires, et qu'ainsi J. J. Rousseau, fils d'un horloger; Talleyrand évêque; Mably, fils d'un officier supérieur de gendarmerie, s'ils étaient venus après Mr. de Broglie, auraient été inhabiles à remplir des fonctions dans la carrière diplomatique et consulaire, 'risum teneatis, amici'? Réparez les bévues d'un homme qui, de l'aveu de tous ceux qui le pratiquent, croit tout voir, avec son lorgnon quoiqu'il (n'ait)[2] jamais appris que les souplesses, les artifices et la pa(ssion?).[2]

HIC. Il n'est bruit que de la Banque des Citoyens (qui va)[2] s'établir dans votre ville. C'est déjà d'un favorable augure pour cet établissement, de vous avoir pour son avocat. Votre influence y sera prodigieuse et je donne d'avance, un démenti à votre modestie si vous osez me dire le contraire; eh bien! Je vous demande, et Mr. Morand se joindra bientôt à moi pour vous demander, d'employer vos bons offices, pour faire obtenir à Mr. Germain, une place d'officier dans l'institution qui vous a choisi, pour être son organe. C'est là, une service capital dont nous conserverons un durable souvenir, eh morbleu! Je ne serai pas, un jour, en reste avec vous. J'ai l'habitude de poursuivre, avec persévérance, les projets que j'ai formés, et mon nom ne se trouvera jamais dans le très volumineux dictionnaire des girouettes.

J'ai l'honneur d'être,
Votre dévoué serviteur—LAKANAL.

P. S. Je vous prie, bien instamment, de garder le silence sur ma démarche qui pourrait compromettre Mr. Germain auprès du Consul.

[2]Manuscript defective.

APPENDIX II.

Hommage[1] à Mr. J. G. Birney administrateur de l'université de l'alabama, par son dévoué serviteur

J. Lakanal, membre de la société de medicine de la Nouvelle Orléans et des principales académies de l'europe.

NOTE.

J. Lakanal, après avoir donné sa démission de la présidence du Collêge d'orleans, en faveur de son gendre, M. Charvet, ancien éleve de la célèbre école polythecnique de paris, s'est retiré, dpuis *six ans*, sur sa belle plantation de la Mobile, qu'il fait prosperer, à l'aide de douze forts esclaves qui lui appartiennent.

[manuscript blurred] il compte au nombre de ses amis, qu'il reçoit habituellement chez lui, tous les citoyens du pays, distingués par leur probité et leurs lumières; les suivants lui rendront, il en est sur, un honorable temoinage.

AVOCATS MM. Acre; Durand; Aisckot; Garow; Chambodouin; Elliott, etc.

MEDECINS MM. Gannard; Cheusse; Corez, etc.

NEGOCIANS MM. Mkloskey; Durand; Robertson; Dunier; Armstrong; le juge Hull; le general Avrit; le colonel Storm, et sans exception, tous les gens de bien. Yertas, amigo.

Lakanal a professé *20 ans* les belles lettres, la philosophie et les mathematiques dans l'université de france.

il possède les langues anciennes et parle, avec facilité, le latin. il connait la langue française, il ose dire à fond, ayant été 18 ans un des redacteurs du nouveau Dictionnaire français, en 2 vol in 4^0, adopté par l'institut, et le corps législatif.

possédant une nombreuse et bonne bibliothèque, et se livrant à l'étude, depuis près de 55 ans, et presque exclusivement, il ose croire réunir, à très-peu-prés nos connossances positives dans les sciences les lettres et les beaux arts;

un grand ouvrage, dans lequel elles sont analysées sous le titre de *Tableau des connoissances humaines à la fin du xviiie Siècle,* a été le fruit de 30 ans de travail et a été adopté par l'institut de france, apres cinq séances de déliberations.

Mr. Lakanal, dans les E U [for Etats Unis] depuis 15 ans, n'ayant pas fait une étude suivie de la langue anglaise, l'a [sic] parle et l'entend imparfaitement, quoiqu'll aít composé un petit Dictionnaire et une petite grammaire à son usage, dans cette langue.

Salve mi Mecaenas; peropto ut quod instituisti, superis bene fortunantibus, feliciter absolvas, et bonis avibus coepta res, melioribus exeat.

tuí deditissimus,
J. LAKANAL.

[1]The spelling and punctuation of the original have been faithfully followed.

The Ferdinand J. Dreer Collection, Historical Society of Pennsylvania, contains a letter written by Lakanal on September 24, 1793, and is accompanied by a fine profile engraving of Lakanal. This letter, which was copied for use in this book by Dr. Dan Thomas, Professor of History in Rhode Island State College, reads as follows:

Paris du 24 7bre
L'An 2e

Recue le 25 7bre
Citoyens,

Je me disposais à me rendre au comité d'agriculture et des subsistances ains que je vous l'avais promis, lorsque j'ai recu une lettre de C. Cassini, par laquelle il m'invitait à me rendre à l'observatoire pour affaires instantes; inspecteur de cet établisseement national, Je me suis vu dans l'alternative ou de trahir mes devoirs ou de me rendre, et mon choix n'a pas été longtemps douteux.

De retour à la convention j'ai appris qu'on vous avait addressés au ministre de l'intérieur: ce n'était là qu'une honnête défaite; c'était vous éconduire poliment, car les lettres des ministres actuelles ne produisent aucun effet auprés des administrations départementales, les ministres n'étant en quelque sorte que les premiers commis du comité de salut public, c'était à lui ou à la convention qu'il fallait recourir.

Telle est aussi la marche que j'ai suivie: après avoir rappellé les services rendus à la République par les citoyens de Fontainebleau, après avoir observé que cette cité patriote était par son généreux dévouement à sa liberté, la rivale de gloire de Versailles puisque comme elle, elle a toujours préféré les sacrifices que commande une grande révolution à l'abondance que versait dans ses murs la cour de nos anciens tyrans, J'ai proposé et fait adopter, malgré quelques réclamations, le projet de décret qui avait été concerté entre nous au comité d'instruction publique; je vous en adresse un collationné officiel.

Salut et fraternité
(Signed) LAKANAL.

APPENDIX III.

THE FRENCH VINE AND OLIVE COLONY

The role of America as a home for the oppressed of Europe began with the arrival of the Huguenots in the later seventeenth and early eighteenth centuries. Following the revocation of the Edict of Nantes in 1685, thousands of the French protestants found refuge in Holland and England; and many of them came to America to the colonies along the Atlantic seaboard. Following the American Revolution in 1789, individuals and groups found refuge in this country. Also many of the French soldiers who had helped in our Revolutionary War remained and made America their home.

Beginning with the founding of Gallipolis and Marietta, Ohio, in 1791, by French colonists, there were numerous attempts to settle French groups in this country: notably, the colony at Asylum, Pennsylvania; the French-speaking Swiss colony at Vevay, Indiana; the French colonies in Genevieve, Missouri, and in Iowa; and the immense landholding of over three hundred thousand acres in Northern New York where Napoleon had dreamed of building a strong French colony which would be contiguous to the French of Canada.

At Philadelphia assembled a number of Napoleon's favorite generals as well as a host of lesser officers, common soldiers, and others who had occupied positions in civil life under the Emperor. At one time it was rumored in France that as many as 30,000 Frenchmen had sought refuge in this country from a vengeful Bourbon rule, but it is not likely that the total reached one-tenth that number. Whatever the number, the problem presented itself of what to do with them.

However sincerely the hearts of Americans may have been disposed to welcome oppressed foreigners to this land of freedom and liberty, there was also the materialistic motive of utilizing them for the advantage of agricultural development. Hence it is not strange that a group of the Napoleonic exiles were encouraged to found a colony for the cultivation of the vine and the olive. Their first thought had been to settle in the Ohio Valley, but they were finally persuaded to settle in Alabama on land that the government had recently acquired from the Creek Indians. The government gave the colonists a grant of land on very liberal terms along the Tombigbee River. A town was laid out and named Demopolis, the county in which it was located received the name of Marengo, and near by were formed settlements named for others of Napoleon's battles, such as Arcola, Linden, and Moscow. Aigleville was named in memory of the Napoleonic standard.

The French Agricultural and Manufacturing Society, as it was originally called, was organized in the fall of 1816 in Philadelphia. It was also variously known as the Society for the Cultivation of the Vine and Olive, the French Emigrant Association, and the Tombigbee (Tombeckbee) Association. Through the instrumentality of the secretary of the company, Simon Parmentier, the proposed colonists obtained from Congress a grant of four contiguous townships, each six miles square, for the cultivation of the vine and the olive. By act of Congress of March 3, 1817, the Secretary of the Treasury was authorized to sell the four townships at two dollars per acre, the whole to be paid for within fourteen years. Philadelphia became the headquarters of the society, and there the shares were subscribed for and the allotments made. General Charles Lallemand was president of the society, and Nicholas S. Parmentier secretary. Eventually Charles Villar, who was general agent of the company, became the first vice president. Count Réal and General Vandamme were interested in the movement, and among the names which appear in the first list of shareholders were Marshal Grouchy and his sons, Generals Charles and Henri Lallemand, General Bertrand Clausel, General Lefèbvre-Desnouettes. Lakanal appeared in this first list, and to him was assigned a tract of 430 acres, the amount of land to which at first each of the larger subscribers was limited.

Through their officials the colonists appealed to Thomas Jefferson to assist them with a plan of government for the proposed settlement. In a letter to William Lee, Jefferson stated his reasons for declining the request:

"No one can be more sensible than I am of the honor of their confidence in me, so flatteringly manifested in this resolution; and certainly no one can feel stronger dispositions than myself to be useful to them, as well in return for this great mark of respect, as from feelings for the situation of strangers, forced by the misfortunes of their native country to seek another by adoption, so distant, and so different from that in all its circumstances. I commiserate the hardships they have to encounter, and equally applaud the resolution with which they meet them, as well as the principles proposed for their government. That their emigration may be for the happiness of their descendants, I can but believe; but from the knowledge I have of the country they have left, and its state of social intercourse and comfort, their own personal happiness will undergo several trials. The laws however which are to effect this must flow from their own habits, their own feelings, and the resources of their own minds. No stranger to these could possibly propose regulations adapted to them. Every people have their own particular habits, ways of thinking, manners, etc., which have grown up with them from their infancy, are become a part of their nature, and to which the regulations which are to make them happy must be accommodated. No member of a foreign country can have a sufficient sympathy with these. The institutions of Lycurgus, for example, would not have suited Athens, nor those of Solon Lacedaemon. The organizations of Locke were impracticable for California, and those of Rousseau and Mably for Poland.

Turning inwardly on myself from these eminent illustrations of the truth of my observations, I feel all the presumption it would manifest should I undertake to do what this respectable society is alone qualified to do suitably for itself. There are some preliminary questions too which are particularly for their own consideration. Is it proposed that this shall be a separate state? Or a county of a State? Or a mere voluntary association, as those of the Quakers, Dunkars, Menonists? A separate state it can not be, because from the tract it asks, it would not be of more than 20 miles square, and in establishing new states, regard is had to a certain degree of equality in size. If it is to be a county of a state, it cannot be governed by its own laws, but must be subject to those of the state of which it is a part. If merely a voluntary association, the submission of its members will be merely voluntary also; as no act of coercion would be permitted by the general law. These considerations must control the society, and themselves alone can modify their own intentions and wishes to them. With this apology for declining a task to which I am so unequal, I pray them to be assured of my sincere wishes for their success and happiness."[1]

In April, 1817, a large group of colonists sailed on the schooner *McDonough*, taking with them an assortment of vines and olive plants which they proposed to cultivate on the lands alloted to them in Alabama.[2] Late one evening in the month of May, a schooner was seen approaching Mobile Point, tossed to and fro by a heavy gale.[3] The increasing tempest threw her among the breakers, and she ran aground. Lieutenant Beal, commanding Fort Bowyer, together with six resolute men, set out in a small boat, and finally reached the schooner. It was the *McDonough*, carrying the French colonists. After some of the colonists had been rescued in small boats, the schooner shifted into deeper water and the rest of the passengers remained on board, ultimately reaching land in safety. For several days they remained at Fort Bowyer, where they were shown every attention by Lieutenant Beal and his companions. A few days later, when they had arrived at Mobile, the French exiles gave Lieutenant Beal a public dinner as a token of gratitude to him for his kindness. After enjoying the hospitality of the little town of Mobile, the colonists prepared to ascend the river to their future home in the wilderness, their final destination being the White Bluffs at confluence of the Warrior and Tombigbee rivers; a location not far removed from the scene of the great battle of Maubila, where in 1540 De Soto and his little band of Spaniards had met and defeated the Indian Chief Tuskaloosa.

Through the good offices of Addin Lewis, Collector of the Port of Mobile, a revenue cutter was put at the disposal of the French colonists, in which they placed a supply of essential stores and such of their household goods as would be necessary in their pioneer homes. It was a glorious spring morning, bright and balmy, when the cutter crowded with exiles was loosed from the wharf.[4] The scene presented a striking contrast to the stormy reception that had greeted the passengers of the *McDonough* at the entrance of the Bay. The narrow wharf was lined with the new-made friends of the exiles. Adieux were waved to the disappearing boat, and cheer after cheer went up from its passengers, who with all the ardor and enthusiasm of their race, welcomed the adventurous voyage of exploration before them. The progress up the river was slow. The trip of the exiles was enlivened by one or two incidents worthy of mention. At Fort Stoddert they enjoyed the hospitality of Judge Toulmin, to whom they bore letters of introduction; and they stopped for a day or two at Fort Montgomery, then in command of General Gaines.[5] At St. Stephens they found a flourishing village with a cultured population—a

[1]Reeves, *op cit.*, p. 37.

[2]Not only did colonists reach the French colony by sea to Mobile, but many of them made the journey overland via the Ohio River. Niles' *Register* of September 6, 1817, says: "By a respectable Indian Agent, now at the seat of government, we learn, that in coming up the Ohio, he met upwards of a hundred Frenchmen, at different times, directing their course towards the new settlement on the Tombigbee."

[3]Albert James Pickett, *History of Alabama* (Charleston, 1851); Thomas Chalmers McCorvey, "The Vine and Olive Colony", *Alabama Historical Reporter*, Tuscaloosa, Ala., April, 1885; Ann Bozeman Lyon, "The Bonapartists in Alabama", *Southern Home Journal*, Memphis, March, 1900: Whitfield, *op. cit.*

[4]McCorvey, *op. cit.; The Times Democrat,* New Orleans, Feb. 22, 1885.

[5]The Captor of Aaron Burr.

sort of Mecca of civilization for the sparse settlements of the surrounding country. After a short rest there, and after transferring to a bargé, they proceeded up the winding rapid current of the Tombigbee. Once or twice a camp was struck on the river bank, while some of the more adventurous of the party made hunting forays into the surrounding country. The occasional white squatter encountered on these expeditions scanned them with no less curious interest and suspicion than did the red deer that came down to the river's brink to slake its thirst. At last the exiles reached the white bluff just below the junction of the Tombigbee and Black Warrior rivers, which, as their future home, was to be the scene of one of the most picturesque chapters in American history.

Some conception of the nature of the wild and dangerous journey which these French men and women had just completed on the waterways may be formed from an account given by William H. Robertson, who became a leading merchant at Mobile, and later U. S. Consul at Bremen, Germany. In 1806 young Robertson had undertaken a journey by boat over forty miles of the route traversed later by the French colonists. In his account, as yet unpublished,[6] he relates a journey by boat from Mobile to Fort Stoddert.

". . . . I at once repaired on board, and commenced ascending the river. I may add almost the first vessel that ever attempted to ascend the river to the point we arrived at.

"So little was the river disturbed at that period I shall speak of, 1806, except Indian canoes, that the water was literally alive with alligators. There was no time about midday that you could not see one to two hundred basking in the sun on the old logs bordering each side of the river. . . .

"We had ascended about 20 miles, with our sails when toward night the wind died away and promising a bright moonshine. The sweeps were employed until about 12 o'clock, when the kedge was thrown over, and she was anchored in the middle of the river. Unfortunately the sweeps were not taken in. Having nothing to do, I brot up my mattress from the cabin, & spread it on the afterhatch, rigging my musquitoe net under the boom where I stretched myself away and to sleep, ignorant of the time when we anchored. Between the hatch & the mainmast, directly at my head, there was a coop of fowls. Toward morning I was awakened by the extraordinary noises of these fowls. In attempting to look out to see what was the matter, I found, as I supposed, one of the sailors laying partly on the edge of my mattress, and on the musquitoe net. After several efforts to wake up the stupid fellow without success I tried the other side, and with no better success. In vexation, I crawled out at foot, when I beheld two tremendous alligators had been laying each side of me, I do not know how long; and I saw besides 5 more on the main deck, and one on each sweep. The moon was still shining brightly, but the men were all sleeping under the awning on the quarter deck, upon which I immediately sprang, and give the alarm, that the vessel was in possession of the alligators.

"All hands were soon awake, and in hot pursuit, no less surprised at the sight before them than I had been, but could not resist a burst of laughter when they saw my two companions on my mattress, who had been so intent up[on] the chickens they had not moved, but were even then preparing to tear away the slats. They were soon however disturbed & returned to

[6]Unpublished memoirs written in decade between 1850-1860. By courtesy of Professor William P. Fidler, of the Department of English, University of Alabama, who is editing these memoirs.

their own element, which occup[i]ed about 10 minutes when the sweep was taken that had formed the bridge for their visit."

On the west side of the Tombigbee the land still belonged to the Choctaw Indians, but the land which the exiles proposed to settle had recently been procured by the United States from the Creeks (Muscogees). It formed a vast forest of trees and cane, broken here and there by a prairie. In the canebrakes the canes were so large that one joint of cane would hold a pint of water, "and travellers were wont to use them to carry water while on a journey." The nearest white inhabitants lived in the Russell settlement which had been founded by a group of Tennesseans near the present town of Greensboro. A few other white settlers lived in Marengo and Clarke counties.

Here at the White Bluffs the colonists set about the work of establishing their homes. They built rude log huts, cleared patches of ground, and took steps toward laying off a town and dividing the lots among the members of the Association. At the request of Count Pierre François Réal, one of the original incorporators of the colony at Philadelphia, the town was named Demopolis (city of the people). Having been accustomed to a Parisian life of ease and luxury, it was hard for these people to adapt themselves to the life of a pioneer in the wilds of the Alabama territory.[7] Unprovided with wagons and teams, and unacquainted with the shifts to which pioneer people are often compelled to resort, they made but slow progress in subduing the wilderness. Provisions were very high priced, and it was a great struggle for those unaccustomed to manual labor to make a subsistance in a foreign land in a wilderness uncleared, uncultivated, and with no near neighbor to teach them the art of agriculture. . . . However, with a soil that produces abundantly with but a little exertion, they managed to cultivate a few patches of soil without knowing upon whose grant they were making improvements, and were enabled to eke out a subsistance with the aid of the money and valuables they had brought with them.

When the town of Demopolis was laid off, in order to secure frontage on the river, two fractional townships were chosen instead of two townships. This was exceedingly unfortunate, as after some time had elapsed and many improvements had been made, it was discovered that the town was not located in the townships which had been secured by the French, and the land on which the town was built had been purchased from the federal government by an American company at $52 an acre instead of $2 an acre as had been agreed on with the French. The contract made at Washington was enforced, and thus the colonists were deprived of their hard-earned improvements.

After George S. Gaines (government land agent at Demopolis, and for whom the still extant and beautiful ante-bellum mansion of the Whitfield family was named *Gaineswood*) discovered that the vine and olive company had made a mistake in believing that the river bluff formed part of their grant, the French settlers moved further to the east and formed a village which they named Aigleville in honor of Napoleon's ensign, the name later being translated into Eaglesville.[8] Here a town was laid off, and as before, cabins

[7]Pickett, *op. cit.*, 1851.

[8]Some years ago there was discovered in a French Château a panoramic wall-paper, painted by hand, under title "The French at Aigleville or Foundation of the State of Marengo." This wall-paper was purchased by Thomas W. Martin, of Birmingham, who presented it to the Department of Archives

were erected and improvements made. In the meantime, a new contract had been made between Secretary of the Treasury Crawford and the Agent of the Vine and Olive Company Charles Villar by which the lands were sold and the tracts of each person were designated. The allotments made at Philadelphia and ratified by Mr. Crawford turned out to be different from those already occupied by the settlers, and disclosed the fact that they were once more to lose their hard-earned improvements, must move still further into the interior, and for the third time build themselves homes in the wilderness. This time they founded the village of Arcola, also named after one of Napoleon's battles.

Marengo County, named for the battle of that name at the suggestion of Judge Lipscomb while a member of the legislature which met at St. Stephens in 1818,[9] was the principal location of the French grant, although it also included parts of Hale and Greene counties, reaching almost to the town of Greensboro. It extended east and south of Demopolis, and included the town of Linden which received its name from Hohenlinden, another one of the Napoleonic battles, made the more famous by the poet Campbell.

Among the many discouragements encountered by the French was the want of wagons and teams, together with the great scarcity of water in the canebrakes. Thus they were compelled to dwell on small allotments, while their more valuable tracts were left unoccupied. Unaccustomed to agriculture and guided by their love of the beautiful rather than the nature of the soil, many of the settlers selected the poorest land. Clinging to the principles of the French Revolution—Liberty, Equality, Fraternity—they refused to own slaves, but imported a number of German redemptioners, paying their debts and passage, and binding them to work until the sum was repaid. While some of these redemptioners were true to their obligations, others disregarded them and often became a burden and expense rather than a help.

Although the French refugees encountered many heartbreaking discouragements and underwent untold hardships, they retained their essential French character, and brought with them to their homes in the wilderness the gay grace and social culture for which the French capital was famous.[10] If the days were filled with work—felling trees, building cabins, grading roads, fencing fields—the nights were given up to pleasure, and everywhere throughout the infant village could be seen and heard evidences that a joyous people inhabited it—handsomely attired women, with gallant escorts, passing in and out of the rude log cabins where they indulged in music and dancing. Some of the refugees had brought with them many things to gratify luxurious tastes; and they seemed determined to enjoy life. Long before they had made a test of grape culture, wines of rare French vintage crowned the boards

and History, State of Alabama, on March 14, 1939. The original consists of five panels with overall length of 42 ft., 9½ in., and is 6 ft., 7 in., in height. A photographic reproduction was printed by Mr. Martin in his book *French Military Adventurers in Alabama 1818-1828* (Birmingham, Ala., 1937). Scenes from the Panorama have also been published in *Travel* magazine, accompanying an article by Hudson Strode entitled: "Bonapartists in the Alabama Canebrake," *Travel,* April, 1938.

[9]In anticipation of becoming admitted to statehood, the territory of Alabama was divided into counties. Alabama became a state in 1819.

[10]Pickett and McCorvey, *op. cit.*

on festive occasions. The surrounding forests abounded in the choicest game, that required little skill in killing or taking. Well cultivated gardens yielded an abundant supply of all kinds of vegetables. With these resources at command, the proverbial culinary skill of the French people supplied the exiles with table comforts. Many of the ladies had brought with them rich silks and laces, and on holiday occasions these took the place of homespun that was worn in the performance of household duties. At such times Demopolis assumed somewhat the appearance of a miniature French town.

Gay and frivolous pastimes did not comport with the frugality and self-denial required for success in pioneer life; but it must be borne in mind that pioneers are rarely made of the material that formed the colony upon the Tombigbee; and it could hardly be expected that men who had been taught to regard social charms and graces as nearest in importance to the glories of war could readily abandon their former customs for the dull thrift of the farmer's life.

As stated, the purpose of the founding of the French colony was not only to furnish an asylum to a group of exiles, but also to encourage the growing of grapes and olives in America. The site in Alabama had been chosen as one very similar in climate and soil to southern France where lay the fruitful olive groves and the vineyards from whose grapes were pressed the famous Bordeaux wines. The colonists in good faith entered upon the cultivation of the vine and the olive.[11] Plants were often imported from Bordeaux, but the newness of the land and the ignorance of the colonists as to the manner of their cultivation, doomed the experiment to ultimate failure. The importations often arrived out of season, and the vines withered away, while olive seed would not germinate. In 1821 the colonists planted three hundred and eighty-three olive trees upon the grant, and a large number in 1824. Every winter the frosts would kill them to the ground, but they would grow out again in the Spring, to be killed each succeeding winter. . . . They succeeded in growing the vine, but the grapes matured too early in the heat of August, and thus no wines comparable to the fine French wines were made. Discouraged in their efforts, the colonists finally turned to cotton, transforming their vineyards and olive orchards into cotton patches, cotton being at that time a highly profitable crop bringing 30 cents a pound.

Their relations with the neighboring Indian tribes were of the best, and oftentimes the Indians were of service in instructing them in the ways of primitive agriculture. The American settlers of the region complained of the Choctaws, but in the French settlements there were no complaints; and although the Indians sometimes became intoxicated, they never gave any trouble to the French.

[11]Pickett, *op. cit.;* J. W. Beeson, articles in the Demopolis *Express,* 1895.

ORIGINAL SHAREHOLDERS IN THE VINE AND OLIVE COLONY

Numbers of the sections.	Numerical Nos. of the Shareholders.	Names of the shareholders.	No. of Acres of each shareholder.
1	1	Meeslier, Bizile	480
	2	Lauret, Louis	160
2	3	Conte, Honore	120
	4	Roudet, Corneille Cadet	120
	5	Vial, Antonie	120
	6	Bujey, Antoine	120
	7	Godemar, Jean Baptiste	120
	A	Reserve	40
3	8	Jeannet, Louis Rene	320
	9	Julie, Pastol	320
4	10	Allard, Henry	120
	11	Combes, Germain	120
	12	Combes, Vincent	120
	13	Sibenthal, Freres	240
	B	Reserve	40
5	14	Perdrauville, Rene	240
	15	Alma, Anselme	120
	16	Salmon, Francois	120
	17	Lintroy	120
	C	Reserve	40
6	18	Schultz, Col. Jean	320
	19	Combe, Col. Michael	320
7	20	Martin, Francis	480
	21	Pelagot, Antoine Zacharie	160
8	22	George, Edouard	480
	23	Viole	160
9	24	Lacombe, Pierre	480
	25	Latapie, Antoine	160
10	26	Richard, Etienne	480
	27	Papillot, Etienne	160
11	28	Frenaye, Jeune Pierre	480
	29	Rivet, George	160
12	30	Boutiere, Jean Claude Benoit	240
	31	Ve. Louise, David	120
	32	Delaporte, Louis	120
	33	Meynie, Jean Ulysse	120
	D	Reserve	40
13	34	Metais, Et. J. B.	240
	35	Mansuis, Luillier	120
	36	Jouny, Louis Michael	120
	37	Vernhes, Jean Vincent	120
	E	Reserve	40

Group	No.	Name	Amount
14	38	Marchand, Louis Pre. Jh.	480
	39	Martin, Amedee	160
15	40	Butaud, Isaac	240
	41	Keller, Jonas	240
	42	Menou, Dieudonne	120
	F	Reserve	40
16	43	Jordan, Col. Ambrose	320
	44	Vorster, Col. Emile	320
17	45	Cadet, Bergache	240
	46	Gallard, Pierre	240
	47	Lafeuvre, Claude Joseph	120
	G	Reserve	40
18	48	Paguenaud, Edouard	240
	49	Transon, Jean	240
	50	Gauny, Nicholas	120
	H	Reserve	40
19	51	Astolphi, Laurent	480
	52	Knappe, Philippe	160
20	53	Grouchy, Col. Alphonse	320
	54	Grouchy, Cap. Victor	160
	55	Pillero	160
21	56	Drouet, Pierre	480
	57	Bailey, Michel	120
	I	Reserve	40
22	58	Lemaignen, Pierre Paul	480
	59	Lerouyer, Francois	160
23	60	Garesche, Pierre	480
	61	Formento, Felix	160
24	62	Faures, Laurent	240
	63	Burckle, Emanuel	120
	64	Coquillon, Freres	240
	J	Reserve	40
25	65	Jackson, Samuel	240
	66	Montelius, Guillaume	240
	67	Boutiere, Francois Gaspard	120
	K	Reserve	40
26	68	Robin, Thomas	240
	69	Nartigue, J. Justin	240
	70	Gerard, Hiacinthe	160
27	71	Follin, Auguste Firmin	480
	72	Follin, Freres	160
28	73	Chapron, J. M.	480
	74	Weill, James	160

29	75	Dupuoy, Nicholas Alex.	480
	76	Manoury, P. Max.	160
30	77	Garesche, V. M.	480
	78	Tournel, Jacques	160
31	79	Martin Picquet, L. J. F.	480
	80	Martin Picquet, Joseph	160
32	81	Robard, Josepr	480
	82	Martin Picquet, Pere	120
	L	Reserve	40
33	83	Auze, Freres	240
	84	Braud, Jacques	240
	85	Barrau	160
34	86	Lecampion, Francois	240
	87	Brechemin, Louis	240
	88	Humbert, Jacques Etienne	160
35	89	Jamet	480
	90	Rigau, Narcisse Pericles	160
36	91	Promis, Guillaume	480
	92	Desmares	160
37	93	Durand, Jean Baptiste	480
	94	Robaglia, Joseph	160
38	95	Garnier, Fils	240
	96	Peniere, Fils Emile	240
	97	Ve. Audibert	120
	M	Reserve	40
39	98	Nidelet, E. F.	480
	99	Cousin, David	120
	N	Reserve	40
40	100	Galabert, Col. Louis	320
	101	Petitval, J. B.	320
41	102	Anduze, Mathieu Bernard	480
	103	Frederic, Louis Auguste	160
42	104	Gubert, J. H.	480
	105	Moynier, Joseph Ariste Theo	160
43	106	Douarche, Col.	320
	107	Grouchet, Louis	320
44	108	Villar, Charles	480
	109	Pagniere, J. Alexandre	160
45	110	Dirat, Louis M.	480
	111	Mondin	160
46	112	Pagaud, Pierre	480
	113	Fallot, Eugine Hiacinthe	160

47	114	Frenaye, Marc. Antoine	480
	115	Lauret, Clement	120
	0	Reserve	40
48	116	Gl. Vandame	480
	117	Angeli, Hiacinthe	120
	P	Reserve	40
49	118	Poculo, Benoit	320
	119	Baltar	160
	120	Moquart	160
50	121	Besson, Louis An.	480
	122	Lemeunier, J. Joseph	160
51	123	Mesnier, Freres	480
	124	Henry, Germain	160
52	125	Cal. Rigau	480
	126	Mariano, Pompee	160
53	127	Texier, Lapomeraye	320
	128	Harraneder, Charles	160
	129	Metaye, Jean Pierre	120
	Q	Reserve	40
54	130	Martin, J. du Columbier	480
	131	Campardon, Bte.	160
55	132	Ravesies, F.	480
	133	Bordas, Elie	160
56	134	Debrosse, Charles	480
	135	Merle, Etienne	160
57	136	Ladurelle, M. F. Aug.	480
	137	Canobio, Francois	160
58	138	Davis, L. A.	240
	139	B. Charles Firmin	240
	140	Montalegri, Hiacinthe	160
59	141	Duval, Jacques S.	480
	142	Bacle, Alexis, Fils, aine	160
60	143	Lakanal	480
	144	Desportes, Leonte	120
	R	Reserve	40
61	145	Tulane, Freres	240
	146	Kimbal	120
	147	Billington	120
	148	Boiteau, Francois	120
	S	Reserve	40
62	149	Leboutellier, Michel	480
	150	Plantevigne	160
63	151	Moncravie, Jacques	240
	152	Brown, F. S.	240
	153	Monot, Charles	160

64	154	Cluis, J. Jerome	480
	155	Ruffier, Ferdinand	160
65	156	Garnier, Pere	480
	157	Simon	160
66	158	Wells & Leelere	240
	159	Macre, Jean M.	120
	160	Dumas, Antoine	120
	161	Dalmazeau, J.	120
	T	Reserve	40
67	162	Fontanges, P. F.	480
	163	Godon, Victorine (N)	120
	U	Reserve	40
68	164	Belair, Louis	480
	165	Sagnier, Henri Antoine	160
69	166	Lallemand, Gen. Charles	480
	167	Valcourt, Aime	160
70	168	Clausel, Gen. Bertrand	480
	169	Blaquerolle	160
71	170	Sary, Jean M. Alex.	160
	171	Gatty, Antoine	160
	172	Ilari, Benoit	160
	173	Milton, Solidor	160
72	174	Carre, Jean Thomas	480
	175	Genin, Charles Franc	160
73	176	Charrassin, Col.	320
	177	Vasquez, Jean	320
74	178	Roland, Jean Francois	320
	179	Pichon, Claude Charles	320
75	180	Charreton, Joseph Lewis	480
	181	Grillet Francois	160
76	782	Texier, Jean	240
	183	Martinet, Pierre Louis	240
	184	Vitalbe, Jean Baptiste	160
77	185	Jogan, Antonin	240
	186	Cavoroc Charles	120
	187	Roster, John	120
	188	Chapon	120
	V	Reserve	40
78	189	Dubarry, John	480
	190	Salaignac, Louis	120
	W	Reserve	40
79	191	Descourt, Leonard Alex.	240
	192	Onfroy, Jean Baptiste	120
	193	Pochard, Angustin Francois	120
	194	Fux, Louis	160

80	195	Stewart, George	480
	196	Gilbert	160
81	197	Sevelinge, Joseph	480
	198	Mane	160
82	199	Richard, George	160
	200	Nardel, Francois	160
	201	Chauvot Charles	160
	202	Plaidaut, Francois	160
83	203	Bono, Charles	240
	204	Tascha	120
	205	Blandin, Jean	120
	206	Azan	120
	X	Reserve	40
84	207	Victoire, Delaunay Josephe	480
	208	Castan, Etienne	160
85	209	Lefrancois, Freres	480
	210	Groning	160
86	211	Pothier, Simon	240
	212	Shubart, Henry	240
	213	Neel, Jean Baptiste	160
87	214	Beylle, Joseph	480
	215	Malozewsky, Const. Paul	160
88	216	Teterel, Francois	480
	217	Pagniere	160
89	218	Dubosq	120
	219	George, Fils aine Edouard	120
	220	Lesueur	120
	221	Dor	120
	222	Maillet, Henry Pre. Ae. As.	160
90	223	Stollenwerek, Freres	480
	224	Vallot, Joseph	160
91	225	Mathieu, Dr. Joseph	480
	226	Allain, Joseph	120
	Y	Reserve	40
92	227	Jeandrau, Jean	240
	228	Caillebaux, Guillaume	240
	229	Nelson	120
	Z	Reserve	40
93	230	Taillade, Col.	320
	231	Olivieri, Joseph	160
	232	Luciana, Pascal	160
94	233	Mal. Grouchy	480
	234	Deschamps, Francois Me.	160

95	235	Baumier, Ceasar	160
	236	Barbe, Antoine	160
	237	Stribaud, Charles	160
	238	Decorme, Charles	160
96	239	Chaudron, Edouard	480
	240	Gilbal, Antoine	160
97	241	Martin, Prosper	480
	242	Desplan, Samuel	160
98	243	Melizet, Francois	480
	244	Corso, Francois	160
99	245	Hamel, Victor	480
	246	Havard	160
100	247	Peniere, Pere J. A.	480
	248	Fanchon, Hre.	160
101	249	Lecoq du' Marcelay	480
	250	Godat	120
	AA	Reserve	40
102	251	Defourni, Col. Fabias	320
	252	Gouillot	320
103	253	Bardaraque, Thomas	480
	254	Conte, Marius	160
104	255	Desfouch, Charles	160
	256	Pascal, Paul	160
	257	Fouasche, Pierre	160
	258	Bernard, Henry	160
105	259	Rapin, Joseph	480
	260	Contardi, Louis	160
106	261	St. Guiron, Jeune	480
	262	Demony, Dominique Victor	160
107	263	Ravesies, Ee.	240
	264	Fournier, Honore	240
	265	Farcy	160
108	266	Champenois, P. J.	240
	267	Savary, Joseph	240
	268	Belmere, pere and fils	160
109	269	Gal. Lallemand, Hy.	480
	270	Prompt	160
110	271	Bayol, Honore	480
	272	Durive, Francois	160
111	273	Conde, Charles	240
	274	Pierce, Freres	240
	275	Laurent, Maurice	160

112	276	Chaudron, Simon	480
	277	Boilandry, Eugenie	120
	BB	Reserve	40
113	278	Arnaud, Camille	240
	279	Deprest, Rene, Freres and Zach.	240
	280	Batre, Charles	120
	CC	Reserve	40
114	281	Belange, Mal. Denis	320
	282	Chasseriau, Benoit	320
115	283	Real, Pierre Francois	480
	284	Panazi, Louis	160
116	285	Eujac, Freres, Mathieu & Alfd.	240
	286	Germond and Reviere	240
	287	Guibert, Hy.	120
	DD	Reserve	40
117	288	Ducoing, Pre.	480
	289	Stephens, Samuel J.	160
118	290	Fourestier, Elie	480
	291	Gregoire, Etienne	160
119	292	Manfredi, Math. Ferdinand	160
	293	Dupont	96
	EE	Reserve	384
120	294	Gal. Lefebre Desnouettes	480
	295	Desroures	160
121	296	Jeannet, George	480
	297	Jeannet, Je.	160
122	298	Dumenil	240
	299	Ducommun, Joseph	120
	300	Parat, F. Romaine	120
	301	Burgues, Jn. Bernard	120
	FF	Reserve	40
123	302	Ve. Demerest	240
	303	Bourlon, E.	240
	304	Lapeyre, Jn. Bte.	160
124	305	Thouron, pere and fils	480
	306	Lavau, Sully	120
	GG	Reserve	40
125	307	Englebert	480
	308	Landevin, Francois	120
	HH	Reserve	40
126	309	Legrix, Belisle	240
	310	Legras	240
	311	Bulliard, Etienne	160

127	312	Pollin, George	480
	313	Fauquier	160
128	314	Emery and Duterte	480
	315	Vogelsang, Daniel	120
	II	Reserve	40
129	316	Gaines, George	480
	317	Murrat, Jean Bte.	160
130	318	Mestayer, Michael	480
	319	Rieger, Gabriel V.	160
131	320	Parmantier, Nicolas Simon	480
	321	Bauzan, Pierre	160
132	322	Vorrhees, S.	480
	323	Fisher	160
133	324	Dufourg, Jean Jacques	240
	325	Dufourg, D. V.	120
	326	Dufourg, F.	120
	327	Lacroix, Rene Francois	160
134	328	St. Guiron, aine Pre. Pascal	240
	329	Farrouilh, A.	120
	330	St. Felix, Jean R.	120
	331	Decave, Marc Lewis	120
	JJ	Reserve	40
135	332	Barbaroux, Joseph	240
	333	Cirode, William	120
	334	Shoeun, Sebastian	120
	335	Gouiran, Joseph Michel	120
	KK	Reserve	40
136	336	Lajonie	480
	337	Truck	160
137	338	Colona, Dornano B.	320
	339	Peraldi, Toussaint	160
	340	Scasso, Vincent	160
	341	Laroderie, Alphonse	240
	342	Savournin, Joseph	240
	343	Balbuena, Joseph	160
	344	Canonge, Pierre Auguste	480
	345	Lucien	160
	346	Tablee, William	480
	347	Torta, Jean	160

B.—List of the Persons who are actually Established at Eagleville, on the Tombeckbee.

Bazile Meslier	492	Veune de Launay	492
Pennieres	492	Defrancois Freres	192
J. Cd. De. Coutiere	246	Jean Jeandrau	246
Jean Francon	246	St. Guiron's Jeune	492
Victor Grouchy	163	Francois Durive	163
Isaac Butaud	246	Jonathan Pierce	246
David Cousin	163	Maurice Laurent	163
Benoit Poculo	326	Charles Batre	123
Boltar	163	Riviere	123
Mocar	163	Lefebre Desnouette	492
Charles Decrosse	492	Michel Metayer	492
Leontine Desportes	123	Nics. Simon Parmentier	492
Billington	123	Saml. Vorrees	492
Francs, Boitau	123	Lajonie	492
Michel Lebouteiller	492	Lucien	163
Simon	163		
Jean Texier	246		9,817
George Steward	492	Viol	163
			9,980

In this list are not included about ten persons established there, who are not on the list or erased from it, and those who have arrived there since five months that I am absent from the colony.

The following are the names of persons established in the colony whose names are not on the list or erased from it, which are, to my knowledge: Prudomme, Fougnet, Guyault, Haez, Mignon, Clement, Joseph.

List furnished by Gen. C. Lefebre Desnouette.[1]

[1]Lowrie, Walter, ed. *Documents, legislative and executive, of the Congress of the United States, in relation to the Public lands, from the first session of the twenty-third congress: March 4, 1789, to June 15, 1824. Washington:* Duff Green, 1834.

BIBLIOGRAPHY

The Lakanal Papers, Howard Memorial Library, Tulane University, New Orleans; The Court House Records, Mobile; Archives of the University of Alabama; Pickett Papers, Archives of History, Montgomery; Unpublished Memoirs of William H. Robertson written in decade 1850-1860.

Commercial Register, Mobile, 1824-37; Gazette de la Louisiane, New Orleans, 1822-24; L'Amis des Lois, New Orleans, 1822-24; Courrier de la Louisiane, New Orleans, 1822-24; Niles' Weekly Register, Baltimore, 1815-1830.

Acloque, A. "Les Contemporains: Lakanal," *Biographie des Hommes du Jour.* Paris, 1841.

Adams, George Burton. *The Growth of the French Nation.* New York, 1896.

Allain, Abbe E. "Étude sur Lakanal," *Revue du monde catholique,* septembre, 1886.

American State Papers. Public Lands. Washington, 1834.

Arago, D. F. J. *Condorcet, a Biography.* Translated by M. A. Henry. Washington, 1879.

Arnaud, G. *Histoire de la Révolution dans le Départment de l'Ariège* (1789-1795). Toulouse, 1904.

Arnault, A. V. "Notes sur Lakanal," *Biographie Nouvelle des Contemporains.* 1827.

Aulard, A. *Histoire politique de la Révolution francaise, 1789-1804.* Paris, 1926.

Aulard F. A. *Les représentants en mission, La Révolution française 1887,* 2e *semestre.*

———*Paris sous la Réaction thermidorienne et pendant le Directoire.* 5 vols.

———*Recueil des actes du Comité du salut public, avec la correspondance officielle des représentants en mission.* Paris, 1889.

Balzac, Honoré. *Le Ménage d'un Garçon.* Translation by Clara Bell under title: *A Bachelor's Establishment.* Philadelphia, 1902.

Barbé-Marbois. *Histoire de la Louisiane.* Paris, 1829.

Barère, Bertrand. *Memoirs of Bertrand Barère, Chairman of the Committee of Public Safety during the Revolution.* Translated by De V. Payen-Payne. London, 1896. 4 vols.

Barnes, Edward. *History of the Wars of the French Revolution, 1792-1815.* Philadelphia, 1835.

Bastid, Paul. "Sieyès et sa Pensée." *Le Temps,* 6 janvier 1940.

Beaunier, A. *Lakanal conspirateur.* Paris, 1910.

Beeson, J. W. Series of eleven articles in the *Demopolis Express,* 1895.

Benoit, Dolive. "Lakanal et le Collège d'Orléans." Unpublished. Baton Rouge, 1937.

Berriat-Saint-Prix. *Note sur deux établissements d'utilité publique fondés à Bergerac par M. Lakanal, pendant sa mission comme représentant, en 1793 et 1794, lue à l'académie royale des sciences morales et politiques, le 24 mai 1845.* Paris, 1846.

Bertin, Georges. *Joseph Bonaparte en Amérique.* Paris, 1893.
Biographical Sketch of Joseph Napoleon Bonaparte, Count de Survilliers. 3rd. édition. London, 1834.
Biographie des hommes vivants. Paris, 1818.
Biographie universelle Michaud, nouvelle edition, t. XXII. Article on Lakanal by I. Geoffroy Saint-Hilaire.
Biot. *Essai sur l'histoire générale des sciences pendant la Révolution française.* Paris, 1803.
Blazy, Abbé Louis. *Quelques lettres inédites du conventionnel Lakanal.* Foix, 1910.
Bouchard, E. *Histoire du collège de Moulins.* Moulins, 1872.
Bowes, Frederick P. *The Culture of Early Charleston.* Chapel Hill, 1942.
Buckle, Henry Thomas. *History of Civilization in England.* New York, 1859-66; 1874.
Buisson, F. *Dictionnaire de Pédagogie.* Paris 1888. 1re partie, t.11. Article on Lakanal by M. J. Guillaume. Republished in corrected and condensed form in the *Nouveau dictionnaire de pédagogie et d'instruction primaire.* Paris, 1911.
Burlingame, A. E. *Condorcet, The Torchbearer of the French Revolution.* Boston, 1930.
C. . . D. . . *Le Champ d'asile au Texas, ou Notice curieuse et intéressante sur la formation de cette Colonie, jusqu'à sa dissolution; avec des renseignements propre à éclaircir les faits, et a venger les malheureux Colons des calomnies qu'on leur a prodiguées.* Paris. n. d. [Presumably around 1819].
Caillet, Émile. "La Tradition littéraire des Idéologues," *Memoirs of the American Philosophical Society,* vol. XIX. Philadelphia, 1943.
Carlyle, Thomas. *History of the French Revolution.* New York, 1851, 1936.
Carré, G. *Éloge de Lakanal.* Sceaux, 1888.
Challamel, Augustin. "Convention Nationale," *Histoire-Musée de la République française, depuis l'Assemblée des notables jusqu'à l'Empire,* 3me édition. vol. I, Livre III. Paris, 1857.
Chaudron, Jean Simon. *Oraison funèbre du frère George . . .* Philadelphia, 1801.
———*Funeral oration of Brother George Washington, delivered January 1, 1800, in the French Lodge l'Aménité.* Philadelphia, 1811.
———*Funeral Oration on . . . George Washington . . . translated from the French by S. F. Bradford.* Philadelphia, 1800.
———*Ode aux Français.* Philadelphia, n.d.
———*Poésies choisies, suivies de l'oraison funèbre de Washington.* Paris, 1841.
Chinard, Gilbert. *Jefferson et les Idéologues d'après sa Correspondance inédite avec Destutt de Tracy, Cabanis, J.-B. Say et Auguste Comte.* Baltimore, 1925.
Choix de Rapports, etc. Paris, 1826.
Claiborne, William Charles Cole. *Official Letterbooks of W. C. C. Claiborne.* Ed., Dunbar Rowland. Jackson, Miss., 1917.
Clamageran, F. *Le conventionnel Lakanal; son administration dans le département de la Dordogne.* Paris, 1875.
Claretie, Jules. "La Statue de Lakanal. Ses écrits posthumes," *Le Temps,* 1er février, 1881.
———"Lakanal et Geoffroy Saint-Hilaire," *Le Temps,* 15 avril, 1881.
Commercial Register for the Country, Mobile, Alabama.
Compayré, Gabriel, *The History of Pedagogy.* Boston, 1899.
Court House Records, Mobile, Alabama.
Craighead, Erwin. *Mobile: Fact and Tradition.* Mobile, 1930.
Darnaud, Émile. *Lakanal.* Paris, 1874.

DAUBENTON. *Instruction pour les bergers et les propriétaires de troupeaux.* 1782.

DAVENPORT, F. G. *Ante-Bellum Kentucky.*

DAWSON, JOHN CHARLES. *A French Regicide in Alabama (1824-1837).* Tuscaloosa, Ala., 1939.

———"Lakanal and Chappe's Telegraph," *The Scientific Monthly,* April, 1945. pp. 322-323.

———"The French in Alabama, The Vine and Olive Colony," *The French Review.* Dec., 1944.

Debates and Proceedings in the Congress of the United States. Washington, 1855.

Decade (La) philosophique, littéraire et politique par une société de républicans. Paris, 1794-1807. 42 vols.

DECEMBRE-ALLONIER. *Dictionnaire de la Révolution française.* Paris, 1866.

DE FRANQUEVILLE. *L'Institut, son origine, ses transformations, son organization.* Paris, 1895.

DERIDOUR, A. *Recueil des actes du Directoire exécutif,* t. I. Paris, 1910.

DESTUTT DE TRACY. *Projet d'Élements d'Idéologie à l'usage des Écoles centrales.* Paris, 1802, 1817-18 and 1824.

DEVIC. *Histoire de la vie et des travaux de J.-D. Cassini IV.*

Dictionnaire des Hommes marquans.

Documents of the Congress of the United States, in relation to the Public Lands, etc., Session of 1829: "Condition of the Tombeckbée Association." Washington, 1860. Vol. VI.

DUPUY PAUL. *L'École normale en l'an III.* Paris, 1895.

DURUY, VICTOR. *Histoire de France.* Paris, 1866, 1913.

DUZER, CH. VAN. *Contribution of the Idéalogues to French Revolutionary Thought.* Baltimore, 1935.

Fête (La) du Collège Lakanal à Treignac. Tulle, 1898.

FONTAINE, J. B. L. S. *Mémoire présenté au Congrès des États-Unis d'Amérique par les habitants de la Nouvelle Orléans.* New Orleans, 1804.

FORGE, A. DE. *Les serviteurs de la démocratie.* Paris, 1883.

FORNERON, H. *Histoire générale des émigrés pendant la Révolution française.* Paris, 1884. t.I.

FORTIER, ALCÉE. *A History of Louisiana.* New York, 1904. 4 vols.

FOURNIER, A. "Lakanal dénonciateur," *Revue des Revues,* 15 mars 1894.

GAYARRÉ, CHARLES. *Audret Dubayet or the Two Sister Republics.* New York, 1882

———*Fernando de Lemos.* New York, 1872.

———*History of Louisiana,* Vol. IV, New Orleans, 1903.

GLACHANT, P. et V. "Une lettre inédite de Lakanal, premier économe du Lycée Bonaparte," *L'Enseignement secondaire* 1er avril 1901, p. 118.

GREEN, THOMAS MARSHALL. *The Spanish Conspiracy.* Cincinnati, 1891.

GROS, J. *Lakanal et l'Éducation national.* Paris, 1912.

GROS, M. "Le Duc et la Duchesse d'Angoûlème dans le Midi," *Mémoires de l'Académie des Sciences, Inscriptions et Belles-Lettres de Toulouse.* Douzième série, II, 47-66.

———"Un Coin du Pays de Foix, *"Mémoires de l'Académie des Sciences, Inscriptions et Belles-Lettres de Toulouse.* Onzieme Serie, IX, pp. 83-91.

GUILLAUME, J. "Lakanal et l'Académie des sciences," *La Révolution française,* 1899, 2e semestre, p. 523.

GUILLAUME, M. J. (ed.) *Procès-Verbaux du Comité d'Instruction publique de l'Assemblée Législative.* Paris, 1889.

———(ed.) *Procès-Verbaux du Comité d'Instruction publique de la Convention nationale.* Paris, 1891-1907. 6 vols.

GUIZOT. *The History of France.* Vol. 8, ch. 18.

Hartmann et Millard. *Le Texas ou notice sur le Champ d'Asile.* Paris, [1819?].
Histoire Parlementaire de la Révolution française: ou Journal des Assemblées nationales depuis 1789. Paris, 1833.
Hyde de Neuville, Jean Guillaume. *Mémoires et Souvenirs du baron Hyde de Neuville.* Paris 1893, 1912. 3 vols.
Institut de France. Paris 1800-1840. 8 vols.
Institut de France: Mémoires de l'Institut national des sciences et des arts, Littérature et Beaux-Arts. Paris, 1798-1805. 5 vols.
Jouin, H. *Lakanal en Amérique d'après sa correspondance inédite.* Besançon, 1904.
———*Lakanal et David d'Angers.* Angers, 1902.
Kendall, J. S. *History of New Orleans.* New York, 1922.
King, Grace. *New Orleans, the Place and the People.* New York, 1907.
Kinkead, Elizabeth Shelby. *History of Kentucky.* Cincinnati, 1896.
Labroue, Henri. *La Mission du Conventionnel Lakanal dans la Dordogne en l'An II (octobre 1793-aout 1794).* Paris [1912].
Lacroix, Paul. *Directoire, Consulat et Empire. Moeurs et usages, lettres, sciences et arts. 1793-1815.* Paris, 1884.
Lakanal, Joseph. "Discours sur l'Education nationale," December, 1792. *Procès-Verbaux du Comité d'Instruction publique de la Convention nationale.* M. J. Guillaume, ed., Paris, 1891-1907. 6 vols.
———"Rapport 17 mai 1793, à l'appui du décret autorisant l'Académie des sciences à nommer aux places vacantes dans son sein." *Ibid.*
———"Rapport sur l'Académie des sciences de Paris, 22 mai 1793." *Ibid.*
———"Rapport de ler juin 1793, à l'appui du décret de ce jour, changeant les noms de quatre communes." *Ibid.*
———"Rapport sur les honneurs du Panthéon à accorder à Joseph Sauveur, 10 juin 1793." *Ibid.*
———"Rapport sur le Jardin national des plantes et le Cabinet d'histoire naturelle de Paris, 10 juin 1793." *Ibid.*
———"Rapport à l'appui du décret concernant la composition des livres élémentaires destinés à l'enseignement national, 13 juin 1793." *Ibid.*
———"Rapport présenté à la Convention le 18 juin 1793, à l'appui du décret appliquant aux écoles militaires les dispositions de la loi du 8 mars 1793, et ordonnant la répartition des élèves de l'orphenilat de Popincourt dans les écoles militaires." *Ibid.*
———"Rapport, 19 juin 1793, à l'appui du décret mettant à la disposition du ministre de la guerre une somme de 5,596 livres pour les dépenses arrièrées du collège militaire de Brienne."
———"Projet de décret . . . sur la réunion du 10 août. 25 juin 1793." *Ibid.*
———"Discours préliminaire." June 26, 1793. *Ibid.*
———"Lakanal à ses Collègues," Paris, July 1793. *Ibid.*
———"Rapport fait par Lakanal à la Convention sur la propriété littéraire et artistique, 19 juillet 1793." *Ibid.*
———"Rapport sur le télégraphe (of Claude Chappe), 26 juillet 1793." *Ibid.*
———"Rapport sur la suppression des écoles militaires. Journal des débats et des décrets. 9 septembre 1793. *Ibid.*
———"Rapport sur les morts du 10 août." April 17, 1794. *Ibid.*
———"Rapport sur la formation d'un jury pour juger le concours des horloges décimales, etc." August 21, 1794. *Ibid.*
———"Rapport sur la translation au Panthéon des cendres de J. J. Rousseau." September 15, 1794. *Ibid.*
———"Rapport sur le manuscrit de Rousseau offert à la Convention par Thérèse Levasseur." September 28, 1794. *Ibid.*
———"Rapport sur l'établissement des écoles normales, 3 brumaire 1794." *Ibid.*

———"Rapport sur l'organisation des écoles primaries, 7 brumaire 1794." *Ibid.*
———"Projet de décret sur l'organisation des écoles primaires, 7 brumaire 1794." *Ibid.*
———"Rapport sur les langues orientales, commerciales et diplomatiques." Paris 1794. *Ibid.*
———"Rapport et projet de loi sur les écoles centrales, 26 frimaire 1794." *Ibid.*
———"Rapport sur une réimpression du *Traité des Moutons* de Daubenton." January 3, 1795. *Ibid.*
———"Décret nommant, sur le rapport de Lakanal, Vandermonde professeur d'Économie politique à l'École normale; also decree after report of Lakanal dedicating 30,000 livres to the printing of works that the Committee of Public Instruction shall judge useful to have delivered to the pupils of the Normal School." February 7, 1795. *Ibid.*
———"Nouveau rapport sur les écoles centrales." February 27, 1795. *Ibid.*
———"Rapport pour l'établissement à Paris de cinq écoles centrales." February 29, 1795. *Ibid.*
———"Rapport sur l'École des langues orientales vivantes, 30 mars 1795." *Ibid.*
———"Rapport sur l'impression d'un exemplaire annoté du Dictionnaire de l'Académie française. 1er jour complémentaire de l'an III." Sept. 17, 1795. *Ibid.*
———"Rapport pour proposer . . . que l'année commencera le jour de l'Équinoxe vrai. 5e jour complémentaire 1795." *Ibid.*
———"Décrets rendus, sur le rapport de Lakanal, . . . pour la création d'écoles primaires de filles, et pour le placement des écoles centrales, 3 brumaire 1795." *Ibid.*
———"Un mot de Lakanal . . . à quelques folliculaires qui ne sont pas avares de mots." Paris an III. *Ibid.*
———"Rapport fait au Conseil des cinq-Cents, par Lakanal, un de ses membres, sur les livres élémentaires présentés au concours ouvert par la loi du 9 pluviôse, an II. Séance du 14 brumaire, an IV." Paris an IV. *Ibid.*
———"Lakanal . . . à ses frères les républicains du département de l'Ariège. Paris an IV.
———"Notice sur J. Lakanal, membre de l'Institut." Paris 1801. *Ibid.*
———"Présentation à la Convention d'un nouveau projet sur l'éducation et l'instruction publique." *Ibid.*
———"Rapport ordonnant que les membres de l'Académie des sciences qui avaient été chargés de divers travaux continueront de s'en occuper," etc. *Ibid.*
———"Rapport à l'appui du décret portant la peine de deux ans de prison contre ceux qui dégraderont les chefs-d'oeuvre en sculpture dans le jardin des Tuileries et autres lieux publics; (aussi à l'appui du décrét étendant l'application de cette peine à quiconque dégradera les monuments des arts dépendant des propriétés nationales." *Ibid.*
———"Rapport précédant le décret nommant Garat commissaire de l'instruction publique, Ginguené et Clément de Ris adjoints." *Ibid.*
———"Exposé sommaire des Travaux de Joseph Lakanal, ex-membre de la Convention Nationale et du Conseil des Cinq-Cents, pour sauver, durant la Révolution, les Sciences, les Lettres, et ceux qui les honoraient par leurs Travaux." Paris 1838.
———"Suum Cuique." Paris 1840.
———"Premiére réponse à la "Note sur la création de l'institut." Paris 1840.
———"Tableau synoptique de la Convention nationale." Paris 1843.
Lakanal Papers. Howard Memorial Library, Tulane University, New Orleans.
Lakanal et Daubenton. *La Révolution française.* 1885. 1er trimestre. p. 735.
LAMARTINE, ALPHONSE DE. *History of the Restoration.*

Lands allotted to Encourage the Cultivation of the Vine and Olive. Communicated to the House of Representatives, Dec. 14, 1818. 15th Congress, No. 287. 2nd session.

LAVIGNE, B. *Joseph Lakanal.* Toulouse, 1880.

LAVISSE, ERNEST. *Histoire de France.* Paris, 1911.

——*Histoire de France contemporaine depuis la Révolution jusqu'à la Paix de 1919.* Paris, 1920-22. 10 vols.

LE GENDRE, PAUL. "Lakanal," *Les hommes de la Révolution.* Paris, 1884.

LEPELETIER, MICHEL. *Oeuvres de Michel Lepeletier Saint-Fargeau, précédées de sa vie, par Felix Lepeletier son frère, suivies de documents historiques.* Bruxelles, 1826.

LUCAS-DUBRETON. *La Restauration.* Paris, 1926.

LYON, ANNE BOZEMAN. "The Bonapartists in Alabama," *Southern Home Journal,* Memphis, March, 1900; reprinted in *Gulf States Historical Magazine,* Montgomery, March, 1903.

MCCARTNEY and DORRANCE. *The Bonapartes in America.* Philadelphia, 1939.

MCCORVEY, THOMAS CHALMERS. "The Vine and the Olive: a sketch of the Colony of French Imperialists that settled in Marengo County, Ala., in 1818." *The Times-Democrat,* New Orleans, February 22, 1885.

——"The Vine and Olive Colony." *Alabama Historical Reporter,* Tuscaloosa, Ala., April, 1885.

MADELIN, LOUIS. *La Révolution.* Paris, 1912. English translation, New York, 1916.

Manuel pour la concordance des Calendriers républicain et grégorien, ou Recueil complet de tous les Annuaires depuis la première année républicaine. Paris, 1805.

MARCUS (TOUSSAINT NIGOUL). *Lakanal.* Paris, 1879.

MARTIN, THOMAS W. *French Military Adventurers in Alabama 1818-1828.* Birmingham, 1937.

MATHEWS, Shailer. *The French Revolution.* New York, 1900.

MATHIEZ. *The French Revolution.* New York, 1929.

MATTHIEZ, A. *Le Directoire.* Paris, 1934.

Mémoires de l'Académie royale des sciences morales et politiques de l'Institut de France. Paris, 1837.

Mercure français, No. 119, Nov. 9, 1793.

MESNARD, P. *Histoire de l'Académie française.*

MICHELET, JULES. Oeuvres complètes. Paris, 1893-99.

MIGNET. *Notice historique sur la vie et les travaux de M. Lakanal.* Paris, 1857.

MOORE, ALBERT BURTON. *History of Alabama.* University, Alabama, 1934.

MORNET, DANIEL. *A Short History of French Literature* (translation of his *Histoire de la Littérature et de la Pensée françaises,* New York, 1935).

NETON, A. *Sieyès (1748-1836) d'après des documents inédits.* Paris, 1900.

Niles Weekly Register. Baltimore, for years 1815-1830.

NOBLE, S. G. "Governor Claiborne and the Public School System of the Territorial Government of Louisiana," *Louisiana Historical Quarterly,* 1929.

——"Schools of New Orleans during the First Quarter of the Nineteenth Century," *Louisiana Historical Quarterly,* 1931.

Notice sur le Champ d'Asile. Paris, 1817.

Nouvelle Biographie générale. Paris, 1859.

PARKER, HAROLD T. *The Cult of Antiquity and the French Revolutionaries.* Chicago, 1937.

PICAVET, F. *Les Idéologues, essai sur l'histoire des idées et des théories scientifiques, philosophiques, religieuses, . . . en France depuis 1789.* Paris, 1891.

PICKETT, ALBERT JAMES. *History of Alabama.* Charleston, 1851. 2 vols. Republished in Alabama, 1896. See vol. II, chapter entitled: "Modern French Colony in America."

POSTEL, R. *Lakanal.* Paris, 1883.
POYER, G. *Cabanis. Choix de textes et introduction.* Paris, 1910.
Procès ou Assassinat juridique de Louis XVI, Roi de France et de Navarre. Paris, 1814.
PROTH, MARIO. *1793 et l'instruction publique, Lakanal.* Paris, 1872.
REEVES, JESSE S. *The Napoleonic Exiles in America.* Baltimore, 1905.
Réimpression de l'ancien Moniteur. Paris, 1847-50. Vol. 32.
REISNER, E. H. *Nationalism and Education since 1789.* New York, 1923.
REMUSAT. *Institut royal de France . . . Funérailles de M. Lakanal. Discours de M. de Rémusat, le 16 fevrier 1845.* Paris, 1845. Published in the *Moniteur* Feb. 17, 1845, and in the *Journal de Bergerac,* April 5, 1845.
"Révolution francaise, *(La),*" *Revue d'histoire moderne et contemporaine.* Paris, 1881-1935.
Revue historique de la révolution française. Paris, Reims, 1910-1923. 15 vols.
Revue internationale de l'enseignement, octobre, 1882.
ROBERT A., ET CONGNY, G. *Dictionnaire des parlementaires.* 1890. Vol. II.
ROBERTSON, WILLIAM H. "Memoirs" (unpublished) written in decade 1850-1860.
ROBINET. *Le Mouvement religieux à Paris pendant la Révolution* (1789-1801). 1896-1899.
ROBINET, ROBERT. *Dictionnaire historique et Biographique de la Révolution et de l'Empire (1789-1815).* Paris, n.d.
ROSE. *Napoleon.*
ROSEBERRY. *Napoleon, the Last Phase.*
ROSENGARTEN, J. G. *French Colonists and Exiles in the United States.* Philadelphia, 1907.
SAINT-HILAIRE, ISADORE GEOFFROY. *Lakanal, sa Vie, ses Travaux à la Convention et au Conseil des Cinq-Cents.* Paris, 1849.
SAINT-PIERRE, BERNARDIN DE. *Études de la Nature.* Paris, 1792. 5 vols.
SANTHONAX (A. Aulard). "Lakanal à Bergerac." *La Révolution française.* 1888, 1er *semestre.*
SARRUT ET SAINT-EDME. "Lakanal," *Biographie des Hommes du jour.* Paris, 1841. t.V., *pre* partie.
SAUZAY, A. "Count Bertrand Clausel," *Nouvelle biographie générale.* Paris, 1854.
SIMON, JULES *"Mon petit journal," Le Temps,* 22 décembre, 1890.
SMITH, Z. F. *The History of Kentucky.* Louisville, 1895.
STERNE, EMMA GELDERS. *Some Plant Olive Trees.* New York, 1937.
STRODE, HUDSON. "Bonapartists in the Alabama Canebrakes," *Travel,* April, 1938.
Sur le proconsulat et moeurs de Lakanal. n.d.
TESTON, A. *Lakanal.* Montpellier, 1885.
THENARD, J. F. "Lakanal électeur en Seine-et-Oise," *La Révolution française 1888,* 1*er semestre.*
THIERS, L. A. *Histoire du Consulat et de l'Empire.* Paris, 1843-49. 9 vols.
TINKER, EDWARD LAROQUE. "Les écrits de langue française en Louisiane au XIX siècle," *Essais biographiques et bibliographiques.* Evreux, 1932.
TOURNEUX, M. "Histoire de l'instruction publique, actes et déliberations de la convention", *Bibliothèque de l'histoire de Paris.* 1900. Vol. III.
Trustees' Records, University of Alabama. Two Lakanal letters. University archives.
VERON, L. *"Mémoires d'un Bourgeois de Paris.* Vol. II.
WELVERT, EUGENE. "Lakanal en Amérique," *Feuilles d'histoire,* 1910.
———"La légende de Lakanal. Lakanal Réorganisateur de L'Instruction publique," *Revue des questions historiques,* Juillet 1908. Reprinted Paris, 1908.
WHITFIELD, GAIUS, JR. "The French Grant in Alabama, a History of the Founding of Demopolis," *Publications of the Alabama Historical Society,* Transactions. Vol. IV.

INDEX